THE LONELIEST PLACES

THE LONELIEST PLACES

Loss, Grief, and the Long Journey Home

RACHEL DICKINSON

THREE HILLS
AN IMPRINT OF
CORNELL UNIVERSITY PRESS
ITHACA AND LONDON

"Thrown for a Loop" was first published in *Aeon*, April 2014.

"Birding on Bleaker Island" was first published in *When Birds Are Near*, ed. Susan Fox Rogers, Three Hills / Cornell University Press, 2021.

"Minefields" was first published in *Catapult*, December 2018.

First published 2022 by Cornell University Press

Printed in the United States of America

Library of Congress Cataloging-in-Publication Data

Names: Dickinson, Rachel, author.
Title: The loneliest places : loss, grief, and the long journey home / Rachel Dickinson.
Description: Ithaca [New York] : Three Hills, an imprint of Cornell University Press, 2022.
Identifiers: LCCN 2022003664 (print) | LCCN 2022003665 (ebook) | ISBN 9781501766091 (paperback) | ISBN 9781501766381 (pdf) | ISBN 9781501766398 (epub)
Subjects: LCSH: Dickinson, Rachel. | Mothers of suicide victims—New York (State) | Parental grief—New York (State) | Grief in women—New York (State) | Suicide victims—Family relationships—New York (State) | Loss (Psychology)
Classification: LCC BF575.G7 D527 2022 (print) | LCC BF575.G7 (ebook) | DDC 155.9/37085—dc23/eng/20220517
LC record available at https://lccn.loc.gov/2022003664
LC ebook record available at https://lccn.loc.gov/2022003665

For Tim, Railey, Clara, and Gwen

CONTENTS

THESE FRAGMENTS I HAVE SHORED
AGAINST MY RUINS

A child's suicide pitches you into a hellish place of fragmentary images, the deepest depression imaginable, efforts to destroy yourself, and an almost complete break with what's happening in the world around you. That was my experience. I wish it upon no one.

Over the past decade since Jack's death, I've written books and articles, none of them about suicide or my experience with it. But I was also working on the essays in this collection. I wanted these essays to chronicle my life after my son's suicide, but the pieces became so much more. It became clear to me that in order to write about the aftermath of a single event, I also had to dwell in the past to seek out some of the messy bits that make me who I am.

The essays in *The Loneliest Places* are arranged in sections. They are not necessarily chronological but are grouped much like the songs on one side of an album would be arranged or like paintings hung for an exhibition. The essays in each section are connected by mood, theme, subject matter, or tone. Or maybe by something else that today I cannot discern.

The result is a nonlinear and sometimes fragmented exploration of my experience with the worst thing that can ever happen to a person. I hope the readers who recognize some of these thoughts, feelings, and behaviors can take solace in the fact that surviving your child's suicide may be messy and will be chaotic, and that there is no right way to move through your new world.

T. S. Eliot wrote the line "These fragments I have shored against my ruins" toward the end of his 1922 poem *The Waste Land*. And while there isn't agreement on what exactly this line refers to, I like to think that the fragments are bits and pieces of our past we should be collecting to help make sense of the world around us. This is what I have done in *The Loneliest Places*.

The Loneliest Places

Cast of Characters

Jane ~ Charles   Daphne ~ William
1929-2011 1930-2018   1917-2011 · 1919-1995

charles Amy Anne Rachel ~ Timothy Janet Maureen
1955   1959 1957 1956   1950   1955   1948

Bailey   Clara   Jack   Gwen
1985   1993   1994-2012 1999

BEGINNING

Autumn, Again

This season brings so many memories. They flood my brain and my heart before I even know what's happening. The mixture of melancholy and beauty, anticipation, and the desire to stop time are at war within me. It has always been this way. I expect this is true of many people.

Great vees of geese cross the sky, their honking sounding like the baying of a pack of hounds in pursuit of a deer. And the numbers of little birds—the ones that hang around all summer—are thinning. No more *cheerie up cheerie oh* of the robin to wake me in the morning. Waves of fattened warblers make their way through the region, and sometimes you'll come across a tree with fruit or berries that is dripping with birds who have stopped to refuel on their way to their southern homes. The mammals are growing their winter coats. The foxes, squirrels, and chipmunks look fat, and the deer who linger in the backyard look healthy.

As a little girl, I remember sitting on the steps of our farmhouse's front stoop as the days got cooler and staring at the bright orange sugar maple tree in the neighbor's yard. I wanted to know how that happened—how those leaves changed color—but was too lazy to look it up in the set of the 1932 *Encyclopaedia Britannica* we had in the house. We loved those encyclopedias because of the beauty of the Art Deco–influenced illustrations and the black-and-white photographs that took us away from the farm as well as back in time.

I don't remember the timing of many big events in my life, but in the story I write in my head, they all come to the front of my brain as happening in autumn—the beautiful season hiding decay and the looming harshness to come. I wallow in my sadness in autumn. I yearn for my mother and my boy. I can see them both so clearly in this season: my mother in her Greek Revival farmhouse showered with yellow and orange leaves from the massive sugar maples in her yard, and Jack as a toddler being pushed by Tim on a tire swing hanging from the limb of an oak tree. As I watch Tim and Jack, I sit at a picnic table at Dryden Lake and take in the hill of flaming sugar maples across the small body of water.

The joy and sadness of living in the place where you grew up and where most of the pivotal events of your life happened become heightened in autumn. You cannot escape or ignore your past. It all comes back as those leaves turn, and the nights get colder. I can drive past my mother's house and see that the leaves are still falling on the roof and covering the yard. I can also go to Dryden Lake and sit in my car and cry as memories of other autumns wash over me.

Sometimes there is no lesson to be learned from trying to understand these experiences and attempting to figure out your relationship to a season. It is what it is. Some people are significantly affected by the shorter days and lack of sunlight in the winter and use a lightbox to simulate the sun to feel better. This autumn experience is my version of seasonal affective disorder, and my car and iPhone serve as my lightbox. I drive the country roads and take pictures. Focusing on capturing a season in photographs manages to keep me one step removed from my seasonal melancholy.

One Night

One night in early February 2012—on a night when the stars shone in the sky and the earth spun on its axis and orbited around the sun with complete regularity—I was at home when I got a frantic call on my cell phone from Clara, our eighteen-year-old daughter, who was a freshman at Cornell University.

"Where's Jack! Where's Jack!" she yelled into the phone.

Then I heard the shot, and ran upstairs and found him lying across his bed with a shotgun next to him.

Several days later, calling hours for our seventeen-year-old son Jack O'Bannon Gallagher were held at the local funeral home. Afterwards—as he handed me the guest book—the funeral director told me this was the largest crowd he had ever seen during a three-hour period. Seven hundred and twenty-six people signed the guest book. People from all over my emotional map—friends, family, soccer players, musicians, teenagers I'd never seen before, teenagers I had seen before, parents, teachers, and neighbors. Many of them had to wait in line for two hours on a dark, dreary, cold afternoon that turned into a dark, dreary, cold evening just to get inside the building. I stood—dressed in black and wearing dark glasses—at the end of the receiving line as far away as possible from Jack's closed coffin, which was surrounded by flowers and photographs of Jack with friends and family. By the time people got to me, they were emotional wrecks. That was my permanent state.

Jack's burial was private. He was buried at 9:30 a.m. on February 10, 2012. My husband, Tim, and I, and Jack's sisters, Railey, Clara, and Gwen, were accompanied by several of my aunts and cousins, and my sisters and their families. We drove into Willow Glen Cemetery on the crest of a hill about three miles from where we live in the village of Freeville in central New York. We stared at our family plot, which would now hold five generations of one family. Fortunately, my eighty-three-year-old aunt Jean was willing to give up her burial spot; otherwise Jack would have been buried alone, and I just couldn't bear the thought of that. Now he would rest next to his grandmother—my mother.

Did the wind blow that morning? Did we have to bundle up and put our hands inside our coat pockets to keep warm? Were there flakes of snow swirling in the air? These are the kinds of things I don't remember. I do remember looking at the coffin in front of me and wondering if Jack was cold—he was dressed in a lavender tee shirt and wore no coat. The funeral home used an ugly blue tarp as a backdrop for the graveside service and the coffin sat in front of that. Then several chairs were set in front of the coffin, facing it. People sat but I don't remember if I was one of them. Words were said but I don't remember what they were. And then we left.

Jack's memorial service at the Freeville United Methodist Church immediately followed the burial. We parked at home because we live three doors down from the small church in what we call the Pink House, a large Victorian with a huge front porch. This house, painted a dusty-rose color, which we had all loved for the decade we had lived there, had become the scene of the crime. The Pink House. "Oh, you know," I imagined people saying. "The house where the boy killed himself."

I kept my eyes, behind dark glasses, on the sidewalk in front of me, looking at all the cracks and heaves in the walkway as we moved slowly from our house toward the church. We had to walk through crowds of people who would never be able to get inside. Our knot of family members had the same effect that a drop of oil has in water—people parted silently and automatically to allow us to walk up the four steps to the church door and enter the vestibule.

I couldn't possibly say anything at the funeral. I had taken Valium to try to control the sobbing and had worried for a couple of days about whether I was even going to be able to walk into the church. I didn't know if I could bear one more overwhelming experience. As my family slid into the front pew, I saw that the altar was covered with white flowers, which I loved. And in the middle of the chrysanthemums and lilies and orchids and tulips was a photograph of Jack that I had taken a couple of years earlier. He's in among the silvery limbs of the big beech tree, peering out from behind a branch and smiling at me, and he is wearing his favorite aqua-colored tee shirt. That enormous beech tree is at the cemetery where we had just buried Jack. As I stared at the photograph of Jack in the tree, I thought about how that tree with its spreading limbs and coppery leaves would be shading both Jack and my mother during the hot days of the summer.

I stared at Jack's photograph as Railey, Jack's twenty-five-year-old sister, came to the lectern to give a eulogy for her brother. At six feet tall and with hair dyed platinum, Railey was a commanding figure in any setting. When she was standing behind the lectern at her brother's funeral, every heart in the room opened and communicated love to her as she tried to tell all of us who Jack was.

"There's no way any of us are going to be able to separate our memories of Jack from our memories of his music," she began. "He was more than a musician, of course—he was a son, a brother, a friend, an artist, and a thinker—but right now, his songs are in my head, and in my heart."

As Railey spoke I stared at the photograph of Jack smiling in the tree that would now be his guardian. Jack's thin white arms clasped around dark limbs that gathered him up and held him tight. An image that would remain frozen in time because I captured it with my point-and-shoot Sony camera. That tee shirt—that stupid aqua tee shirt with the silk screen pattern of cassette tapes on the front of it—a shirt I would at some point fold and then roll up tightly and pack into a box of keepsakes for Jack's girlfriend Isabel who lived in London.

"In Little League, Jack made his mark not as the amazing fielder, or the terrific sportsman," Railey said, "but as the boy who would spend entire innings crouched near the ground, searching for four-leaf clovers, singing Handel's Hallelujah Chorus at the top of his lungs . . . He didn't score runs but was still the player that everyone talked about.

"It's important to remember Jack's music. It was something he loved and devoted himself to. His voice was clear and true and full. He played many instruments, nearly all of them self-taught, and loved them for their variations and individual strengths, and he loved the ways he could blend his voice with each of their distinct sounds.

"His music was the product of a lot of work and an uncommon dedication to a beloved thing. Jack's friends were much the same. I have never known anyone as unfailingly devoted to his friends as Jack was.

"It was as a young man that he found ways of capturing his particular view of the world, and I feel so lucky that we have photos and art and songs as artifacts of his life, which so clearly defied logic and convention.

"I will never be able to figure Jack out," said Railey. "But the things I do know, and will always keep, are his humor; the way he would quietly sing when he was driving; how his eyes would twinkle when he found something genuinely funny; how he remained staunchly true to his own code; how incredibly special Gwennie was to him; his love of gross food; his sure place in a family made of individuals; and how much I miss him."

When I read over the names of those who had been in the church that day—many of whom had also been at calling hours—I saw the name of his pediatrician, many of the teachers Jack had had over the years, the founder of the Ithaca Children's Choir which Jack had sung with since third grade, friends of Jack's from all around the region, members of my family from up and down the Eastern Seaboard, Tim's sister from California, Tim's best friend from Alabama, two friends of mine from New Jersey, the superintendent of the school, Jack's sweet girlfriend Isabel, and the list goes on and on and on.

It's tough to know where to begin a journey through the world of grief. Was it when Jack was born? When we discovered his dark side? When he died? And wherever we choose to start—whatever we choose to call the beginning—it will always feel like a mistake. The world of "what ifs" and "I should haves" is insidious and creeps into your thinking before you know it, eroding what little sense of reality you have left. Basically, you have to keep that irrational world out as you navigate through a landscape of loss without being given any tools. No compass to guide you along your way. No bridges to cross rivers of tears. For me, the journey began in an instant—a signpost that marked both the ending and the starting point—the end of Jack's life and the beginning of our life without Jack.

Jack was an enormously complicated kid with an IQ over 150 who excelled at everything he did. He was handsome; musically, artistically, and academically gifted; a kid with an easy smile and lots of friends. He also abused over-the-counter medication, and he embraced a kind of nihilistic philosophy and was always ready to say "That doesn't matter—nothing matters" when you tried to engage in political or social discourse. He showed a certain naïveté about the human condition. I remember getting into one of those arguments with him about voting as November and a general election neared. "I'm never going to vote," he said. "But that's really silly," I replied, and then tried to point out the power of one vote, particularly on the local level. The conversation ended the way it always did—"That doesn't matter," he said. "Nothing matters."

How do you tell people that your son just killed himself? I knew I had to call my sisters Amy and Anne and tell them, and I completely dreaded it. I can still remember my sister Anne sobbing on the phone as I choked out the news and her saying over and over again, "Oh, Rachel . . . Oh, Rachel."

And then you have to take clothes over to the funeral home.
And then you have to pick out a casket.
And then you have to notify the colleges he applied to that he has died.
And then you have to be seen in public at calling hours and the funeral.
And then you hope you can be left alone.

Three weeks after Jack's death, Jack's sisters Clara and Railey and his best friend, Will, organized an evening of music—a remembrance concert—at a large community space in Ithaca. I was so angry they had done this because I didn't want to have to go anywhere and I knew I would have to be there. I wasn't even sure what this event was going to be. I just knew I had to go because Railey and Clara were going to sing.

I had spent every waking moment since the memorial service sitting in a big green armchair that stood in the corner of the front room of the Pink House. I kept myself wrapped in an old red quilt taken from my mother's house after her death. I was in a state of being and not being—dwelling on the past and absent from the present—and almost unable to open my eyes. Having to go anywhere—having to leave my Green Chair in the Pink House—was like torture. I was sure I would drown in my own tears.

Tim persuaded me to get in the car on the day of the concert, and he and Gwennie—who was now a very sad twelve-year-old—and I headed to Ithaca. I fretted and almost felt sick several times as we drove the ten miles southwest out of the hills that guide Fall Creek to Cayuga Lake.

This community room had a stage on one side, and someone had put out about a hundred folding chairs. I sat in the very front row wearing my dark glasses because my eyes were so puffy and red, and I knew I would be crying for much of the time. At one point I turned around and saw that hundreds of people had crowded into that room—friends of ours, friends of Jack, friends of Railey and Clara and Gwen—and I was stunned. Each musician was allowed ten minutes onstage. Several of them sang and played songs that Jack had written. Many of them sang songs that they had written. They played banjo, guitar, cello, and piano. Two of them did a modern dance, moving across the floor in front of us in leotards and holding scarves that floated in the air as they twisted and turned to music.

Sitting there listening and watching, I knew this is what artistic teenagers do best. They show their angst and emotions in a very public setting. Every word is heartfelt and sung badly or beautifully from some inner space reserved for the distressed and bereft youth. They loved Jack. And they loved the idea of Jack—a complicated, artistic singer who could make an entire room fall silent with his powerful baritone voice. They hated what Jack had done to himself. And they hated what Jack had done to them.

Railey and Clara performed several songs together at the end of the evening—Clara playing guitar and Railey singing harmony—their voices sounding the same and yet not the same because they are siblings. The two of them standing there, looking so confident. They were pitch-perfect and even in their own distress were consummate performers—at ease onstage, cracking wise, and throwing themselves into singing the songs they'd chosen. They were Jack's sisters. They all shared the performance gene that ran through both families. It was a breathtaking moment punctuating a long evening of earnest performances.

And then, after the concert, because they were teenagers, most of them left without saying anything to Tim and me. It was just as well.

Thoughts You Have While at Your Son's Funeral

In the spring of 1994, Tim and I drove through a tremendous snow squall in the middle of the night to get to the hospital. Odd for mid-April, we thought. About half an hour after Jack's birth Tim started looking at the clock and I told him to go home where my mother was watching eight-year-old Railey and Clara, who was a week shy of turning one. I looked at my beautiful baby boy—and he was beautiful—and was so happy he was joining our family. For the first couple of years of his life, we called him Happy Jack because that blond-haired, blue-eyed boy was always smiling.

It's funny the things you think about when you're sitting in the front pew at your son's funeral. At one point I wondered where his little pink-and-purple glasses were that he wore when he was three. One eye was starting to cross—what they used to call lazy eye—so the ophthalmologist suggested we try glasses for a while to strengthen the eye muscle. We let Jack pick out his own frames. He immediately picked out the pink-and-purple ones. They were labeled as being for girls—and had some girl's name written on the inside of the one of the bows, like "Jessica"—but that was immaterial because he loved them and we loved him.

Jack was on the playground at the elementary school adjacent to our house. When he was in first and second grades there, I used to sit out in the backyard with a book when the weather was fine just as the kids came out to play. Although I couldn't see the kids because the playground was beyond a hedgerow, I could hear them and above all I could hear Jack's husky voice because it carried. Often, he'd be singing one of his favorite songs—he went through a Britney Spears phase at about that same time. Then, inevitably, I'd hear the stern voice of the playground monitor saying "Jack Gallagher!" just as my son was about to go off the rails.

And those flowers. All of those white flowers surrounding your photograph on the altar, Jack. Who are they all from? How will I be able to thank the people who gave them to us? Or, more appropriate, who gave them to you? I can't tell at the moment. Who are those flowers for?

Where are those four-leaf clovers you picked in the outfield during Little League games? I know I stuck them in a book, but what book?

He would start playing an instrument—guitar, banjo, keyboards—at about midnight and I don't even know how long he'd play into the night. The long dark night when he should have been sleeping. Can I ever hear the sound of a banjo again? And his strong baritone voice singing songs he loved from Coldplay and Wilco and Mumford & Sons and whoever. Jack's songs are what I called them. I don't want to hear any of his songs again.

Those boys and girls in his life. Gathered over a short period and yet lifelong friends. I don't feel like I really know any of them well and now so regret that. Why didn't I pay more attention to Jack's friends? They loved him, and he loved them. Now they'll drift away and take part of Jack with them—a part I never knew and I'll never know.

I remember a long school bus ride to Saratoga with a bunch of art students when Jack was in sixth or seventh grade. He had won an art award and his piece was going to be on display, and he wanted me to be there. When the day came, I felt sick, but I went anyway. I kept popping ibuprofen on the bus to manage a terrible sore throat and fever. We walked around the big gymnasium where all the art projects were displayed and talked about the pieces. He wanted to be with me. I felt like it might be the last time he would want to be with me to celebrate one of his accomplishments. He was at that embarrassed-but-still-happy-to-be-with-me stage.

Oh my god. What has he done to all of us?

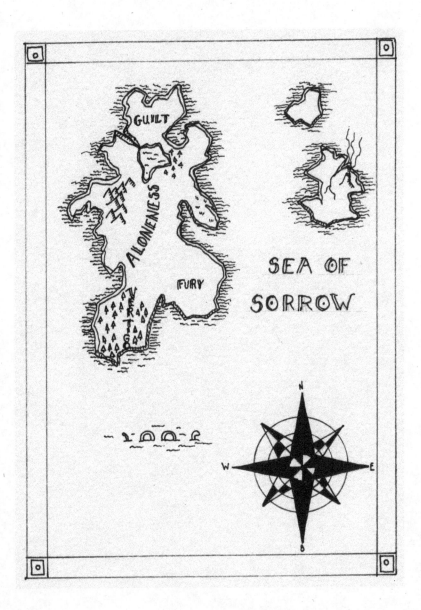

Withdrawn

Running Away

For about fifteen years before Jack died, I made my living as a travel writer. I'd been to places that at one time verged on the exotic like Tibet and Iceland, and had sold stories to numerous publications including some that paid real money. For several months before Jack's death, I was working out the logistics to fly to the Falkland Islands.

Five weeks after Jack's death, I left home and traveled ten thousand kilometers—about six thousand miles—to that remote archipelago in the South Atlantic. It was thirty years after the 1982 conflict pitting the Argentines—who had invaded the islands—against the British, who sent warships, troops, and fighter jets to protect their overseas territory. When I made my final plans in January, I wanted to travel to the Falklands to witness the anniversary of what the rest of the world tended to view as a silly little war. By the time I got on the plane to go to the Falklands via Santiago, Chile, I was frantic to leave my own world and enter another.

Jack's suicide knocked me, my husband, and Jack's sisters into a parallel negative universe of moving shapes and shadows lacking substance.
I spent most of my days sitting in the Green Chair wrapped in the old
red quilt from my mother's house. My husband built fires in the fireplace
next to my chair and I'd watch the flames consume the wood until it was
red embers and finally cold, dark ashes. I couldn't read—couldn't focus
on the page—and although I recognized words, they made no sense. So
I sat and watched the fire and dwelled on the night Jack died. I thought if
I could run through that scene a hundred or a thousand times, then maybe
it wouldn't seem so shocking. Maybe I would get used to the reality of
his violent death and would then be able to rise from my chair and walk
through the haunted rooms of the Pink House without sobbing. Maybe
then I would be able to travel thousands of miles from home to a place
I was convinced would be restorative.

I knew people in my family thought I was crazy. I learned that my
sisters had been talking to each other on the phone—one in favor of me
traveling and the other thinking it was a bad idea. I knew I was a topic of
conversation at the local diner where my aunts and cousins met for breakfast every Wednesday morning. And there I was, not joining them in the
nearby village of Dryden, unable to leave my chair, yet finalizing a trip to
the Falkland Islands. I think my husband was so frightened about my near
catatonic state that he embraced my desire to leave, to carry through with
plans made before our son died.

The rest of the family doesn't understand, I thought. *They don't understand my need to be gone.* My need was to be out of that house, that scene
of the crime. My need to leave the ancestral village was strong enough to
break my paralysis because everywhere I looked, I searched for the ghosts
of the people who would not be there—my mother, my son, my aunt and
uncle, and my grandparents. I had to leave the ghosts. *The people who
are left will just have to let me go,* I reasoned. Instinctively, I knew that by
going away I might be able to reclaim a part of myself that had been frozen.

After my husband left me at the curb of the Syracuse airport, where
I would take a flight to New York, I felt enormous relief. I knew from that
moment forward no one would know me. No one would know my backstory or the grief-stricken family I'd left behind. My village would mean
nothing to anyone during my days of travel. There was no sad house in
their memory, or Green Chair, or old red quilt. Although there might be

dead people moving like shadow figures through their lives, they would not be the ghosts of my mother, who died a year earlier, or my son.

Nobody knows me. Don't cry. Don't think about Jack. Don't cry, don't cry, don't cry. These would be my mantras for the next two weeks.

As I sat on the thirteen-hour flight from New York to Santiago, Chile, I remarkably thought about what lay ahead and not about what I was leaving behind. I pulled out a guidebook to the birds of the Falkland Islands, which I studied for a while. I had always found that watching birds brought a measure of peacefulness to my mind. I also brought along *The Voyages of the Penelope*, an account by Roberto Herrscher, at one time a teenaged Argentine conscript who spent months during the 1982 war on a sailboat named the *Penelope* confiscated from a Falkland Islander. The *Penelope*'s job was to deliver cans of petrol to Argentine troops who were scattered around the islands. Herrscher was by 2012 a well-known journalist living in Barcelona, and I was fortunate to meet Roberto—a short, red-headed, blue-eyed Argentine—when I attended a talk at Ithaca College about his book and the Falklands War while I was planning the trip. He gave me his copy—which had been translated from Spanish into English by a Falkland Islander—because I was unable to find a copy anywhere in the United States. I asked Roberto for a list of people he thought I should meet, which I then tucked between the pages of his book, which I leafed through as the plane cruised above the Caribbean Sea.

As I settled into the trip, I carefully went through the motions of how I thought a sane journalist would approach the assignment. I would eventually land in Stanley, the capital city, armed with the bird guidebook, my Argentine account of the war, and Roberto's list. I had also done enough reading to know the basics: that the archipelago lay three hundred miles off the tip of Argentina in the frigid waters of the South Atlantic. Three thousand people lived in the Falklands, most of them in Stanley. The rest share the islands with about ten thousand sheep and millions of birds. It was a desolate place, and appealingly so.

I had to stay overnight in Santiago before catching a morning flight to the Falklands. At 4:30 in the morning I was awakened by a violent shaking and the sound of deep rumbling. At first I thought the building under construction next to my hotel was collapsing, but within seconds I knew it was an earthquake. And I did exactly what you're not supposed to do. I sprang to look out of my fourteenth-story window and watched the workmen run out of the construction site across the way yelling to one another as the partially completed building continued to sway. I felt giddy and reckless at experiencing what I soon found out was a quake registering 7.1 on the Richter scale. Here was something completely outside human control and I was in the middle of it. I had felt out of control for so many weeks that to have something even greater than my own grief grab me and shake me, along with everyone else in the city, made me feel very much alive.

Later that day, when I landed in Stanley, the Argentines were once again making noises about trying to reclaim the Falklands, which they called Las Malvinas and considered their territory. In some ways it was difficult to accept their argument because the islands have been populated since the early nineteenth century by descendants of English sailors and Scottish sheep farmers, and when you're there, it feels more British than many places in Britain. *Maybe I'll get stuck here*, I thought as the rhetoric of the Argentine media heated up. Maybe there will even be another so-called war. *I could even live here*, I decided: flags are flying, teatime is sacred, and the barkeeps know how to draw a good pint.

Thirty years ago, when Argentine forces invaded the islands on April 2, 1982, they believed they were there to liberate the islanders from the clutches of Great Britain. Things had gone to hell in Argentina, and by opting for military action, the junta-controlled government led by General Leopoldo Galtieri hoped to mobilize the long-standing patriotic feelings of Argentines toward the islands. This was a thinly veiled effort to divert public attention from the country's chronic economic problems and rampant human rights violations.

This move and its justification shocked the Falkland Islanders, who didn't know they were being oppressed by the British and had no interest in being liberated. Ten weeks later the Argentines left the islands in defeat after being thumped by British forces dispatched by Prime Minister Margaret Thatcher. Although short in duration, the war was brutal, and among the fatalities were 649 Argentines, 255 British service members, and three civilians. Stanley was occupied for the duration. I never even considered the harsh reality of a war when I was naïvely wishing it upon the islands.

"Why do you want to go there?" one of my sisters asked before I left. "And why aren't you scared?" I knew that last question was really a statement about how she felt. She was scared, but not of a possible war—she was mostly afraid that I wouldn't return; that I would find a way to stay there. I tried to explain this was something I had to do for myself and that the political rhetoric coming out of Argentina as early as January made it more likely that I'd find a good story. I couldn't share with her that for me it was about getting to someplace wholly unfamiliar. I knew the landscape of home. The Falklands were a complete mystery to me and I didn't know what was going to happen and, frankly, I didn't care.

I traveled around those islands—island hopping they call it—in a little red prop plane that could transport about eight or nine people at a time. It landed on rocky pastures and the slopes of hillsides where there was always someone in a Land Rover waiting to meet those getting off the plane. Most of the tourists to the Falklands come by small cruise ship and disembark for four hours or so to look at some penguins and sea lions and then go on their way, so I felt like I was doing something special. By the end of my week, I had gotten to know the people like me, the ones who had come for the week, because our paths crossed again and again—on the little red plane, in guesthouses, and walking through Stanley. One day, while a fellow traveler Pietro and I were having a pint in a pub in Stanley, he asked me how many children I had, and I burst into tears. I didn't know how to answer his question.

I visited several islands, including Bleaker, Carcass, Sea Lion, and Saunders, and spent most of my time walking. It was March and the tourist season had just ended as the Falklands headed into autumn. The weather was cool—like our autumns in upstate New York—and often brisk because of the omnipresent ocean breezes. I kept mostly to myself. I woke before dawn to be outside as the sun pushed up out of the ocean and lit the rocks and the cliffs and the fields with a brief golden glow before establishing itself in the sky. I followed narrow sheep paths through the diddle-dee (the Falkland Islands version of heather) and the short grasses. I waded through and got lost in great clumps of soft tussac grass that grows to be eight feet tall, taking comfort in the green sea that surrounded me and held me close. I watched penguins, albatrosses, and endangered striated caracaras. I saw black-necked swans and flightless steamer ducks.

I was chased by skuas, huge predatory birds that didn't want me in their territory. I spied elephant seals and sea lions basking on rocks at the edge of the crashing sea. The animals were so different from what I was used to, yet the landscape was familiar. Some would describe it as bleak and barren—there are no trees—and many would find it featureless. But to me it was reminiscent of the Outer Hebrides with a bit of central Wyoming thrown in—two places I had spent some time in and had grown to love over the years.

Sometimes, as I wandered, I would think about my mother—it was safe to think about her in this landscape because she would have hated it. Where I saw undulating grasses and seabirds lifting from ledges on cliffs, she would have seen nothing. Without trees she would not have felt anchored to the earth. Her death was expected but her absence was crushing and filled me with sadness. Jack's death just a year later was shocking and cruel. He sometimes crept into the edges of my thoughts, although I tried hard to keep him out. Jack's memory and that of my mother were, no matter how they complemented each other, so different. I pushed against the memory of his sweet singing voice and his ever-present whistle, afraid that once he wedged himself into my consciousness, I would never be able to shake him loose.

On Sea Lion Island was a lone grave—a solitary headstone surrounded by a low white picket fence, put there, I presume, to keep out the sheep. The owner of the guesthouse told me it was the grave of a German man who came to this island in the late nineteenth century and was driven insane by the isolation. At the extremity of his instability, he killed himself. Then the owner prattled on about how the German couldn't be taken to Stanley and buried in the churchyard because he had committed suicide. I felt sick and I'm sure all the color drained from my face as she was telling me this. I tried to make myself think about other things—the birds flying overhead, the waves crashing against the rocks, the tussac grasses swaying in the relentless wind, the sound of a penguin braying. I took several pictures of the grave on the tiny island but could not make myself walk right up to the low fence to look at the headstone. I thought that if I didn't know his name, maybe his suicide never really happened.

Driving across the big island that holds Stanley, on a road that alternates between rutted two-track dirt and compacted gravel, I found the landscape looked more dramatic. Rivers of rocks—they call them stone runs—spill down the sides of small mountains with jagged quartzite peaks. It looks primordial, like the earth is readjusting herself. Then I saw them. The minefields. Miles and miles of land fenced off with barbed wire. White signs bordered in red with black skulls on them and the word "MINE" written underneath were posted every hundred yards or so. The Argentines placed tens of thousands of land mines around Stanley in 1982 and in their panic to defend the land they had just seized, they didn't keep maps of where they put them.

This is what the Falkland Islanders live with. Beaches adults used to play on when they were children are off limits because you would have to traipse through a minefield to get there. Walking to the hills around Stanley is dangerous unless you take the one road out of town that's cleared of ordnance (though flanked by the marked minefields). For a visitor, it was a shocking reminder of the mayhem and fear created by even the smallest of wars, and I found myself taking pictures of the minefield signs and rusting pieces of military equipment, like the big 105 mm artillery guns used by the Argentines against the British which I stumbled across on some of the remote ridges. To the residents, the scars, materiel, and unending dangers of wars just are. They are artifacts of their recent past and part of who they are. Much like, I realized, the photographs of Jack around the house. My own personal minefields.

One morning Patrick Watts, my guide for the day, collected me from Bennett House, my B&B in Stanley, and drove me out of town, past Government House and the site of the old barracks, the first two places attacked by the Argentines when they invaded thirty years ago. I was reminded as we drove out of town that the more I got to know Stanley—and the Falkland Islands—the more I was convinced that I was in pre-Beatles Britain. People don't lock their doors, and everyone here flies the island's flag—a Union Jack in one corner and the coat of arms of the islands placed next to it on a field of blue—from their cars and lapels.

I had asked for a tour of Mount Longdon, a 172-foot-tall ridge within view of the capital city and the site of the bloodiest battle of the Falklands War. We drove out of town on a paved road, which disintegrated into gravel, then headed overland around peat beds and through patches of diddle-dee. Up we went, climbing the side of a hill and parking on Wireless Ridge. Patrick—a tall, lanky man with a hawk-like nose and close-cropped gray hair—was wound tight and walked at a brisk pace.

It was a cool, blustery day on the ridge, and we walked over to the almost vertical slabs of quartzite where Argentinian soldiers holed up for two months during the particularly nasty and cold winter of 1982. We looked at an abandoned 105 mm artillery gun, rusting on the ridge, which had once been able to take out targets on the side of the mountain across the valley. The Argentine soldiers would find spaces between the slabs of rock and then build up another side with boulders to provide a three-sided shelter. And there they stayed—cold and hungry—waiting for something to happen.

We headed to the adjacent ridge—Mount Longdon—and parked at the base of the hill. The wind had picked up, and when I opened the door of the Land Rover, it nearly blew off. As we walked up the side of the ridge, Patrick took me through the battle, blow by blow. Britain's 3 PARA (the Third Battalion of the army's Parachute Regiment) attacked an entrenched Argentine B Company on the night of June 11, and fierce fighting raged for about twelve hours. Crosses were placed where each British soldier fell, many adorned that day with red poppy wreaths and messages. A curious Falkland thrush, a pretty soft brown bird the size of our robin, followed us up the hill, flying from rock to rock. Patrick pointed out Argentine positions, as the thrush kept pace, many still very visible and scarred from grenade and phosphorus attacks. In "the bowl," an Argentine stronghold on the mountain, about a dozen foot-high white crosses were clumped together. Patrick said they had been placed where Argentines had been killed, but that young fellas from town would come up occasionally and rip them out.

Patrick has been up the ridge hundreds of times and has taken veterans from both sides onto Mount Longdon, trying to piece together the elements of the chaotic battle. We wandered over every inch of the mountain, jumping into Argentine shelters and pulling out bits and pieces of wire and tarp, fabric and canteens. I stood at another 105 mm gun and tried to imagine manning that gun as I looked across the valley. Rivers of stone ran down the side of the mountain, leftovers of a previous ice age. Gray skies were breaking up and, as I stood at the rusty gun looking at Stanley in the distance, I got a chill realizing I was standing on the bloodiest battle site of the war. Many here resorted to hand-to-hand combat as the final Argentine positions collapsed.

By the end of the battle, twenty-three Brits had been killed and forty-seven wounded on Mount Longdon. Thirty-one Argentines were killed on the slopes; 120 were wounded; fifty were captured. Several days after the battle, Patrick, who then ran the radio station in town, was asked to come up to the foot of the mountain to witness the mass burial of the fallen Argentine soldiers in several large graves.

"Words were said, taps were played—it was done properly," he said. These bodies were later moved to the Argentine cemetery in the little settlement of Darwin on the island of East Falkland.

The thirtieth anniversary was bittersweet for people like Patrick Watts, who lived in occupied Stanley during the conflict and who, since the war, has spent many years trying to make sense of what happened on these islands. The violent past can be as remote as the South Atlantic. Or, for me, as close as my son's bedroom.

Every person I talked to who was old enough to have memories of the war eventually told me where they were and what they were doing thirty years earlier. I found John Fowler, the man who translated Roberto Herrsher's book into English, in the *Penguin News* office in Stanley, where he served as part-time editor of the weekly newspaper. He took me to lunch at the only real restaurant in Stanley and, as we ate and drank beer, he told me about his experiences during the war.

Fowler was then superintendent of education, and most of the children in the Falklands came into Stanley for public boarding school. After the Argentines invaded and occupied Stanley, he put together a convoy of Land Rovers to get those children to ferries and back to the relative safety of their homes. His story—like the stories of the three hundred residents who decided to stay in occupied Stanley—was about obsession with fortifying their homes against bombings and dealing with the Argentine authorities. It seemed as if every day brought a new edict by the occupiers, like insisting that Spanish was now the official language, although few of the Falkland Islanders spoke it. Or when they tried to make the islanders drive on the other side of the road like they did in Argentina, which was abandoned after one week of pure chaos. To Fowler, this feeling of being trapped in an absurdist play was exacerbated by long periods of boredom broken only by sporadic radio coverage and the handful of VHS tapes that were surreptitiously circulating through the community.

The only Falkland Islanders, almost all loyal Brits, killed in the weeks of that war were slain by a British shell, fired from across the harbor, which fell short of its target. It ripped through Fowler's house, killing three women and injuring others, including Fowler. He still has a piece of shrapnel in his leg, his own intimate memento of war. As he was telling me about the day the bomb dropped—in an almost dispassionate way—I realized I was looking at someone who has lived with grinding guilt. He had not been able to keep safe the people who had come to his house for protection. I stared at him as he told the story—a story that clearly had become a set piece for him—for it was now evident I was immersed in a community that was suffering from collective PTSD. Running away from the scene of my own trauma—my own home where I had not been able to keep my son safe—I had stumbled into a place that had been trauma- tized for thirty years and where every home was a relic of war. With the anniversary of the war noted in the national and international press and the heated rhetoric coming from the president of Argentina, some of them were stepping right back into the place they thought—they hoped—they had left long ago.

As we ordered our second round of pints, Fowler told me that on June 14, 1982, when the British troops invaded Stanley, "everyone was absolutely knackered, worn-out, drained, and inadequate to welcome troops. They were weary, with blackened faces and filthy. At one point when two hundred Marines came down the road," he said, "I was the only one there, limping past. I gave a little wave. During the final two or three days of the occupation the electricity and water supplies were damaged. We had had a long period of snow and freezing temperatures and thousands of feet had compressed the slush on the roads into ice, and there was so much filth and abandoned stuff everywhere. We were walking on abandoned ammunition. Twenty-four hours before and for forty-eight hours after the British came to Stanley all the rules broke down and there was chaos. There was looting." He paused then added, "I didn't know if the world would ever be the same."

I kept my head down as I transcribed what he was telling me. When he got to his last line—*I didn't know if the world would ever be the same*—I looked up at John and saw in his face that for him the world never was the same after the war. He carried the weight of that war and of those women's deaths with him wherever he was.

And I knew then I was looking into a mirror. I realized that we dragged our world—the land of regret—with us and, like Fowler, no matter where I went in my attempt to elude the ghosts of my past, they would forever be my traveling companions.

Adirondack Anniversary

My husband and I managed to go to Garnet Hill Lodge in the Adirondacks for several days on our twenty-first wedding anniversary. We drove into the Adirondack Park, a place our family has for decades loved as a vacation spot, and wound through deep pine forests and past blue lakes. It was the beginning of August, and each village was packed with visitors buying supplies for their stay or looking for the nearest ice cream stand. We headed up a narrow paved road, then up and up a narrower dirt road until we found the lodge sitting on a hilltop with a spectacular view of a sliver of Thirteenth Lake and the mountains behind. Kind of a funky old place—a year-round hotel with lots of cross-country skiing trails cut through the surrounding forest. That's something I love about the Adirondacks—the mixed forests of eastern white pines and delicate yellow and paper birches (which always look like they're about to snap in two), and then the hardwoods like maple, ash, and oak trees. The summer canopy has varying shades of green and leaves of different sizes that let the sun and rain filter down to the leaf-littered ground.

As solitary travelers who sometimes travel together, we have a way of being together that can be like toddlers engaged in parallel play. Tim and I both brought small stacks of books and were content to sit in Adirondack chairs on the lawn and read, read, read. I felt that we both visibly relaxed while on our break. Some of the sorrow drained from us and washed downhill toward Thirteenth Lake.

We have now been married longer than either set of our parents were married to each other. We are growing old together. I've watched Tim's hair turn white and thin. He's watched my hair grow gray. We've gained weight, gotten wrinkles, acquired aches and pains, and have stashed pairs of reading glasses around the house. We've had a very good marriage, probably because we both travel so much, and rarely venture out with each other. We've each been to Iceland three times but never at the same time. Tim travels for work—he's the editor of *Living Bird* magazine at Cornell's Lab of Ornithology and writes about conservation efforts that take place around the world. One of us almost always stays home because the kids and animals need to be taken care of. Our tag team travel means we have time to think about and miss the other person. The parent at home takes on the role of making sure the children get to school or soccer or music or play rehearsals. Makes sure they have the food they want to eat stocked on the shelves. (Clara once accused us of not having any food in the house—just ingredients.) Makes sure they are safe and sound and relatively happy. One thing we didn't know how to do after twenty-one good years was to be alone together.

In an Adirondack chair on the lawn overlooking Thirteenth Lake, I spent most of the day trying to figure out how I felt. It was like holding a needle between my fingers that I periodically poked into my thigh to see if it still hurt. Tim gave me a card and a couple of little presents. I gave him nothing. I was too invested in figuring out my feelings to think about his. Was I sad? Would I cry? Was I too distracted to read? Could I keep the sound of Jack singing out of my head? Me, me, me—what was I feeling?

Over the previous six months, since Jack's suicide, I had become so self-conscious. I felt that everyone was looking at me, trying to gauge where I was in my grief. If I sat on my front porch and read the paper, I knew that people in the cars driving past were looking at me. I knew that they knew. I was self-absorbed and unable to distance myself from those feelings. I knew I was becoming hermitlike and tried to make myself leave the comfort of the overstuffed Green Chair and walk out the front door and head down the street once a day but was not always successful. My only salvation was in getting away from Freeville—away from my home—and going someplace where no one knew my story or cared. I was convinced that I would get better only by leaving, and I spent a lot of time thinking about how to make that happen.

That day—that weird anniversary day marking the steady joy of my marriage and the violent shock of Jack's death—while sitting in an Adirondack chair on the hotel lawn I thought again of Coldplay's song "Fix You." That was a Jack song. He listened to it, he sang it, he performed it. Tears streamed down my face as I thought of it and him, and I sobbed because none of us had been able to fix him. I sobbed because he did not learn from his mistakes and perhaps neither had I.

The last night we were at Garnet Hill Lodge a family came to dinner, and after the meal, while the adults drank wine in the dining room, the two boys went outside and played on the rope swing that hung from an eastern white pine right outside our bedroom window. The boys were about seven and four, and the older one spent most of his time pushing the younger one on the swing. The younger boy would laugh and ask to be pushed higher; after a while, the swing came to a stop and the two boys fell into a conversation that revolved around bathroom humor. It sounded so familiar. In them I saw Jack and Clara. The younger boy's voice was eerily similar to Jack's voice at four—kind of loud and low, and a bit gravely and squeaky at the same time, particularly as he got more tired.

I stopped reading my book and lay in bed listening to the boys talk and kid around on the hotel lawn until well after dark. I finally closed my eyes and wallowed in the melancholy way their voices made me feel, wishing it would never end.

Clara and Jack Sing a Duet

It was the first full day of school for Gwen—her first day of eighth grade—and I was going to spend that fine early September day at home getting some writing done. I sat on the porch, with the dog Skeeter gnawing on a rawhide bone behind me, and proceeded to look at my emails and check my Facebook account, avoiding the work of writing. I saw on Facebook that Clara had posted a video of her and Jack singing at her high school graduation in June 2011. They performed Simon and Garfunkel's "*Old Friends*," and, as Clara wrote on her Facebook page, this was the best gift Jack could have given her.

I was not there that day in 2011. I was in Ireland at a writing conference. I had won a travel writing contest, and this was the prize. Although I knew I'd miss Clara's graduation, I thought this would be just the first of many ceremonies for her. She was headed to Cornell in the fall, and that seemed like a graduation I wouldn't miss. Plus, Jack's high school graduation was a year later. Plus, I was coming back from Ireland to pick up Clara so that we could head out to Germany to tour the country and watch some Women's World Cup soccer games. I was a good parent managing the necessary compromises of life.

In the year since that graduation, I had traveled a road gutted by potholes of regret, but I never intended to have Clara's graduation be one of them. I didn't particularly like these ceremonies. I always felt as if I were channeling Mrs. Bridge (from the Evan S. Connell novel) at these ceremonies—an awkward middle-aged woman who never knows how to act appropriately. I didn't dress properly, didn't know how to behave or feel in these formal and ceremonial settings, and was painfully aware that I might be embarrassing or disappointing my children by doing either too much or too little. I looked around me at families who were well put together—mothers who obviously didn't buy all of their clothes at Walmart or Target; mothers who got their hair done or at least cut on a regular basis; mothers who weren't overweight and who wore dresses or skirts; mothers who seemed to like wearing at least a dab of makeup; mothers who didn't seem most comfortable in hiking boots, black sneakers, or black Tevas. I wanted none of that to matter for me or my kids, but I knew it did.

Sometimes my children looked at me—particularly Jack and maybe Gwen—and I'd catch a glimpse of disappointment or embarrassment in their faces. I was now Joanne Woodward in the movie adaptation of the Connell novel *Mr. and Mrs. Bridge* when, playing Mrs. Bridge, she accompanies her son to the Eagle Scout ceremony, only she hasn't been told what is expected of her. She is an outsider in her own son's life, and he makes her painfully aware of that fact when he doesn't give her a kiss during the ceremony. I was Mrs. Bridge again and again and Jack was her son. That was made clear to me by Jack's exclusion of me from some important moments of his life. Times when he sang solos, was celebrated, went to parties that should have included family members, didn't invite boys over to our house, and preferred to spend his time at his friends' houses on the weekends. I always knew on some level that I was the awkward mother and that Jack was the embarrassed son, as seen through Connell's mind's eye, but I somehow believed that both of us would grow up and get beyond this stage. That we would learn from our mistakes and get out of the painfully humorous movie we were in.

We didn't.

Watching the video of my children singing was heart-wrenching. I wasn't there. Tim was, though, and he taped the performance. I did not hear them perform together. I did not see Clara sitting in her cheap white rayon graduation robe unzipped so she could play her guitar more easily or Jack in khakis and a blue Oxford shirt with the sleeves carefully rolled to just above the elbow. Siblings so completely comfortable sitting in a sweltering-hot packed gym performing for their classmates and family members. Their voices were oddly the same but yet very different. They were two musicians with a job to be done.

It had been seven months since Jack died, and he still didn't have a headstone.

Seeking Permission from Donald Hall

I am having a hard time again. I upped the dosage of my antidepressant from 20 to 40 mg about ten days ago because I was having such a tough time getting through the day. For about a week I didn't cry at all. And I was thinking that was a good thing. But I don't know if it is or it isn't. I am so tired of crying. It's exhausting to always be on the brink. I think I am getting better at controlling the crying in public, though.

This morning I sat down and read Donald Hall's *Life Work*. I read it in one sitting. He wrote this book in about three months in 1994 in the farmhouse where he lived and that had been in his family since the 1840s.

In *Life Work* he looked at what his family did for work over those years, from farming to running a dairy to delivering milk to doing office work to writing poetry. He looked at the men and the women who dwelled in that farmhouse and considered what work meant to them and to him. While writing the book, Hall was diagnosed with liver cancer and had one-third of his liver removed. He didn't know what his doctor's prognosis was, but he expected to die.

Hall didn't die and the book was reissued in 2005, a decade after the first printing. In the foreword he wrote for the 2005 edition, Hall revealed that his wife, poet Jane Kenyon, had died of leukemia the year after *Life Work* was published. He wrote that after her death he experienced six years of hard grief during which he was unable to work—to do the very thing that defined him.

Although I loved reading about the stalwart New England workers, the foreword spoke to me. I felt that Hall was giving me permission to be consumed by grief. I realize I am always seeking permission from various sources—relatives, friends, strangers, and now, Donald Hall—to be grief-stricken. Maybe what I do is not expressly seeking permission from others; I am looking inward to grant myself permission to be grief-stricken. I don't want to see people. I don't want to be brave. I don't want to have to think about anyone else. Hall gave himself the freedom to fall down and be consumed by grief. Today that seems to me to be a great gift.

It's just not fair. Why did Jack do this? Why did he plunge me into this hell that I don't know if I will ever be able to climb out of?

THE GREEN CHAIR

THOUGHTS

Guns in the Attic

We still have guns in the attic. We also have all of Jack's belongings in the attic, which are stored under a large blue tarp. The guns and Jack's stuff share space in a beautiful unfinished attic with chestnut beams and dormer windows providing four views of the village below. Although I know why Jack's things are in the attic, I don't know why the guns are still there. On the rare occasion I even recognize the fact of their existence, I then think it wouldn't have mattered if Jack had a gun or not, so the gun itself turns into something unimportant to me. Even as I write down that sentence, it strikes me as crazy.

I don't want to go into the attic and look through Jack's things, although as I write this he's been dead almost four years. I might be able to discover clues about why he decided to kill himself. About why he chose to use a gun. About why he was the way he was. But it still feels like prying. And although I'll find the sad remnants of the sum total of a seventeen-year-old boy's life under a blue tarp, at this moment I'm not sure that picking up every piece of paper and scrutinizing Jack's scrinched lefty handwriting will give me any clues to what I've come to believe was an impulsive act. But then I think about the gun and the fact that he had to buy or find shotgun shells. That moment, a little after 8:00 on a Monday evening, was the impulsive act. But the plan was in place before that moment.

Deer hunting season started today, which means for the next three weeks I won't be taking morning walks along the trail through the swamp that lies behind our house. The sounds of shots come early, at the crack of dawn when light is creeping over the horizon and begins to shine between the trees, and animals and humans start to stir. Although close to Ithaca and Cornell, Freeville is far away in many respects. This is rural central New York, which celebrates deer hunting. When I was a kid, and hunting season started on a weekday, students who went hunting on opening day were excused from school. And there have always been hunters' breakfast specials where diners and firehouses open their doors at 5:00 a.m. to serve stacks of pancakes, bacon, eggs, sausage, and coffee to anyone getting ready for a day in a tree stand. These hunters' breakfasts are also a treat for the insomniacs who populate every village and town and are looking for something to do before dawn.

During deer hunting season the deer act crazy—like animals that are running for their lives. They're easily spooked and run across roads and through yards, wild-eyed and panicky looking. Seeing them in such an agitated state makes me feel sick. During other times of the year, we bitch and moan about there being so many whitetail deer in our area that you can't grow a garden without an eight-foot-high deer fence surrounding it. And conversations in local nurseries often begin with *What kind of perennials won't the deer eat?* But during hunting season most of us put our heads down out of guilt at the knowledge that we want these animals dead. We try not to make eye contact with the freaked-out deer that careen and crash through the brown-upon-brown autumn landscape. We have homeowners and gardeners who want the herds culled but lack the stomach for the shooting and killing.

I do not come from a family of hunters. I do, however, have a thick red wool coat—made by Abercrombie & Fitch in about 1920—that my grandfather called his hunting jacket. And we do have a double-barreled shotgun made by Ithaca Gun that was cut down to accommodate my grandfather's small stature, so I guess, on the basis of that evidence, he might have hunted ducks at one time. That was literally a hundred years ago and not within my memory.

When I married Tim, he brought oiled and cleaned guns—working guns—to the marriage. I never paid much attention to what they were or where they were because they were out of sight. The guns were, I believe, somewhere in the attic with my grandfather's Ithaca Gun shotgun and were not stored with shotgun shells anywhere nearby.

Tim was and is a hunter. Even though he owns guns, he spent the first two decades of our marriage hunting with falcons. This was not like the deer hunters I grew up with. He did not wear camouflage and blaze orange when out in the field. Rather, he dressed like an English gentleman with his oiled Barbour coat, tweed cap, and green wellies. When he was out in the field with his bird, he had a whistle around his neck and a falcon on his gloved fist. And while the familiar deer hunters looked like they'd stepped from the pages of *Field & Stream*, Tim looked as if he'd stepped from the pages of *Gray's Sporting Journal*, which covers sports like falconry, fox hunting, beagling, and fly-fishing. He's originally from England and when he goes back there to visit falconers, he fits right in.

The falcons were also housed in the attic of our big pink Victorian house. At one point we had three falcons—a kestrel, a merlin, and a peregrine—and each of them lived in an enclosure built around an attic dormer window. There were times when one of the falcons would begin calling and the others would join in and our house sounded like the set of a National Geographic nature program. I would venture a guess that none of my kids had friends who were taught how to feed falcons dead day-old chicks and pieces of quail.

I never thought about the guns for those decades because I was enthralled with the world of falconry. It seemed to me to be a terribly noble sport. I disassociated it from hunting—forgetting that the point of flying a bird of prey was to hunt—until Tim would come back from the field with a wild duck caught by his peregrine Macduff in his game bag. For about a decade, each Thanksgiving dinner would begin with barded strips of extremely lean dark duck meat from birds caught by Macduff. I spent many days in the field with Tim and Macduff, and watched as the falcon flew high above Tim's head waiting for Tim, the falcon's hunting partner, to flush game. For the falconer that meant trying to get ducks to rise from a pond, which they were reluctant to do when they saw the falcon flying above them. Then, if all went according to the falconer's plan, at least one duck, slightly panicked by Tim beating the tall grasses and lured by open sky, would take its chances. This is what the peregrine is waiting for. Macduff would take aim at that duck, tuck his wings to his sides, then plummet toward earth with the speed of a meteorite. It always looked like a fair fight and, unfortunately, at that moment often the earworm Disney tune from *The Lion King* about the circle of life ran through my head. Maybe that's how I explained hunting to the kids. I don't remember. The peregrine would then either connect with that duck and inevitably kill it, or it wouldn't. On most days, the odds were in favor of the duck getting away.

After Macduff died at the age of fourteen, Tim started going gun hunting for game birds with a friend from Ithaca. They'd take their shotguns and their dogs—Tim took Skeeter, our English springer spaniel—and would head to the edges of the forest and follow the dogs through the brushy, scrubby fields where ruffed grouse, pheasant, and woodcock liked to hide. Tim never came back with much in his game bag, but Skeeter would bound into the house with his fur matted with burdocks and prickers, and a goofy dog smile on his liver-and-white dog face. As with falconry, in this contest of bird versus gun, many birds lived to fly another day.

I believe the act of hunting for Tim was much more about thrusting himself into nature than about killing something. It was also about sharing time in the field in partnership with an animal—in this case, Skeeter. I think he loves to read nature's signs by taking note of the vagaries of the weather and of the wind, and understanding the habitat most preferred by his prey. He reads the sky, scanning for soaring raptors, and hears the songs of birds that he can identify by ear. Perhaps it's similar to me taking my morning swamp walks, although I don't carry a falcon on my fist or a shotgun—barrel broken open—draped over my arm. I always try to notice who's there and who's not—different species of duck, geese, heron, and woodpeckers. And last summer I watched as the young green heron and the family of Cooper's hawks learned to fly and hunt within the confines of the swamp. These are the experiences and stories I return with from the field.

This, you see, was the culture of our family and our particular relationship to hunting. Shooting the gun is almost beside the point. The gun, the dog, and the falcon were ways to get close to nature.

Maybe this essay isn't about hunting at all but is really about the attic and what still lies hidden in a corner behind a disused falcon's enclosure. Or maybe it's about what you don't know and can't imagine as a parent, and your complicity in a tragic event. Or maybe it's about what you know and what you don't know and asking yourself the question that others are surely asking about you—*Didn't you know that having guns in the house is dangerous?*

Our family's story will be forever seen as a cautionary tale. By having guns in our house, we unwittingly provided the tools that led to our own son's death. It never occurred to Tim or to me that our teenaged son Jack might root through the attic and uncover an old single-shot shotgun Tim hadn't used since he was a boy. That Jack would then purchase or obtain shotgun shells for the gun. That he would hide the gun in his room with the shotgun shells. That he would shoot himself with the gun when his teenage-boy brain was not processing thoughts rationally because of drugs and hormones. That he would shoot himself because he was mad at his girlfriend and us and the school that had sent him to the emergency room earlier that day. That he would shoot himself to teach us all a lesson. I can almost hear him say, *I'll make them regret the day they didn't pay attention to me.*

Maybe Jack believed we had provided both the motive and the means of his destruction. Should I have put more emphasis on the gun? Maybe I should have acted like Rhett Butler in *Gone With the Wind*, who shot Bonnie Blue's pony after she fell off its back and broke her neck. He shot that pony because he himself had provided the means of his daughter's destruction by buying her the pony. His guilt required a sacrifice. Maybe I should find my grandfather's double-barreled shotgun and throw it in a fire or bury it in the backyard or run over it with my car. Maybe symbolic destruction of the kind of object that led to Jack's demise will bring me some peace.

But I don't think it will. Jack chose to kill Jack, and his choice of his father's shotgun was the ultimate *fuck you* to his parents.

I try so very hard not to accept the blame that he surely heaped upon us for his death. My failure, I believe, doesn't have to do with having guns in the attic. My failure is in not knowing death was even a possibility. Phrases like *ignorance is no excuse* run through my head as I repeatedly ask the question *why, why, why?* The answer, unfortunately, may be as simple as because he wanted to and because he could.

The People Who Stayed

Today we took a Sunday drive to Skaneateles, a village about thirty-five miles away that sits on the northern end of one of the smaller Finger Lakes. I suggested we do this last night as the Labor Day weekend stretched out before us with few plans to interrupt the quietness of the Pink House. Gwen, Tim, and I headed out of the village around 11:00 a.m. I had asked Railey to join us, but she had other plans, and Clara was in Washington, DC, with the Cornell women's soccer team. So, it was just the three of us.

As we headed out of Freeville and entered the countryside of fields of corn and buckwheat and soybeans punctuated by large red barns and Greek Revival farmhouses, I thought, *What a beautiful part of the country we live in.* Sure, some of the farmhouses have been covered with vinyl siding, and there are far fewer barns than I remember as a child, but if you're willing to squint your eyes and forgive barnyards filled with rusting farm machinery and the occasional trailer, then you can concentrate on the geography itself, which is strongly determined by the glaciers that once overlay this area. Rounded hills squashed together, ponds, roadcuts revealing layers of gray limestone and shale, and open fields dipping down to long narrow lakes all pointed on a north-south axis. This is the landscape of home.

The sky was a dark blue with small, very puffy white clouds painted with wisps of gray. As we approached Skaneateles Lake, I could see that the color of the water reflected the sky's deep blue. The largely hardwood hedgerows and forests had lost their summer greens and had faded as if they knew they were headed into their moment of glory and were saving up their energies for the bursts of red, orange, and yellow. What must it be like to be a tree? To know that your leaves are expressions of pure energy and work like little factories to absorb light, and as the days grow shorter and the light weaker, your leaves are done. The abscission layer develops at the end of the stalk, starving the leaf of nutrients and breaking down the chlorophyll, which usually masks the carotenes and anthocyanins. Now it's their turn to shine as they create the color. Once the leaves drop, all that energy stays within the trunk, nurturing it until the light gets stronger and the days grow longer, and the cycle can begin again.

I want that kind of cyclical energy. If I could, I'd gladly lose my appendages as adversity closes in. Then I would hold close and tightly guard only those feelings that will help me endure my time of weak light, my time of darkness.

Or am I like the leaf itself that will be cut off from the branch by an encroaching membrane that creates the abscission layer? Will I gradually fade then drop away to create a nourishing decaying layer of humus that will eventually nourish someone else? Or am I the trunk of the tree jealously storing my nutrients until I can grow strong again and push through this darkness, which envelops me daily? The landscape of central New York, my home, provokes such thoughts.

We often took Sunday drives when I was a kid. It was the only time during the week when my family was all together. My father was working construction jobs, which ran for six days a week. Later, when we moved from Ludlowville to Freeville, he worked construction as he also tried to run a little farm. It was nonstop labor—something always needed fixing, milking, or planting. We took one family vacation to Maine during that period, and I don't even know how we pulled that off. What I do know is that I was sulking most of the time because I was thirteen, didn't want to go, and was determined to let my parents know they couldn't make me like it. Two things I distinctly remember is my mother getting out of the car somewhere in Massachusetts and peering into the windows of John Greenleaf Whittier's house, and then me somewhere in Maine, standing on a large rock next to the ocean wearing my paisley Nehru jacket—shoulder-length blond hair being whipped by the stiff breeze off the early autumn Atlantic Ocean—contemplating my extreme angst.

No matter the responsibilities that kept us grounded in Freeville, without fail, our family did take that Sunday drive. We'd pile into the car, kids squished into the back seat, bouncing up and down as we flew over gravelly washboard roads that connected the villages of central New York. My mother and father sat in the front smoking cigarettes and talking. As kids, we knew it wasn't about the destination—it was about the drive itself—and we tried to make it as much fun as possible for ourselves. It was probably the only time my parents ever talked meaningfully to each other because they were trapped in close proximity in that heavy American-made Buick. I have no idea what they talked about, though.

When Tim, Gwen, and I headed out to Skaneateles that morning, I thought it was about the destination—something to do, someplace to go with the promise of a nice lunch at the other end—but it also turned out to be about the journey. As we drove on the country road above the east side of Skaneateles Lake, we passed the boyhood home of John D. Rockefeller, and I knew if we took the other route back, via the village of Moravia, we'd pass within a stone's throw of the boyhood home of Millard Fillmore. I don't know why these accidents of history and geography struck me that day, as I've passed by these two places dozens of times, but for some reason, they did. Fillmore became the thirteenth president of the United States and is known for the Missouri Compromise and the Fugitive Slave Act of 1850 and is generally ranked among the bottom five presidents in any kind of poll. Rockefeller became the filthy-rich robber baron, founder of Standard Oil, and by all accounts the richest man in the world at the time. His father was a philandering ne'er-do-well bigamist who taught his sons to "always trade dishes for platters."

What was it about this part of central New York that nourished these two men who rose to prominence on the national stage in the nineteenth century? And if you go about ten miles farther west from the village of Skaneateles, you'll find the boyhood home of Brigham Young, and twenty miles beyond that is the childhood home of John Smith, founder of the Church of Jesus Christ of Latter-day Saints. Historian Whitney Cross called this part of New York State the Burned-over District—a part of the state that burned bright with religious enthusiasms and kind of out-there nineteenth-century thinking, including spiritualism, phrenology, and communal societies.

Years ago, I took a drive alone to Skaneateles. It was also an autumnal day, maybe in late September, so the drying corn stalks were just beginning to rustle in the wind, and the tops of the sumacs were starting their showy blaze of red. I checked for birds along the drive but didn't see much beyond starlings, Canada geese, and some mallards sitting on a pond. The village of Skaneateles features a long pier extending from a sweet little park with a bandstand. The pier is used by fishermen and people wanting to get a better look at the lake and at the homes lining the lakeshore to the southeast and southwest.

I walked along the pier and saw a young man standing at the end. He was holding a fishing pole, and his line was in the water. He was watching the line, and I didn't want to bother him, so I stood, iPhone camera in hand, and faced the other direction to watch two small sailboats tack back and forth across the lake. They were going at a good clip, cutting through the choppy blue water, their white triangular sails leading the boats at thirty-degree angles. The leaves of the sugar maples that covered the low hills defining the edges of the lake were beginning to shimmer gold and red and orange, and the sky that day was a brilliant blue. It was one of those glorious autumn days in upstate New York—the kind of halcyon day travel magazines tout to visitors as if these were the only kinds of days we locals ever see.

An older man in a black tracksuit and polar fleece jacket walked up to me and asked if I'd taken any pictures of Teddy Roosevelt's summer house. "Where is it?" I asked. He pointed to the huge Greek Revival house with a massive pediment supported by four large pillars—it's a couple of hundred yards down the west side of the lake and sits on the crest of the hill with a sweeping lawn that comes right down to the water.

I stared at the house and couldn't believe I didn't know this fact. "When was he there?" I asked. The man told me this was his summer home during his presidency. "His first term as president or second?" I asked. I can be such a jerk sometimes. "Oh, I don't know that," he answered. "But this was his summer home. And over there"—he pointed to a modern house on the east side of the lake—"is where the Clintons stay when they come to town." I looked at the one-story rectilinear gray house, and my mind took in the almost two hundred years of architectural difference between the two places. *If this is progress,* I thought, *I don't really like it.* The man piped up, "They haven't been here lately because they're both so busy." *Uh, yeah,* I thought.

I got all excited because I couldn't believe I didn't know Teddy Roosevelt's summer home was basically in my central New York backyard. Then I started to think about it. I knew about Sagamore Hill and Oyster Bay. Why hadn't I heard about this? Because it turned out the guy was totally wrong. Roosevelt Hall—the name of the Greek Revival house—was owned by a cousin of both Teddy and Franklin Delano Roosevelt. Teddy came through Skaneateles twice on the train—may even have stepped off the train once—but that's it. FDR actually came to Roosevelt Hall to check on something for his cousin, who was out of town. But Franklin knew he was not well liked in this Republican stronghold of Onondaga County, so he didn't tarry.

Why do we have this need to believe that so-and-so slept here? I love that part of us, but I do wonder what's behind it. Is it because we are all storytellers, and if we invoke the name of a president or celebrity then the story will have more resonance? Or is it because we're a country of liars? I think it's the latter. Most of the time, we don't intentionally lie, but we see nothing wrong with either stretching the truth beyond the breaking point or passing on unverified information.

Little towns in my part of central New York love to perpetuate a good half-truth and trade on the gullibility of people. The Cardiff Giant—a ten-foot-tall figure carved out of a block of gypsum in the 1860s and passed off as a petrified man—came from this neck of the woods. Mark Twain spent his summers south of here in the city of Elmira. L. Frank Baum, who wrote the Oz books, was born down the road in Chittenango. These are all obvious examples of purveyors of tall tales, half-truths, and scams. But what I love are the examples of rumor turned half-truth turned truth—the mostly unintended slip from fact to fiction. This is what happened with the Teddy-Roosevelt-slept-here story. We want to believe stories like that. We love to mythologize our collective brushes with celebrity.

About twenty years ago, the then president of Taiwan was driven through our little village on his way from the Syracuse airport to Cornell. I got the kids, and we stood on the sidewalk with some of the other neighborhood kids and waved at the presidential motorcade as it blasted through Freeville. The next morning when I was standing at the bus stop with the kids, one of the neighbor boys was all excited because, as he put it, "I saw the president's car come through town yesterday!" I explained it had been the president of Taiwan, but he insisted it was the president of the United States.

This is how rumors turn into half-truths and then turn into truths. I'm sure in fifty years we'll be hearing about the day the American president came through Freeville and stayed at the local bed-and-breakfast.

This part of the state has also always embraced freethinkers, vagabonds, ne'er-do-wells, and anyone else who wanted to try to scratch out a living in the glacial till. I put my father's family squarely within that vortex of ambition. While my mother's side of the family has lived within a stone's throw of Freeville since my fifth-great-grandfather received a tract of land for his service in the Revolutionary War, my father's family arrived in central New York in the late 1920s. My grandfather—my father's father—came east to attend Cornell after studying at Deep Springs College in California. He and my grandmother very soon bought a dairy farm in Virgil, New York, about ten miles from where I sit in the Green Chair. It was the beginning of the Great Depression, and that little family eked out a living on the farm. My grandfather was involved in GLF— the Gulf League Federation—which worked like a dairy cooperative and was headquartered in Ithaca. He then started the Free Farmer Movement, which advocated farmers cut out the middleman entirely and sell directly to the consumer, and for those efforts he received death threats and mysterious deaths of cows on his farm. It wasn't a big step for the disillusioned advocate to turn his energies to something bigger—the John Birch Society—and after all their kids left home, he and my grandmother moved to California, where she had been born and where he could be closer to more John Birchers. Like central New Yorkers of almost a century earlier, my grandfather headed west when he became disgusted with the viewpoints and politics of his neighbors. Like Joseph Smith and his followers, my grandfather was searching for a place of like-minded individuals where he would not have to bend to the opinions and beliefs of those he disagreed with.

This is how my father grew up. Hearing his father go off on the government and railing against pinheads and suffering disappointments when he could not make others see his point of view. My father's parents were part of the movement of people who left.

So here we are on this autumnal day, remnants of my little family, driving through a landscape littered with the relics of dreamers and schemers. A landscape that is both my past and my present. A landscape filled, at the moment, with corn just beginning to brown at the edges, and ditches filled with goldenrod, purple loosestrife, chicory, and Queen Anne's lace. Pastures with black-and-white Holstein and soft brown Jersey cows eating the early autumn grass. Deep-blue fingers of lakes cutting through the rounded hills like blue veins that travel up the inside of your arm. Nineteenth-century villages full of Greek Revival houses and sad dilapidated grocery stores and drugstores and gas stations that manage to hang on.

What do the people who live in these villages do? Like me, many I'm sure come from generations who have never traveled more than ten miles from where the family first settled. We are not like Millard Fillmore, John D. Rockefeller, Brigham Young, John Smith, or even like my grandfather, who got fed up with central New York and went as far west as he could while remaining on the continent. We aren't even like my father, who left his family—my family—when I was a teenager and whom I found myself characterizing as a migrant farmer, address unknown, when filling out a financial aid form for college. I remember saying to the financial aid officer who wanted a legitimate address for him, "You can't get blood from a stone."

My little family are the people who stayed. We are the people who take Sunday drives through the landscape of our past and our present. And some of us, like the kid at the bus stop or the man on the pier, make up a good story from a half-truth. A Sunday drive is just a Sunday drive—we pile into the car and pull out of the driveway and leave home—but we always come back to what we know. We watch the seasons change through the windows of our car. We acknowledge the villages as we travel through them—Groton, Locke, Moravia, New Hope, Sempronius—and sometimes make stops to take photographs that reinforce the already iconic images in our memories. A photo taken each autumn of the same farm with the same blazing red, orange, and yellow maples surrounding it. A winter photo of the pier that juts into Skaneateles Lake during a snow squall. A photo of the field of sunflowers. These are the photos of the people who stayed. Photos that in the past would have been stuck into albums with dates scrawled across the bottom or on the back.

Because we are the people who stayed, our pasts and presents converge and can get confused. Some of us feel changes in the built or natural environment more keenly—the loss of a barn due to neglect or the prospect of hydraulic fracturing coming to this part of New York can make us take to our beds. *Why can't things stay the same?* we think. *Why can't we keep traveling through the landscape of our childhoods while jumping up and down on the Buick's floorboards, catching whiffs of cigarette smoke and snatches of conversation coming from the front seat?*

Sunday drives take you away—and while driving through the countryside, you can be wherever you want to be in your head—but eventually, as in my case, you head back home. That brings you back to the present. For me, it was back to the Pink House and the dog and the rescue parakeet. Back to making dinner and to thinking about what Monday morning might bring.

Back to the Green Chair and the red quilt and a world without Jack.

Train Robbers and Pinkertons

In 2014 I applied to Goucher College's MFA program in creative nonfiction. I chose Goucher's low-residency program because it was the only program at that time that dealt exclusively in nonfiction. My perception of MFA programs in other places was that the nonfiction track was tacked on and the real stars were the poets and then the novelists. I wanted the nonfiction writers to be the stars.

The two-year program had about twenty-five people in it, and we worked with five faculty members. We came together twice a year for ten consecutive days each time. Each semester we had a different faculty member, whom Goucher called mentors, to directly supervise our work. So over the course of the MFA program you had at least four different mentors, each of whom had their own way of approaching nonfiction. Between the in-person residencies, we had weekly meetings with our mentors and classmates.

The program took me out of my head and let me focus on something other than myself. Of course, I assumed my thesis would be about Jack, but my first mentor immediately disabused me of that notion. He was right. I was way too close to the event to write about it in any coherent way. So I had to choose a thesis topic before the end of the first semester. I decided it would be a historical subject so I could dwell in the world of archival research, where I felt comfortable. I was also determined to expand my thesis into a book, so I sought a topic worthy of tens of thousands of words, and which would spark a reader's imagination.

One afternoon I pulled up a history website and began to search by date. I chose 2016 as a possible publication date of a book and then looked backward fifty, seventy-five, one hundred, and 150 years from that year knowing that a book about an anniversary had a better chance of being published. I was familiar with all of the events listed on the website until I got to an 1866 entry: the world's first train robbery took place in Seymour, Indiana. That didn't make sense to me because I assumed that the world's first train robbery would have been decades before and would have taken place in England. Within fifteen minutes of jumping into the research rabbit hole I knew I had a subject about which little had been written, and I found myself intrigued.

I dove into the research, which took me to the online version of a dusty basement filled with archived newspapers. I followed the story of the Reno Gang, who lived in and around Seymour, through headlines in the local papers, smaller stories in Chicago papers, and even notices in the *New York Times*. I made research trips to Seymour and befriended a local historian who fed me reams of information.

When I was researching my book, I was not wallowing in despair. My brain shut out all other information that wasn't pertinent to trains, train robberies, counterfeiting, midwestern gangs, the Civil War, the Pinkerton Detective Agency, and the history of vigilantism in the United States. There was barely room for grief. I knew I was getting too intense when I felt compelled to write a whole chapter about the different railroad rail gauges in the mid-nineteenth century. I was happily obsessed. That chapter did not make it into the thesis or the book.

I think my family was relieved that I now had something concrete to occupy my mind and my time. My days were spent reading and writing, throwing myself into research. The thesis was written, the MFA was obtained, a contract for a book was signed, and the book was written and published. This all took place over three years during which I did not dwell on Jack to the exclusion of everything else. And I did not dwell on myself. I channeled the nervous, anxious, overwrought energy into the task at hand. I now had a legitimate reason to get into my car and drive away from the Pink House and the Green Chair.

Hope Is a Strange Invention

For years after Jack's death, I felt hopeless. It was exhausting to feel that way because it meant dragging myself through the days without any clear reason why. Hope gives you the reason why—it's about believing in a future. I could see no future in 2012 or 2013 or 2014 and even 2015. I embraced hopelessness. Even the tiniest tasks like getting out of bed and maybe taking a shower felt monumental. I didn't leave the house unless I was cajoled or shamed into it. I missed funerals of longtime Freeville residents because I couldn't face walking into that village church where I'd last sat for my son's memorial service. I made myself go to middle school concerts my youngest daughter, Gwen, participated in because I knew I had to, but I sat in the back row so I could leave and go sit in the car when I couldn't take the poignant sights and sounds of children singing.

If you're just trying to get through the day, you really can't muster the energy to read about hope and then figure out how to find some. It seems like a stupid endeavor. I knew that if I really wanted to locate hope, one option would be to sit in a church on a Sunday because someone was always talking about it. But in church the inevitable twinning of hope and faith to someone who has never had faith is an equation for despair—a setup for failure—because you're led to believe that you can't embrace one without the other. I think the equation for hope in a church might look something like Hope = Faith + Openness. Sundays I stayed home, too.

Thinking of hope in terms of a c = a + b equation is not novel. In the early 1990s, Charles R. Snyder at the University of Kansas in Lawrence developed what he called hope theory. His equation was Hope = Agency +

Pathways. A person with hope has the will and determination to achieve goals (agency), and the ability to see different strategies to reach those goals (pathways).

How does hope differ from optimism? As I sat in the Green Chair and thought these deep thoughts, I wondered if affecting a glimmer of optimism might lead me toward hope. To me, optimism meant smiling every now and then and lifting the veil of despair just enough to be able to see that there might be a future. It was Snyder's hope theory without half of the equation. You didn't have to fuss around with developing Snyder's pathways, plotting out how to get to hope. I kind of liked that. I imagined it would be like sitting in a boat without a sail and letting the waves push you inevitably toward Tahiti. I would optimistically believe I'd get there but wouldn't provide the means to make that happen.

Maybe hope is more basic. Maybe it can be boiled down to biological determinism: hope means always choosing the path to live. We see this with all organisms. Choosing not to live can happen only if hope is gone. To me biology is too basic and unsatisfying an explanation. Emotion and free will surely have some part in the hope equation. Perhaps pure hope occurs at the juncture of the two—the place where free will meets biology.

Would knowing about the variants of hope theory right after Jack's death have made me think about and embrace hope? Or would I then have concluded that hope is merely a human construct—or to use Emily Dickinson's words, "a strange invention"? If the latter, I could allow myself to disregard the theory and quit questing after hope. I knew then and now that I am more apt to be swayed by poetic words and beautiful sentences than theories. I was not going to be argued into anything.

My reading in the first year after Jack died was done with fury. I sought out books about suicide and death of other people's family members. Not prescriptive ones that ended with the author sitting in a circle of lost souls, but books where the authors took their time rolling around in their grief. My favorite during that period was *Wave* by Sonali Deraniyagala, a professor of economics at the University of London. Her husband, two young sons, and parents were lost in a devastating tsunami in Sri Lanka. She was the only one in her family group to survive. Deraniyagala spent the next several years out of her mind with grief. She drank, took pills, tried to cut her wrists, raved, and staked out and harassed the tenants who had moved into her dead parents' house. She wanted to die. I understood all of this. She did not go back to her home in England for over four years because time had stopped on the day they left for vacation. She couldn't face the objects of their everyday life: small boots lined up near the door, her sons' jackets, muddy cricket bats, theater tickets for a show they were never going to attend. I understood this as well. As I read *Wave*, I nodded in assent each time she demonstrated the depth of her devastation and hopelessness.

Donald Hall frequently wrote about the death of his wife, Jane Kenyon, and his grief. In his poem "Kill the Day," he wrote:

In the second year, into the third and fourth years,
she died again and again, she died by receding
while he recited each day the stanzas of her dying:
He watched her chest go still; he closed her eyes.
Without birthdays, she remained her age at death.
The figurine broke that clutched its fists as she did dying . . .

And in "Midwinter Letter" my heart broke again as Hall ran through a litany of objects that belonged to Kenyon. I knew what that felt like as I looked around my house and saw reminders of Jack in every room.

Remembered happiness is agony;
so is remembered agony.
I live in a present compelled
by anniversaries and objects:
your pincushion; your white slipper;
your hooded Selectric II;
the label basil in a familiar hand;
a stain on flowery sheets.

Gradually, I realized I had been too focused on agency—the will to move toward hope—and not enough on how to get there. Before I could even consider hope, I had to figure out how to survive, not necessarily for myself but for the effect choosing not to live would have on my family. I had to flip the equation and concentrate on creating pathways for living before considering chasing the way to hope. Hall burrowed inward and was able to reclaim his voice. Deraniyagala utterly lacked a family to live for. I was lucky: my family had been wounded but remained. I realized it was only through travel that I began to inch away from that dark, dark place where the future was unimaginable. My pathway, unlike Hall's, led outward.

The need to escape was my strongest impulse after Jack died. I didn't know where I'd go, and it didn't matter, but at least I would be away from the house where my son killed himself. Although I could physically move forward, I couldn't do so emotionally. I wasn't able to embrace or even know what hope was. My realization was that that did not matter. Survival, with its bravado and faking, came first. Until I was able to temper the constant desire to flee, I believed I would never have to think about the future.

When I traveled, I thought only about the immediate present and how to get from point A to point B. I embraced what I could do in the place I was visiting. I'd take photos, talk to people, and try to understand the culture and landscape that surrounded me. It was like I was two people: one couldn't leave her house, and the other was an inquisitive chronicler of place who did not care to return home. It was easier to survive when traveling. This was possible because I always carried with me my hard-and-fast rule that Jack could not inhabit a space that was unfamiliar to him. He was not allowed to deviate from this rule. I did not want to see him unexpectedly as a shadow figure rounding a corner or hiding among a group of boys goofing around. Avoiding familiar landscapes was the only way I could figure out how to make this happen. That's one reason why I traveled to places like Italy, Ireland, and the Falklands. Ghost Jack had to stay home.

Paradoxically, I needed to master and gain control over the desire to run away. This was easier to do when I wasn't at home, so I traveled. When traveling, I stopped feeling like I had to run away. This was a problem.

Snyder's hope theory told me how to get to hope but I was reluctant to embrace the equation. Hope theory needed to lead me back home. What I was doing was leading me away from home. Over time I hope I will be able to sort this out. I hope I will be able to visit familiar places—and live in the Pink House where Jack died—without dread, restlessness, and a constant desire to run away.

Broken

VERTIGO

Thrown for a Loop

In my dreams, I walk like a normal person. I even run and skip. Sometimes I jump rope. I went through a whole series of diving dreams—making the perfect approach on the diving board, then the heavy step that vaults you into the air, twisting and turning and performing a perfect forward dive with a double twist. I entered the water like a red-hot poker through ice cream. Toes pointed. No splash.

These are dreams of ego and yearning. They often involve actions I once performed unconsciously, when a desire to execute a function was easily and instantaneously transmitted along neural pathways to muscles, ligaments, sinew, and bone, creating movement.

Brain. Eyes. Inner ear.

In my new world, the keys have been mislaid, and I spend my days trying to find them.

April 15, 2013, would have been my son Jack's nineteenth birthday. He had been dead for fourteen months. His three sisters, my husband, Tim, and I had dinner together, then they went to the cemetery. I didn't. I sat in my wooden chair in the living room—the chair that belonged to my grandfather, with the carved seat and the woven hickory back—and drank glasses of merlot from a bottle of wine that sat on the table beside me. I didn't want to think about Jack.

The family returned from the cemetery, and when I stood up, the room spun violently. I fell back into the chair, confused, then tried to stand again. I couldn't. I put my head down and held it in my hands. I told Tim I couldn't move. I could hear myself speaking through my hands, but the words didn't sound right. I began to sweat profusely and felt like I was going to vomit. Tim brought me a pan, put it on the floor at my feet, then asked if I wanted help getting upstairs. I mumbled for him to leave me alone.

I slept in the living room where I collapsed and lay on the small oriental rug in front of the cold fireplace, wrapping myself in the old red quilt. The next morning Tim was alarmed that what he had hoped was a spell had not passed, and said I should go to the doctor. How would I get there, I mumbled, making sounds oddly unlike my words, when I can't even lift my head off the floor? It would require an ambulance, and I didn't want to ride in an ambulance. I asked for the pan, lifted my head off the floor, and vomited.

Tim went to work in Ithaca—there was nothing else to be done. Our youngest daughter, Gwen, went to school. I told them I was fine. I stayed on the floor. If I moved my head up above my body, I was smacked by a violent spinning sensation. I couldn't really open my eyes because the light made them hurt. I lay there, on the floor, and thought, *this is it—my life will never be the same.*

Gwen came home and worried, she called Tim to tell him I was still on the floor. Tim left work early and managed to get me upstairs to bed by holding me and with the additional aid of a walking stick I'd bought for hiking. I asked for sunglasses to keep out the light and lay in the semi-darkness, trying to block out all the scary things I was thinking. *It'll never be the same, I've had a stroke, I am going blind, I don't want to think about it.* Gwen and Clara and Railey came upstairs and I was aware of them standing at the end of the bed looking at me. I know they were scared. I tried to tell them, with my slurred words, that everything was going to be okay, although I didn't believe that myself.

It was a week before I finally went to the doctor's office. By that time, I could kind of focus my eyes and could walk upright so long as I didn't lift or turn my head. The few people I'd spoken to in the past week said some version of the following: Oh, my aunt Mabel had this and went to the chiropractor who did a simple head turning thing and she was all better. I could kind of read on my iPad by wearing my dark glasses and enlarging the page, and with a tiny bit of digging into vertigo on a couple of medical websites, I figured out my friends were all describing BPPV (benign paroxysmal positional vertigo), a kind of vertigo that occurs when small crystals in your inner ear are knocked out of place. A particular set of head movements called Epley maneuvers repositions the crystals, and you often feel instantly better. But BPPV is characterized by vertigo being brought on or intensifying when turning your head in one direction, while my vertigo symptoms were constant. It didn't matter what direction I turned my head because it was all bad. I self-diagnosed myself with vestibular neuritis because I'd had a cold right before the vertigo set in, and I read that sometimes a virus could cause the symptoms I was enduring.

After an MRI scan ruled out a stroke, multiple sclerosis, and a brain tumor, my doctor went with my diagnosis of vestibular neuritis. Vestibular: meaning relating to or affecting the perception of body position and movement. Neuritis: meaning inflammation of a peripheral nerve or nerves, usually causing pain and loss of function. In short, I was experiencing the physical embodiment of being thrown for a loop.

For several months I did vestibular rehabilitation therapy, and I spent a lot of time walking down a hallway turning my head side to side, or up and down. I liked to go left, it seemed, which meant whenever I tried to walk straight, I'd veer in that direction. Sitting and lying down were fine, but walking was a challenge. I could tell that the neural pathways signaling from my eyes to my brain to my feet were out of whack on the left side. Mark, the physical therapist, told me that a body works very hard to compensate for the loss of any particular neural pathway and that, over time, the right vestibular nerve would figure out how to read the signals that should be traveling up the left nerve. A miraculous theory, I thought, as I lurched down the hallway, hands out to fend off the approaching wall.

Before vertigo, I had established myself as a travel writer, making up to a dozen trips a year across the United States and abroad. Fleeing home and responsibilities to find meaning in other places and cultures was always my drug of choice. The second I got into the car to head for the airport, I looked only forward.

In the run-up to the vertigo attack of April 2013, our family had suffered a terrible year with the deaths of my mother and Tim's mother, and Jack's suicide. Everything I had been was now called into question: daughter, daughter-in-law, mother.

After Jack died, I felt more compelled to travel. Sometimes I felt like my house was keeping me anchored in despair, and the only moments of peace were on trips to far-flung places where no one knew my backstory. I could run away from my sad sack house and my sad sack family and momentarily forget my fury at both my failure and Jack's betrayal. As Tim held the children even closer, terrified he'd lose another, I fled.

I spent ten days in the Falkland Islands, where I discovered an entire generation trapped in the throes of collective post-traumatic stress disorder thirty years after the Falklands War. I recognized the look people in the Falklands had, the way of storytelling, the desire to talk and to not talk. I felt like these were my people; they'd gone through a terrifying time and come out the other end, but they would never again be whole. When I returned to Freeville, I talked so much about the Falkland Islands that my children and Tim grew afraid I was going to move there. I told them I would bring them with me, and we could all start over away from the house and the village my family had lived in for five generations. They didn't want to leave. Their instinct was to hold on to the fragments of their lives and try to piece them back together.

I sought out the loneliest places. I looked for locales where Jack had never been so that there was no chance of running into him in my mind. I needed to reorder my world; to reestablish a kind of balance.

The diagnosis of vestibular neuritis is a diagnosis of exclusion. If it's not this, then it must be that. It affects only about eleven thousand people in the United States. Much of the work on trying to understand the disease is being done in Germany. The vestibular rehabilitation therapist said that it could take up to six months for the symptoms to clear up and that, after that, I'd be fine. His calculation was based on the theory that your undamaged vestibular nerve will fully compensate for the loss of function in the damaged pathway. The health literature about the disease says something different. The recovery rate of peripheral vestibular function falls between 40 and 63 percent, depending on the use of early onset treatment with corticosteroids. I didn't get corticosteroids, which I guess explains why my peripheral vestibular function on the left seems to be about zero. And for whatever reason the right vestibular nerve didn't fully compensate and take up the slack.

Vestibular neuritis is a disease of confusion and imprecision that seems to be further exacerbated by anxiety and stress. You are in a mental fog and feel unbalanced because of the disease, or because the mental fog and unbalance are caused by the anxiety of worrying that you'll be in a mental fog and unbalanced. A neat tautology, with your health and mental state tightly bound.

It's been years since the initial attack. I've been in cognitive therapy, physical therapy, and even took a battery of tests at a balance clinic at the University of Rochester seven months after the first symptoms. At one point, the technician tried to fake my inner ear into a state of sickening imbalance by squirting cold, hot, then icy water alternately into each ear. My left vestibular nerve did not respond at all to this onslaught of stimuli. I left the office feeling discouraged and depressed. My sister Anne told me to get used to it; this is now your life, she said. She has multiple sclerosis, so I felt guilty for feeling that the sensation that I was walking underwater was a trial.

Most of the time I look like I am walking straight but my head tells me something different. I've learned how to fake it, deceiving the world and sometimes myself. The self-consciousness of unsteadiness affects my every move, and I often ask my family if I am lurching. Days are planned out in terms of how far I will have to walk. Sometimes I take my walking stick since uneven surfaces can throw me off. My fear of falling has skyrocketed, and I've stayed in the house for days during the winter because I'm afraid to walk on the snow and ice. Still, I survive.

Balance comprises three things that have to work together. First, proprioception (from the Latin *proprius*, meaning one's own, individual, and *perception*) is the sense of the relative position of neighboring parts of the body and the strength of effort being employed in movement; or, knowing how to get all the parts of your body to move in a coordinated way through the world—location, orientation, then movement. Second, your vestibular system is the sensory system that informs your brain about where you are (in the most elemental and physical sense) and then adjusts for balance and motion. Finally, balance depends upon visual inputs, so if your vision is screwed up, you're going to have a tough time feeling balanced.

With my initial attack of vertigo, my eyes developed nystagmus, a condition in which the eyes rapidly move back and forth (similar to what happens during REM sleep). This weird movement made it difficult to focus on any one thing. I remember looking in the mirror and watching as my eyes shifted back and forth. It was disconcerting and embarrassing at the same time. I wore dark glasses for about six weeks because I could not look at anyone without feeling out of sorts. I realized that I didn't know where to look. My eyes became sensitive to light (photophobia), so the sunglasses helped with that as well. When I was riding in cars, the combination of the nystagmus with the visual chaos of trees, houses, and buildings rushing past made me want to vomit, so I'd keep my head down in the passenger seat, eyes shut tight.

Several years later, my vision is in flux. Sometimes I need glasses, sometimes I don't. There are times when I turn my head and see trails from the image I'm looking at, and sometimes things appear segmented like I'm looking at an old film slowed to reveal motion frame by frame. My eyes are registering the action just a split second behind what's taking place. This disconnect often feels exaggerated when I'm looking at the ground while I walk, which causes me to stumble. Being out of balance began to feel permanent.

Dr. Regine Tschan, lead author of a 2011 article in the *Journal of Neurology* that followed sufferers of vestibular disease into recovery, reported on a study that explained, to me, why I felt the way I did. Tschan did an initial study of fifty-nine patients with some kind of vestibular disease, putting them through a battery of tests measuring resilience and psychological well-being, then did a one-year follow-up study with the same patients. On the basis of their answers to initial questions, she was able to predict which patients would be at risk for developing secondary somatoform vertigo and dizziness (SVD), "an underdiagnosed and handicapping psychosomatic disorder leading to extensive utilization of health care and maladaptive coping." She pointed out that few long-term follow-up studies focus on the assessment of risk factors and concluded that patients should be screened for risk and preventive factors, and offered psychotherapeutic treatment if they were shown to have insufficient coping capacity to prevent secondary SVD.

Tschan's study confirmed that what I feel is real to me, which in some ways is a relief. But a 2007 German study in the same journal about phobic postural vertigo, which is characterized by dizziness in standing and walking despite normal clinical balance tests, also rings true. "Patients sometimes exhibit anxiety reactions and avoidance behavior to specific stimuli," the authors wrote. In a year-long study, vestibular rehabilitation exercises, pharmacological treatment, and cognitive behavioral therapy (CBT) were randomly used on dozens of patients, with the finding that CBT had the least significant long-term effect.

It's clear to me now that no one has the answer. No one knows how to fix something that is literally and figuratively in your head.

People talk about searching for and finding balance in their lives. I want to hit them with my walking stick. Their choices revolve around finding balance between work, family, home, and self. I yearn to have those choices. To me, balance is more primal and elemental. I long to wake up in the morning and know that this will be the day when I will think clearly and walk confidently. When all the synapses will be firing along the right neural pathways. When my anxiety about moving through the world won't hold me back. When I can drive to the airport and board a plane and walk through a place that's new to me. When I can navigate once more a landscape of foreign hills, desolate plains, and wild seashores. When I can once again think of myself as a travel writer.

I still catch my daughters and husband watching me. I know I terrified them with the first vertigo attack; I could see the fear on their faces when they came into the bedroom to offer me food and company. This look eventually got me out of bed. If left to my own devices, I might have wallowed in my misery for much longer. Oddly, I think this condition helped all of us put our grief in another place, at least for a while. Now there was something else for the family to focus on; my children became adept at reading the cues if I was feeling stressed or anxious, and they would urge me to take it easy. I still haven't visited the cemetery after that *annus horribilis*—where I buried my mother and son side by side in the family plot. But I know when I muster the courage to do this, I will be lurching toward the headstones with what is left of my family by my side.

Why I Stay

The days and nights are getting cooler, and I find I've fallen into a familiar pattern of lethargy mixed with ennui. I sit in my Green Chair, and look around the front room, and notice that all the books and surfaces have a visible layer of dust on them. I care—in that I noticed—but I don't care enough to do anything about it.

I sit and look at a huge basket that holds all of the cards we received after Jack's death. I think I will want to read them again someday.

In the middle of the night, I wake and start googling medical malpractice and wrongful death. I read all the horror stories on each lawyer's website. I skip the man-versus-bus and man-versus-heavy-equipment and zero in on medical malpractice. I read about hospitals maiming and killing patients as a result of human error. A slip of the knife; too much anesthesia; misdiagnosis. Wrongful death in so many forms. I look at the settlement amounts—$1 million, $6 million, $500,000—and I start building my case against every professional who ever interacted with Jack.

I'd start with the elementary school teacher who made him sit in the hall half the time rather than deal with him. I didn't know that was happening because neither she nor Jack told me until spring, when I visited the classroom, and one little troublemaker of a girl pointed to a desk in the hall and said, "Do you know whose desk that is?" in her sweetest voice. I looked at her in puzzlement. "That's Jack's desk," she said.

That teacher sent us a long, heartfelt note when Jack died, written, I presume, out of guilt.

I'd build a case against his friends who knew he was abusing drugs but didn't reach out to an adult for advice. Then I'd have to forgive them in the end because they were just kids. (And all of us had drug-abusing friends when we were growing up and would never have snitched on them to their parents or our teachers.) I also would not get much of a settlement from any of them.

I wanted to drag his therapist into court and grill her about those months of sessions when she dealt with Jack the liar and Jack the trickster. I would zero in on her phone call with the psychiatric nurse at the hospital, and ask her why she thought it would be okay for the hospital to let this lying, drug-addled boy with suicidal tendencies out of their sight. I would exile the psychiatrist, the psychiatric nurse, and the ER doctors to Siberia without a trial. I would assess their bank accounts for good measure. I wouldn't want to hear what they had to say.

I save the harshest judgment for Tim and myself. We didn't know what was going on with Jack. No parent can be excused for that. Monetary damages are not practical so our punishment is that we continue to live in the house where our boy shot himself. We have to look at photographs of a happy, smiling towheaded lad on a swing, holding a fish, singing with the children's choir, walking along a path in the woods. We must live with the books he read and the artwork he created. We are sentenced to live with the faint echo of the sound of him singing and whistling. We are forbidden to take his clothes out of his bureau.

Every part of me screams, *get out, get out, get out.* But I stay and Tim stays. I deserve to live in this house. Dwelling here is just compensation for my regret, anguish, and love. Inside these walls I listen to my son. I love him and judge myself. I still hear his voice—now just a whisper.

When I no longer hear Jack, I hope I have the courage to leave.

The Ways in Which I Fall

I was in a car with my sister Amy and cousin Jan, and we were on our way to Maine for a five-day stay in an Airbnb situated on a cove. We're in the

time of coronavirus, but Maine, for the time being, was letting New Yorkers into the state without making them quarantine for two weeks or present a negative COVID test. We seized the chance to travel.

The place where we were staying was down an unpaved road the width
of a bicycle path. Down and down through the sugar maples that crowded
the road's edges and whose yellow and orange fallen leaves left a carpet
for us to follow. We could catch glimpses of Harpswell Cove through the
trees. The house was beautiful. Built into the side of a steep hill, it was
three full stories with porches running the house's length on two of them.
There was, however, no bedroom on the main floor of the house.

As I dragged my bags from the car, I considered the possible sleeping
arrangements, both of which required tramping up and down narrow sets
of stairs. I knew that would pose a problem. My knee hurt, my ankle
hurt—both had tiny tears in ligaments or the meniscus and were fluid-
filled. I could imagine the ways in which I would fall. A remnant of my
vestibular neuritis attack years earlier, or was my fearful apprehension
provoked by something else?

I've always imagined myself falling. When I was between the ages of
four and ten, we lived in a big Federal-style house in a hamlet not far from
Freeville. In our backyard ran a creek and the top of a thirty-foot waterfall.
We played in that creek and on top of the falls. We would stand there with
neighbor kids who always told us in somber tones about the boy who fell off
the top of the falls a couple of years earlier. Of course, in their account, he
dashed his head on the huge blocks of limestone at the base of the falls and
died. We stood and listened as the water swirled around our ankles—during
the summer months, the creek shrank to just about nothing—and imagined
the scene. I could never get too close to the top of the falls—maybe I stood
a yard away from the edge—because I always imagined myself falling. Or
did I imagine myself jumping—being pulled by some unseeable force? Either way, I was falling, falling, falling, but, in my mind, I never hit the water
or the rocks. I don't know where I imagined myself ending up. This was,
I think, the beginning of imagining the ways in which I fall.

Experiencing a severe form of vertigo, and having to go to physical
therapy several times a week for months to learn how to balance and walk
straight, have only exacerbated this fear/desire to fall. Yet in spite of this,
I insist on traveling.

In recent years I have visited Iceland twice, for a month at a time.
I go in the winter months because I want to experience the darkness

and northern lights, but while there, I live with the constant fear of falling because of snow and ice on walkways and streets. I become trapped in the cabin where I stay, which appeals to me. (I make a virtue of my limitations.) If I have to walk a hundred yards to the store—a walk that includes going down and then back up the knoll on which the cabin is perched—I have to gear myself up for what will be a journey. I have learned to bring a walking stick and ice grips for my boots to aid me in the simplest excursion.

First, in my mind, I fall and slide down the knoll into the road. Then, if I don't get hit by a car or bus, I crawl to the sidewalk and manage to make my way over the pile of snow that's been thrown there by the snowplow. Because people don't plow or clear their sidewalks, I walk in the knee-deep snow, thankful for what will be a soft landing should I fall. Ahead lies the treacherousness of the little store's parking lot, which is always a sheet of ice. It's almost too much. Those who don't fall and don't think they'll fall cannot imagine the mental gymnastics it takes to get me off the knoll, to the store, then back to the cabin.

When I visited the south rim of the Grand Canyon a couple of years ago—a place I love in theory—it was a nightmare. In my mind, the path was far too close to the edge of the canyon, and I felt I was being pulled into its depths. I wondered if I would think about traveling back in geologic time, as I plunged toward the Colorado River, before I died.

Every time I have to take the dog out at home, the narrow back steps from our kitchen to the basement and the door to the backyard become a perilous journey. I am convinced the dog will pull me to my death. It could happen. But in my mind, it happens often because I think it makes some kind of sense that I have to die in the same house in which my son died.

At some point, falling became synonymous with failing. It's only a letter's difference, and falling is the failure to remain upright and in place. Although the falling is an act of missed perception, failing covers a broad swath of intentional decisions. The failures add up quickly. Failure to lose weight. Failure to read more. Failure to clean the house. Failure to keep in touch with people. It's my version of death by a thousand cuts—emotional death by a thousand failures.

The biggest failure of all was that I failed to keep my son alive. I failed to recognize the seriousness of what I mistakenly viewed as normal teenage angst. I failed to keep our family whole. Everything else recedes into the background when I think of the magnitude of this failure.

Unlike falling, a scenario for Jack's suicide was not something I ever imagined. In my falling scenes, I never hit the ground, water, or pavement. I just imagine the act of falling; it is terrifying but never arrives at final disaster. With Jack's death, there was no time to write the script for something that wasn't even a possibility. What some might consider my overactive imagination failed me completely. I never, in my mind's eye, saw the edge, his slip, the worst.

I ended up while in Maine sleeping on the couch on the first floor. That meant I could also rise each day of our visit before dawn to stand wrapped in a blanket on the east-facing porch as the sun rose. I took too many pictures of a rapidly changing sky. My sister and cousin, cozy in their bedrooms, often missed this spectacle of dawn. As I gazed and snapped images, I did stand back from the porch rail because it was a good twenty-foot drop to the shingle beach below. The beauty of the sky did not force out the palpable fear that I was taking the plunge. Every time I passed the door that led to the downstairs, I pulled it shut because when it was open, an indefinable something was beckoning me to fall down those steep steps. And in my mind, if I fell down those steps, I knew, as in my dreams, I would be tumbling and doing fancy cartwheels and would never hit the floor.

restless

RAGE

Let Me Be Frank

In my unconventional approach to surviving a child's suicide, I managed to avoid doing what every professional or book on the topic said to do. I did not go into group therapy or attend a support group. I acknowledge that many people have a need to share, and they often get great solace from hearing how others are dealing with the same thoughts and feelings they are themselves confronting. That was not for me.

You might be thinking, *Ah, she was not ready for the wisdom of the group. She will get there.* But you'd be wrong.

I'd given myself permission to walk this unconventional path. I maintained that I did have a support group; it was just made up of people who were dead or fictional. For several years after Jack died, I had grown close to characters in books and on television shows. These were my people, my group.

Let me explain.

For months after Jack died, I couldn't read, I couldn't think straight, and I didn't want to talk to anyone. I didn't leave the house. I shuffled from my bed to the Green Chair in the front room. I intrinsically knew that was not a healthy place to be, but I couldn't figure out how to be anywhere else.

My world had shrunk to the dimensions of that chair. It was the heart of winter when Jack killed himself in 2012, and I sat in the Green Chair, day after day, wrapped in the red quilt from my mother's house, and watched the embers of the fire that Tim kept burning for me in the fireplace right next to the chair. Sometimes I'd look out the window toward Main Street, but I was looking through four snowflakes that Jack and Gwen cut out of paper about a week before Jack's last Christmas. Gwen's three snowflakes were not finely cut, but Jack's was intricate and lacy. I taped those snowflakes to the window in the front room right before Christmas of 2011, and there they remained. My view of the outside world both then and now is obstructed (or is it enhanced?) by having to look beyond those four snowflakes.

I pulled a table up to my chair, placed my computer on it, and started searching through television shows to watch on Netflix. I needed something that would provide a total escape. We hadn't had cable television since 2001, and consequently I hadn't seen a lot of shows, so outside of *Frasier, Seinfeld,* and *The Waltons*—shows I had always loved and made my kids watch—everything else was new to me.

Given my past viewing history and what I knew I used to like, I chose the most improbable show to watch: *Battlestar Galactica.* I may have selected the show, which ran from 2003 to 2009, because there were seventy-three episodes to watch. I was sucked in from the opening shot, watching episodes from morning to night. Then I watched them over again. I traveled on that aging battlestar through the space-time continuum with President Roslin, Starbuck, Apollo, Dr. Baltar, and Commander Adama. I was in a world that was nothing like the world I lived in. They were battling Cylons, and looking for Earth and a way to save the human species. I was looking for a way to save myself—viewing the human endeavor writ large and with a space twist.

Battlestar Galactica is firmly within the sci-fi subgenre of space opera, which means it's set mainly or entirely in outer space and involves risk taking as well as chivalric romance. According to people who know more about genre television than me, there's usually conflict between opponents possessing advanced abilities, futuristic weapons, and other sophisticated technology. All true of *Battlestar*. I love that the technology shown on the *Galactica* itself is extremely retro, including dial telephones and stand-alone computers. This use of supposedly outmoded technologies was on purpose, as I remember the storyline, as a way to thwart an enemy's attempts to take over any of the systems.

I became fascinated with Starbuck and President Roslin. They were both women with power—Starbuck a pilot and Roslin the president of what was left of the human race—and they were both flawed. Starbuck's ego and quick temper often put her in conflict with others. Roslin was battling cancer and determined to hold on to power and appear strong no matter her physical state. Starbuck became, at times and as the series progressed, harsh and quick to judge and intractable. I recognized my former self in both of these women—drawn to power, with a quick temper, and intractable once a decision had been made. As I watched episode after episode of *Battlestar Galactica,* I yearned to collect at least bits of my former self—to try to stitch together a new patchwork me—but that would require moving from the chair, which I wasn't yet ready to do.

I don't remember how or what we ate during those *Battlestar Galactica* days. I know I didn't go to the store, and I have no memory of cooking. Maybe we had Chinese food and pizza every night. Maybe we ate cereal. I don't know. My imperfect memory will not let me dredge up that information. I can remember specific scenes from *Battlestar* and what the background music sounded like, but I can't zero in on even one domestic scene in the Pink House. I was absent even though I was present.

I moved on from *Battlestar* to any kind of British detective show, including *MI-5* (called *Spooks* in Britain), *Inspector Lynley, George Gently, Endeavour, Luther, Rosemary & Thyme, Miss Marple, Cadfael, Inspector Morse, Prime Suspect, Midsomer Murders, Wallander, Sherlock, Grantchester, Broadchurch, Happy Valley, The Bletchley Circle, A Touch of Frost, Vera, Whitechapel, Jack Taylor,* and *The Fall.* I also watched detective shows from other countries, including *Top of the Lake, The Bridge, The Killing, Elementary, True Detective,* and *Criminal Minds.*

There were two things about these shows that completely drew me in. First, they were fictional police procedurals. And at the center of each of these shows was a brilliant and complicated character. The crime, almost always a murder, will eventually be solved. Detectives established timelines, sifted through evidence, and collected statements. They drove around urban landscapes in late-model sedans, wheeling around corners, eyes always darting as they looked for some action on the streets. These detectives were curious, obsessed, dark, and misunderstood by their colleagues, and most definitely held at arm's length by the public. They didn't do particularly well with people—they were snappish and impatient—but there was grudging admiration from their superiors for their work.

These were my people, and I thought they would be Starbuck's and Roslin's people too. As I watched them solve crimes on the small screen, I was solving the mystery of Jack in my head. After they stood in dumpsters and pawed through garbage looking for a receipt, in my head I went to the attic to sort through Jack's pile of homework papers, looking for a clue as to his state of mind. As they canvassed neighborhoods and talked to friends and neighbors of the deceased, in my imagination I was talking to Jack's friends Will and Joe and Keith and Isabel. I had to keep watching show after show because, although the television detectives could solve murders and crimes within the space of an hour, my investigation was never complete. There were always more corners of my brain to explore. There were clues to be ferreted out from the cerebellum's deep folds and the cerebral cortex. So long as I kept binge-watching, the file on Jack remained open.

Between television shows, I read mostly nonfiction and some poetry. I tended to be attracted to beautifully written worlds of grief or sorrow. Donald Hall, Joan Didion, Helen Macdonald, John Wickersham, Terry Tempest Williams, Katherine Boo, Rachel Cusk, James Baldwin, Emily Dickinson, Hilary Mantel, and Mark Doty. *Suck me into your story*, I would think as I opened a book and turned to the table of contents. *Make me forget my story, or if you can't do that, make me remember my story in a new way.*

These writers, along with my television detectives and the crew of the *Galactica*, were also part of my virtual support group. In my mind, they met and talked to one another. I listened to their conversations behind the two-way mirror in a police station because that way, it was never about me—they could not see my red-rimmed eyes or gray hair or grief-furrowed face. I was the voyeur. I only watched and listened.

Let me be frank. This is where I've been, and this is where I wanted to be. At some point, I felt like I was with friends and colleagues (yet I noticed they never took my advice). I saw crimes solved and difficult people begrudgingly admired. I saw the bit of arrogance in the way my detectives operated, then fleeting looks of hurt and abandonment when they were excluded from others' lives. *Buck up, Holmes, Luther, Linden, Holder, and Endeavour*, I scolded. *You're the real deal. Those other idiots are just two-dimensional television cops.*

Members of my immediate family didn't seem to be alarmed because, after all, I was not saying these things aloud to the screen. I just sank deeper into the Green Chair and watched it all, and waited for the inevitable solution to the crimes. At the same time, in my head, I tried to solve Jack's crime against himself.

Angry at a Dead Son

I haven't written anything about you in over a month. You missed the presidential election—Obama won by a comfortable margin, but it was a squeaker right up till the votes were counted. You would have said, "It doesn't matter—nothing matters." Getting into political discussions with you was always unsatisfying. You'd hold your staunch libertarian views then capitulate with "It doesn't matter." Things do matter. Individual acts can have deep, deep impacts. Just look at what you did to this family.

You missed Clara's soccer games at Cornell. That's okay since you never took any interest in her sports anyway. But your presence and subsequent absence did have a profound impact on her. After her last game at the beginning of November, she told her coaches she couldn't play soccer anymore because it made her unhappy. She somehow associates soccer with you. Maybe she believes that all the time we spent with her took away from time we should have spent with you.

You missed Gwennie getting dressed up for her first dance. She chose a lovely aqua-colored cotton dress from T. J. Maxx with a couple of wide stripes around the hem. She straightened her hair, put on a silver necklace and dangly silver earrings, and black flat shoes—she looked beautiful.

You missed Gwennie's and my birthdays. Hard to celebrate anything when your child is dead, but Gwen is only thirteen, and I don't want her to constantly be overshadowed by your absence.

You missed Thanksgiving, which was a low-key affair because of you. See, now everyone thinks about you all the time. Is that what you wanted?

I drove past the cemetery the other day by mistake. I always try to take another road from Freeville to Dryden to avoid the place where you are buried. That day I didn't. I slowed down and looked past the Victorian cast-iron gate painted maroon and white and noted the beech tree that is the sentinel for all of my family members, including you.

Since I was a little girl, I have visited that beech tree several times a year. On Memorial Day, as you know, generations of our family gather within the shade of that tree to tend the family plot. We first weed and then we divide the irises that flank the large Genung headstone. Labor done, while one generation sits on the grass and talks about everyone who's buried in the plot, you all—the younger generation—gather around the tree and begin to climb. I have hundreds of pictures of all of you, year after year, in the tree— skinny arms wrapped around smooth silvery branches and big fresh coppery leaves of spring obscuring your faces. As you all got older, it wasn't how high you climbed, it was about finding a comfortable spot to sit, with your back against the trunk, so you could, I assume, contemplate the enormity of it all.

Now, when I drive past that cemetery and spot the beech tree, all of those memories immediately startle me with sadness, and choking sobs come out of my mouth. I can't stop them from erupting with a violence. I think of you, singing at Mom's graveside just months before we would find ourselves sobbing at your graveside. Now you're buried next to your grandmother, who I know you loved. Neither of you has a headstone yet, and I'm not quite sure why. Maybe, lacking that final formality, I don't really have to acknowledge your presence in the family plot. Maybe I didn't want to ground you with the weight of that stone. Maybe I didn't want anyone else to know where you were—I wanted to keep you for myself just a little longer and not share you.

Grief. What the hell do I know about grief? I know that it sits like a block of granite on my chest. It's like being held underwater, and holding your breath and struggling until you finally have to give in. It's like wanting to lie down in a snowstorm and let the cold envelop you until you feel the false warmth that prepares you for death.

I know that it makes me incapable of thinking about anything else—everything is in relation to my grief. (How will I feel? How should I feel? Can I walk into that building without crying? Can I ever see children singing again or a concert band playing without crying?) These aren't things most people have to think about every time they leave the house. I know grief is a universal experience, yet when you're in the middle of it, it doesn't seem like anyone else can possibly understand what you are going through. My single goal is to not burst into tears every time I see or hear or think of something that reminds me of you, Jack.

The Gentle Arts

The other day a friend of mine used the term *rage-quitting*, and because my head is largely still stuck in 1999, I wasn't familiar with the phrase. I thought she said *rage-quilting*. I thought about that for a while—imagining the awesome quilt I'd make, wondering if the awesomeness of the quilt was directly proportional to the rage I felt. I have a lot of rage.

Later that night, I wondered if perhaps the phrase should be broadened. Thinking I should stick with the needle arts at which I am moderately skilled, *rage-crafting* would encompass quilting, knitting, and needlepoint. Maybe even tatting.

I am most adept at rage-knitting. I've been doing it for years. About two decades ago, I told all the kids and my husband to prepare for a

Walton Family Christmas. I initially made the pronouncement because I was so sick of all the crap the kids wanted from Santa. But when I think back to that time, I know the real reason was that I was broke. The diatribe against commercialism was a way to recast the I-cannot-afford-to-spend-$100-per-kid-times-four truth of our life in the Pink House back then.

Back then, in my early rage-knitting days, we were watching videotapes of the first couple of seasons of *The Waltons*, the show from the 1970s about an Appalachian family during the Great Depression. I love the first couple of seasons. If you watch with attention—you can discount the long cloying shot that concluded each episode, where the camera pulls back, and you see the exterior of the house with the front porch and stars twinkling in the black, black Virginia sky, and you hear all the children and the parents say good night to one another from the various bedrooms ("good night, Mama; good night, John-Boy; good night, Mary Ellen," and so forth)—you'll meet a family replete with wonderfully complicated relationships. John-Boy, played by Richard Thomas, is desperate to grow up, get off the family farm, and go to college to learn to be a writer. He puts on his round wire-rim glasses and writes in his journal at night before going to bed. Most days, he is aspiring and pretentious, he's human. The rest of the family is similarly troubled in routine ways. The seven barefoot kids walk to school on the dusty road. They bicker and pick on one another. Jealousies flare, and alliances are made and broken and remade. John-Boy, the oldest, yells at all of them. Mary Ellen, the oldest girl, yells back. It is family.

I think my kids were fascinated by the everyday poverty, much the way I was when I first watched the show. Christmas for the Waltons meant presents were made or bought for fifteen cents at Ike Godsey's general store. There were no Volcano Blowouts or Happenin' Hair Barbies under the scraggly tree cut down and dragged home from the woods. Knit scarves and sweaters and hats and little wooden boxes and chairs and very cheap bottles of perfume all changed hands. All those Waltons liked what they received.

Somehow, I knew my kids wouldn't like their handmade gifts. That didn't stop me from doing that first Walton Family Christmas. I knitted pathetic scarves for my children, although that was not my intention. I had grown up with a knitting mother and watched as sweaters took shape with the industrious click-clack of her needles. Not that my mother didn't go through her own craft phases. There was the sixties, and her angels made from folded *Reader's Digest* magazines with Styrofoam heads then spray-painted gold. And who could forget her sophisticated Williamsburg phase in the seventies when she stuck cloves in rows on oranges then set them on the mantel to shrivel. She wasn't particularly crafty, but she tried. She could, however, knit up a storm. So I assumed, wrongly, that there was a genetic code for knitting that I surely had inherited.

I bought lovely skeins of wool in various shades of heather and knitting needles, and then I cast on my stitches for a scarf. I didn't count the stitches because it didn't occur to me to do so. I thought you just kept knitting until the scarf was long enough.

I could soon tell the first scarf I worked on was pathetic, yet I could not seem to stop. When I sat down to knit, I would tense up, and every stitch showed a variation in tension—too tight, too loose—and my creations were simply terrible. I used expensive wool. Then I tried cheap acrylic yarn. It didn't matter. Each time the end result was a wreck. The rational side of my brain said, *put down the needles and walk away.* The irrational side wouldn't let me do that. It dawned on me that while I was knitting, I was thinking, and clearly any tension or problem in my little world showed up in my projects. The puzzling part is that I kept knitting, producing four ill-formed scarves.

On Christmas Day, the kids opened their presents from me—uneven scarves in shades of gray (for that's what heather really is). They were all on the verge of tears, and I could read the thought bubbles over their heads: *Why me?* and *All I wanted was a nine-dollar Barbie.*

Spurred on by my initial failures, I began to furtively watch people knitting in public places. Those people could knit and talk. All I wanted to do was knit, in silence, one decent scarf. I then watched a YouTube video about knitting and discovered I was knitting backwards.

At one point I abandoned my needles and took up needlepoint. It seemed like the only skill needed was the ability to count. I could do that. (I could even do algebra if it was required because I was reading *Algebra for Dummies* so I could help one of my kids pass the course.)

I imagined re-creating medieval tapestries complete with scenes of gentlewomen holding fierce falcons on their gloved fists. Or I could make something simpler, like a small piece consisting of intertwined Celtic designs. These pieces would be like works of art and would take more concentration than the knitting, meaning I might keep my tension-inducing, rage-producing thoughts at bay.

Fail. I had discovered another rage-craft. Did you know that needlepoint also shows tension? That it's hard to do and that the requisite skills go beyond basic counting? And that there's a reason you don't see a whole lot of it around because it takes f o r e v e r to complete one project? I made pincushions decorated with the most uncomplicated Celtic design I could find. When I finished, I realized that the color combinations were terrible—weak mustard and watery blue—and the final products looked like mistakes from the nineteenth century but lacking the nostalgia that can make poor craftsmanship appealing. And who even uses a pincushion? My therapist suggested I was really making voodoo dolls. Perhaps.

Fast-forward to fifteen years of rage-crafts littering my house. Some are so bad—like the red-and-purple-striped scarf that both gains and loses stitches in unequal proportions I knitted after Jack died—that they remain hidden at the bottom of bags holding balls of yarn. Worse, for my family, some poor pieces are in dresser drawers or propped up on bookshelves as pathetic displays of my craftiness.

I've tried to analyze my behavior. First, what compels me to embark on these projects? Then, where do I go wrong? My projects encapsulate both technical and psychological problems. To untangle these might take years.

I think the impulse is good (although my children might disagree as they open yet one more failed project each Christmas). Intellectually, there is a desire to keep the gentle arts alive. Realistically, my projects prove that the Industrial Revolution happened for a reason—not everyone could keep their family clothed and warm by their own hand.

The practical problem lies in what's going on in my head when I'm doing these projects. I suspect most people use knitting as a way to relax and don't think about much of anything while they're doing it. Or they're knitting by muscle memory and are watching television or talking while their beautiful, even stitches flow like a gentle waterfall from their needles.

Rather than taking me out of my head, these crafty projects put me squarely in whatever part of the brain controls the emotions. Every project, stitch by stitch, describes the death of my mother and the death of my son. They show money anxieties and dark depressions. They express my desire to withdraw from a world of people where I have to make small talk and be engaging. They exemplify my struggle to maintain human connections.

The scariest projects, at least to me, like the red-and-purple scarf and a half-finished needlepoint project of red poppies, are pure rage. Rage about things that are out of my control. Rage at the things that can't be undone. These projects lie hidden in the Pink House but not destroyed.

Now that my children are older, they've grown more tolerant of the projects they receive on Christmas morning. I think they're beginning to understand that this is my personal therapy. Jokes are made. Mittens the size of catcher's mitts are tried on then quietly placed in the pile of hand-made items from Mommy that will never be used. I also notice that they make no effort to discard these pieces. Now, as adults, they recognize each is a record of something important and unnamable.

This year I was thinking of trying quilting—I have a vision of how beautiful the quilt will be with its luscious jewel tones in velvet—but then I remember that I'd be cutting a million pieces of fabric. I can already see the path leading to my failure. The sewing would give me way too much time to go into my head, inevitably producing the five-hundred-hour project known as the rage-quilt. If I could create a quilt as beautiful as the crazy quilts made by lonely women on the prairie, I would gladly put in the time.

These gentle arts seem to be how women have always shown their fury, depression, loneliness, and rage. Their outlet was in the work of their fingers, and the results can often seem like controlled—very controlled—craziness. (Have you ever seen petit point?) Like them, I have the desire to create but lack the skill to produce in practical form what lies locked in my mind.

Maybe it's time to set aside the needles and thread. I don't trust myself with a band saw or whittling knife, so maybe I'll make miniature Adirondack chairs out of wooden clothespins (I bought one of those for five bucks from a guy on the street) or scale replicas of Greek Revival houses from craft sticks. My hope is that working with wood and glue won't tap into the deep well of emotions accessed by the needle arts. Maybe, just maybe, summer camp projects will make me happy and clear my mind.

Mourning and Melancholia, Rejected

In his essay "Mourning and Melancholia," Sigmund Freud suggested that mourners have to reclaim for themselves the energy they have invested in the deceased loved one. To this end, grieving is the process of reclamation. When you lose a person you were close to, you have to reassess your picture of the world and your place in it—you are creating a new world that does not include the deceased. The more your identity is wrapped up in the deceased, the more difficult the mental work. This notion hit me like a ton of bricks.

In my fitful efforts to move forward—to be able to survive—I'm still inhabiting the world that includes Jack. He's around the corner, he's upstairs, he's at school, he'll be home soon. He'll be home soon. These are the thoughts that I've worked to push from the front of my brain. I couldn't control where they'd come to rest. I knew that those thoughts were not dispelled. They now reside in the recesses and folds—half-dormant, waiting to come forward when triggered by a thought, a smell, a song.

My world still includes Jack. That's why I can't go into the supermarket where he briefly worked because I will be trying/not trying to catch a glimpse of him in his long-sleeved gray store polo shirt. Where is he? In the back, stacking boxes? Carrying groceries to someone's car? When I walk into the high school, which I can't avoid because my youngest, Gwennie, is there, I slink down the long hallways almost hugging the walls because I believe/don't believe he's there. Being in the auditorium is torture because he doesn't have to be there, for the empty space still rings with the sound of his rich baritone singing voice and his explosive tympani playing.

He's in the car listening to Mumford & Sons and Bon Iver, and he's singing along and drumming on the dash. He's in the kitchen cooking up a concoction that involves incongruous, and to me unappealing, ingredients. He's at the cabin in the Adirondacks, little camera in hand, taking macro shots of butterflies and flowers. He's playing the guitar in his room, strumming loudly and singing even louder. He's recording songs onto his computer. He's on the couch, feet tucked up, petting our springer spaniel Skeeter (who loved him). He's playing some silly game on the Wii with

Gwennie. He and Clara are preschoolers fighting in the back seat of the car and I feel like I am going to go out of my mind if they don't stop. He is nine and singing at the top of his lungs up in his room, his voice climbing higher and higher until it escapes the house and swirls around in the stratosphere. He's in the backyard digging a garden with me, and we're talking about what to plant.

I'm always driving him places until one day he can drive on his own, and then I worry until he's back home because he is not a great driver. He said he wanted to drive across the country with some friends after graduation—I told him I would make that happen. I was so proud of him, and I was so scared for him. I may not have been the mother he wanted, in his shallow teenage way—I wasn't slim and beautiful—but I was his staunchest advocate and ally when things got tough. And he knew that. I know he knew that.

Our worlds were and are still entwined. Jack was never out of my thoughts when he was here, and he's still in my thoughts, although now it is Shadow Jack—a boy who lurks on the edges of things and is just out of reach. He's behind doors or moving through the house in my peripheral vision. "Jack?" I'll say, then burst into tears.

After my mother died—a year before Jack—she was always in my mind. For months I expected her to call me on the phone and say "Rachel?" Always a question for a greeting. I couldn't drive down the side street in the village where her Greek Revival farmhouse sat, filled with all of her things that my sisters and I had yet to go through. I half-believed she would be sitting on her back porch, a cup of black coffee next to her and a notebook in her hand. I was so, so sad for months.

I remember that last Christmas with her—my sister Amy and nephew Sam fetched her from Bridges, her assisted living home, and took her to my cousin Nancy's house, two doors down from the Pink House, where we were having the holiday dinner and relaxing for the afternoon. When the car reached Nancy's place, the family came out to the driveway and transferred her from the front seat of the car to her wheelchair, which we then carried up the steep front steps and into the house. My mother was terrified as we went up those steps, feeling like she was going to fall any second, assuming that we were going to let the wheelchair slip and drop her. She hadn't been eating well for a couple of weeks, but she tucked right into that food. Roast pork, mashed potatoes, gravy, sweet potatoes, green beans—it was as if she sensed this was going to be her last meal, and she wanted to taste all of it. And she did.

That Christmas dinner *was* her last meal. She didn't eat anything but a bite of this or a taste of that for the next month. Amy and I were frantic to get her to eat, but she would have none of it. She got smaller and smaller, and her voice—now just a whisper because of the rheumatoid arthritis—got softer and softer. Amy and I talked to her about bringing in hospice. My mother resisted for about a day, then agreed. And once she let them into her room at Bridges, she never looked back. She loved the palliative care and being in a little fog because of the morphine. She had fought against the pain of her arthritis for forty years, and now, for once, she was not in pain.

My mother wanted to plan her own funeral service. I couldn't get the movie *Imitation of Life* out of my head when she said that, and all I could think about was the character Annie saying she wanted an elaborate funeral procession including a hearse drawn by six white horses. I brought a Methodist hymnal with me the next day when I visited, and we began to go through the hymns. I'd flip a page to a hymn I knew she liked, sing a few bars, and she'd say yes or no. We did that for over an hour, and then she looked at me and said, "What about 'My Country 'Tis of Thee'? No one sings that anymore." I gave her a puzzled look and then realized that she just wanted to hear me sing some more songs.

My mother didn't want to see anyone except her sisters and her daughters during those last two weeks. I was there when her sisters Jean and Millie visited for the last time. Jean, who looked like she was going to jump out of her skin, stood at the foot of the bed, and Millie—tiny Aunt Millie—went and sat by my mother's head so Millie could hear my mother's soft whisper of a voice. I don't remember what was said, although I can imagine Millie saying, "Well, Jane, this is it," in her funny, pragmatic way.

We had time to prepare for my mother's death, and it was still wrenching.

Tim's mother died two months later. She was in her nineties and living in California, descending into dementia for the final couple of years of her life. Fortunately, Tim and his sisters were with her when she died. Our children had lost both grandmothers, and we had lost our mothers, within the space of two months. Tim and I were plunged into a deep sadness which we tried to modulate because of the kids. Each of the kids had forged their own relationship with my mother, who lived at the other end of the village. My mother fostered a love of classic movies in all of them but particularly Railey and Jack. I would drag my mother to watch Clara play soccer and basketball—sports in which she had no interest—but she loved watching Clara, who made running look beautiful. And little Gwennie spent a lot of time in the car with my mother and me as I took us on long drives through the countryside. Their relationship to Tim's mother was a long-distance one because she lived so far away. But they loved her and the time they got to spend with her.

A year later, Tim and I had lost both of our mothers and our son.

There are times when I defiantly do not want to redefine my world as a world without Jack. I am not ready to reclaim anything, as I've had to do too much of that lately. Let the ghosts in. Forget Freud. Make the fleeting glimpses real. Let them all come to my dining room table where we will have a scrumptious meal of beef bourguignon, a casserole of sweet potatoes with apples and maple syrup, French-cut green beans roasted in the oven and basted with olive oil and herbs, and slices of warm homemade apple pie served with cheddar cheese for dessert. And we will talk about what everyone's been doing. We can talk about my mother's childhood in Washington, DC, and Tim's mother's childhood in Sheffield, England, and Jack's childhood in this very house. While we sip our coffee and pick at our pie and nibble on the cheddar cheese, Jack can play his ghost banjo, and my mother can request songs for him to play and sing.

Tim and I will sit back and relax for the first time in a very long time, for at that imaginary moment—and just for that moment—we will be happy.

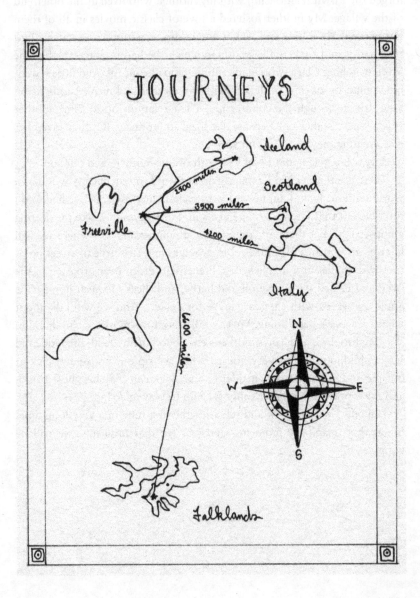

TRAVEL

Pursuit of Aloneness

Snow pelted the filthy windows of the train car. It was getting dark out-side, and through a scrim of coal dust and splotches of snow accumulat-ing on the glass, I could still make out a herd of Highland cattle standing, backs to the storm, looking like miniature mastodons with their shaggy orange hair partially covered by snow. I put my head down on my back-pack and tried to get comfortable on the hard wooden seat. I knew it would be hours before the train reached Thurso, the northernmost rail station in Scotland.

It was 1978. I was twenty-one. I was living in Edinburgh for an aca-demic year with a vague concept about what I was doing. My official charge from the Thomas J. Watson Foundation, which wrote me a check and sent me on my way, was to do a self-directed study about James Hut-ton, the eighteenth-century father of modern geology. I went to places that inspired him, wrote of my experiences of these places in a journal, described the rock formations in some detail, and then, in the same journal, painted some watercolors.

In January 1979 I purchased a month-long BritRail pass and decided I'd live on the train. I took the long hauls at night—I didn't care where it went—so I could do something approximating sleep, then would explore wherever I landed in Scotland, England, and Wales the following day. It was exhausting, and I spent a lot of time in train station bathrooms trying to get cleaned up. I ate out of grocery stores and bakeries—living on cheese and bread, meat pies, and the occasional apple. I sat in numerous tea shops reading and waiting for trains. And once I stayed at a youth hostel somewhere in the Highlands. That's the day I thought I would go mad if I didn't sleep in a bed and take a hot shower in the morning.

When I moved to Edinburgh the previous August, I rented a room in a flat with a couple of other outsiders. Many of my days were spent walking through neighborhoods filled with blocks of attached Georgian houses. Other days I walked up and down the side of the remnants of an ancient volcano—Arthur's Seat—now just a knobby hill creating a natural barrier to the city's development to the southeast. I'd stand on top of Arthur's Seat, arms wrapped around the geographic marker lest the constant gale-force winds send me tumbling down the basalt cliffs. As I hung on, I took in the 360-degree view of the region, including the city and its royal castle perched on a nearby hill. Views of the Firth of Forth always made me yearn to go down to the docks and climb aboard the first ship sailing out of the harbor. Instead, I'd head toward my rented flat, buy a baked potato loaded with cheese and ham from the potato truck on the way, then stop in the local pub to smoke cigarettes, drink lager, and listen to a Scottish band that liked to think they were from New Orleans. "I'm a gonna look you up when I get to New Orleans," said the banjo player who always tried to chat me up during their breaks and was a dead ringer for a rheumy-eyed Dylan Thomas.

The BritRail pass was my ticket out of a living situation that had become so depressing that I knew I had to leave, at least for a while. My Iranian flatmate, a tiny exuberant mustachioed man with a Japanese girlfriend who spoke no English, had just been called back to Iran. The Iranian Revolution was unfolding and Ayatollah Khomeini had returned to Tehran, and the funding for my Iranian friend to carry on his Western-style engineering studies at the university had been yanked by the anticolonial government. He and his girlfriend spent most of their nights at the disco drinking exotic-to-Scotland Carling Black Label beer. When word came that he had to leave, he was rightly terrified about what he'd find back home and worried about how he would be treated.

My other flatmate, a man from Greece, was in Scotland for the socialized medicine. I don't quite know how he swung that. He was a big guy with a bald head and a soft voice, and he had a brain tumor. For the first couple of months I lived there, he seemed okay. Then he went to the hospital, and it looked like he wasn't coming back. His brother came from Greece, packed up his room, and I never saw either of them again.

I think that month spent on the train might have marked the beginning of my penchant for running away, because it was clear I was running away from a situation I didn't feel I could handle emotionally. Later, when I examined my family history, I saw that I was not the first to flee. I just figured out how to make money while fleeing.

A couple of decades after my time in Scotland, I went to the *Ithaca Journal* and asked to see the editor. I presented him with my big idea. I told him he should hire me to write a column about my village. When he got done laughing, he asked me why he should let me do that. "Because you want to sell papers in my part of the county," I said. "Compelling argument," he offered. "What would you write about?" I took the index card out of my pocket and said, "Sweet corn, the creek, and my morning walk." I was hired. That is when I learned how to write. For five years I wrote that weekly column, and within a year, they were advertising my column on the front page above the fold, and the editor said they sold more newspapers on Monday, when my column ran, than on any other day.

About three years into my stringer gig, I decided I wanted to earn a dollar a word instead of a penny a word. I heard of an exclusive travel writers' conference happening in the Hudson Valley and applied with basically no clips to support my claim to be a travel writer. They must have had a late cancellation because I was accepted and met with editors from big magazines like *National Geographic Traveler* and *Travel + Leisure*. What impressed me even more was talking to the other travel writers about what they did and how they marketed themselves. They said, "I write about adventure travel," "I write about soft adventure," "I write about spas for the luxury market." I knew I needed to create a niche for myself, so when asked, I said, "I write about birds and birding." Silence. I told all the editors that's what I did, and that's when the editor from *Travel + Leisure* said, "Blech. I hate birds."

Within a couple of years, I worked my way up the magazine ladder of prestigious publications and was being asked by public relations companies to make trips to their clients' properties in the hope I would write about them. There was no official quid pro quo. It was really the only way a travel writer could get a story unless they were independently wealthy or wrote exclusively for the big magazines that had travel budgets. I soon learned how to say no to most of these requests. No, I do not want to go on a death march through every venue in Branson, Missouri. I do not write about entertainment. And no, do not send me to that luxury hotel with the new multimillion-dollar spa because I would never write about a spa. I began soliciting offers from tour companies set up for birders or small ship adventures that would be sailing in bird-rich areas. That's how I got to Siberia—to see birds endemic to the Russian Far East like the spoon-billed sandpiper—and to the Outer Hebrides to visit a puffin colony and to watch young common murres flutter down from their cliff nests to join their parents in the sea below. Birds were my ticket.

These trips took me away from home maybe six times a year for as long as a month at a time. I traveled alone. I loved it. When people found out I had four children, they would often ask who the children were staying with. I simply said, "They have a father."

After I was struck down by vestibular neuritis on what would have been Jack's nineteenth birthday, I spent weeks in bed, wearing dark glasses, which calmed my vision, and listened to episodes of *Frasier*, a television show I'd watched so many times I didn't have to look at it to know what was happening on-screen. I also dwelled on all the things it seemed I wouldn't be able to do again—things that had previously defined who I was. I wouldn't be able to read. I wouldn't be able to walk on the path that ran behind the village and took me past the swamp filled with several species of ducks and Canada geese. I wouldn't be able to walk to the field where the old crab apple trees in the spring dripped with migrating warblers. I wouldn't be able to drive a car. I wouldn't be able to walk through an airport to get on a plane that would take me away from my home.

I thought about standing on a beach in the Russian Far East, watching two cranes lifting high in the air above the tundra engaged in an aerial ballet featuring outstretched wings and dangling legs. I thought about lying down in the grass on the edge of a cliff and watching puffins fly into their burrows just below me, mouths full of small silver fish to bring to their young. I thought about being chased by a skua with a six-foot wingspan that dove at my head because I walked too close to its territory. I thought about sitting on a white sand beach and watching penguins riding in on the surf then running up onto the beach on their way to their nesting ground. At that moment, I foresaw a future in which I would move through the world closed off from the world, as if walking through a perpetual fog.

For a couple of years after Jack died, while I was also dealing with vestibular neuritis, I spent much of my time sitting in the Green Chair in my living room and watching thousands of hours of television courtesy of Netflix, Amazon, and Hulu. I started with *Battlestar Galactica* just because I could. An inspired choice for someone paralyzed by grief and further isolated by vertigo. My living room became an analog to the *Galactica*. I, too, was hurtling through space, trying to save myself.

I cared about nothing, especially not myself. Later, I tried to figure out if I was acting selfishly, or was I self-absorbed? Po-tay-to, po-tah-to. I drank too much. I did not go outside the house for weeks on end. I had no desire to see anyone I knew because I didn't want to try to make them feel better when they stumbled, awkwardly expressing condolences and concern. I didn't want to be on the receiving end of the pitying look. I knew I looked terrible and felt even worse, and I didn't care.

Poor Gwen was only twelve when her brother Jack died. His other sisters, ages eighteen and twenty-five, had already left the house. The only thing that could rouse me from a self-pitying stupor was watching my youngest daughter trying to navigate the world. She went to school every day when I couldn't even get out of the Green Chair. I knew that all of her teachers were focused on getting her through the school year, and I appreciated that, especially because I was not of much help. Often when I looked at Gwen, I would begin to cry because of the cruelty of her brother's death. My tears were true expressions of care for her. My husband, Tim, went to work every day and spent the rest of his time trying to make life easier for the rest of us. I think I terrified him because he could not figure out how to make me better. So he settled for shopping, making meals, worrying about the girls, and doing the chores. I appreciated all he did but I could not and did not care to help.

I spent so much of my time in the Green Chair that I began to examine the geography of the living room. Every piece of furniture in that room was from someone in the family—an accumulation of relics that had grown over the past two decades. An old oak desk, a large primitive wooden cupboard, and the Green Chair had been dropped off by my sister Anne. The small maple writing desk, a cherry drop-leaf table, and numerous paintings were from my mother's house. The hickory wood chair was from my sister Amy. Everything my eyes rested on was an import into my world. Nothing was of my choosing. When had the Pink House become the repository of Dickinson and Genung heirlooms or, more accurately, the dumping ground for the family detritus? Even the wallpaper had been put up by my cousin when she lived in the Pink House. I hate that wallpaper. I began to hate all of it. I wanted to walk out the front door spilling kerosene from an old kerosene lamp (another relic), and then throw a match behind me.

My life, which had once encompassed the globe, had shrunk to a Green Chair in a Pink House filled with family castoffs. I was suffocating and in psychological danger of being buried under the weight of all the stuff.

I told Tim I did not want to live in the sad Pink House any longer. I wanted to move, preferably to Maine. I spent hours on Zillow sending listings of cottages on rocky shorelines to Tim. He indulged me for a while then said he couldn't imagine moving from the Pink House, the family home for two decades. I couldn't imagine staying.

I felt like I had to make a decision about whether to be alone or to be in a family. That analysis is likely too harsh. Can't a person do both? I was sure my family members would not wall themselves off from me should I choose to leave. It was easier and more gratifying for me to think about the act of leaving in black-and-white terms. In my mind, I was either living six thousand miles away in the Falkland Islands or sitting in the Green Chair in my living room. Either way, I wouldn't have to navigate choppy emotional seas while trying to manage my happiness versus the happiness of others for the living room of the Pink House had become its own forlorn isle in a remote sea of sorrows.

A friend of mine, who also suffers from vestibular neuritis, reminded me that stumbling around is the way we discover things. Oh, there's the curb, there's the edge of the sidewalk, there's the uneven patch in the backyard. I think of stumbling as the way cartographers often discovered landmarks. You wouldn't know a swamp was there unless you stumbled upon it.

Even ensconced in the Green Chair I was adventuring in unlikely ways—figuring out who I was, what family meant to me, and assessing the value of this home in this village. I could not map my own world without curiosity and stumbling into the act of discovery. I'd come to know what lay around the Green Chair, and now it was time to venture further—time to find more landscapes to fill what seemed like an unfillable hole within me. Different landscapes were like the old linen napkins I saved from my aunt Millie's house after she died. I stitched imaginary landscapes of volcanoes and raging rivers and wild seas onto those napkins, changing them from utilitarian pieces of fabric to art. I might have invented a new rage-craft. Someday, I thought, I might sew them together to create a map of discovered landscapes from within myself.

What would it mean to travel alone as a woman in her mid-sixties? As I've aged and endured everything that's been thrown my way, I've become much more aware of my limitations and sometimes powerlessness. All I can control in the world is myself, but I've proved to myself that I can't even do that well. I'm overweight, have a chronic case of tendinosis in both Achilles tendons, deal with occasional fogginess from vestibular neuritis, and have to take a handful of pills every day for an underactive thyroid, high cholesterol, high blood pressure, and low potassium. Oh, and pills for the grinding depression and anxiety. Perhaps this makes me more anxious to get away now because I can imagine a future in which it will be even more difficult for me to navigate the world.

I want to release myself from the punishment. I've had enough of stitching landscapes onto napkins while sitting in the Green Chair. I want to insinuate myself back into the world of travel writing in hopes that I can put the Pink House and Green Chair behind me or at least back in their proper place as part of the world and not the whole of my world. Traveling will take me away from here, even though I know grief will be my constant companion. Grief has become familiar and doesn't frighten me and no longer forces me to stay anchored. Grief encourages me to leave, to follow my pursuit of aloneness.

December Snow

It's been snowing all day. I've shoveled the walk twice and also shoveled a path through part of the backyard for our springer spaniel, Skeeter, to run through. I tried to imagine his eighteen-inch-high point of view while doing it. We have about a foot of snow on the ground, and the huge Town of Dryden snowplows pass about once an hour, throwing snow and slush up onto the space between the road and the sidewalk. I know from past years that this will harden into a concrete-like substance that, over time, becomes black with the cinders, salt, and dirt that come from the road.

The children are becoming nocturnal. Gwen and Clara are still in bed—or at least still in their rooms—and it is almost two in the afternoon. I don't care because I'm not about to get out on the road to drive them anywhere. I've gotten more fearful about driving in terrible weather, and I realized today as Tim was leaving to take his sister Janet to the airport that I didn't want to go with them. Tim said, "Is it because you don't want both parents in the car?" and it struck me that that was indeed the reason. What if something happened to both of us? Our children could not bear that catastrophic loss, so I won't put myself in a position to tempt the fates.

The snow is falling straight down in medium-sized flakes that accumulate quickly on the already snow-covered branches. From my chair, I can see the locust tree in the front yard. The snow gives volume to the branches, making them look twice as large as they really are, endowing the normally delicate tree with the illusion of heft. The snow on the Norway spruce trees on one side of the driveway pulls those branches down down down so you instinctively duck when driving past them.

Clara is finally astir and is playing a Grizzly Bear song I associate with Jack. As the sound of it comes wafting down the stairs, I feel sad. I want to get over this musical association problem I have. Jack is gone. I can't do anything to change that. But of all the music in the world, I don't know why Clara has to listen to what I think of as Jack's music. Then I realize that she might be listening to it precisely because it is Jack's music. There is nothing to do but listen and remember.

I still live in the land of regrets and can't seem to free myself because part of me believes I deserve to live there. Until I want to free myself, there is only present and past. Being stuck in the land of regrets means you cannot envision the future. You don't want to envision the future because in that future, there will be no Jack. At least a present that includes feeling bad when I hear a song, see a picture, or think of an interaction keeps me connected to the reality of Jack.

In the future, Jack does not exist.

In this little snow globe of a world where we find ourselves today—a world where I sit in the Green Chair next to the fireplace with four Christmas stocking hangers on the mantel and look out on the same snow-covered locust tree Jack would have seen from his room—I remain fixed in present and past. I don't want to imagine a time when the roads will be clear, and I will have to leave my chair and get into the red SUV and drive up the driveway knocking the snow from the pine boughs. I don't want to do anything.

I know I'm supposed to be getting better, but to me, it's just another day to endure. Another day without Jack. Another day of looking for some bad television to watch to take my mind off the future that I don't want to be real.

Merry Effing Christmas

Two days before Christmas, my sister Amy sent a text saying she was going to make the four-hour drive to Bradford, Pennsylvania, to visit my father in the nursing home. She then asked if I wanted to send anything with her. Some deep-seated daughter guilt took hold, and I texted that I would be happy to accompany her if she wanted the company. She did, so I went.

I gathered up some things to throw into a gift bag for Christmas— an old, soft flannel shirt of Tim's, an embroidered picture I had done of flowers in a garden that I put in a little brown frame, some socks, and a photograph I took of a wintry blue-and-pink sunset that reflected and glistened off the snow between rows of corn stubble.

My feeling about my father has always been ambivalent. When he was in the family house with my mother, he was a bigger-than-life presence with the good looks of a lesser movie star and the mouth of a smart aleck. He and my mother were married for nineteen and a half years before he left us on the rundown farm that was mortgaged to the hilt, with a sizable barn with a half-shingled roof and an addition of one big room onto the old farmhouse that was two-thirds finished. He left my mother and us for a diner waitress in the North Country. We were teenagers and not that sad to see him go. But the effect of his leaving on my mother was devastating. This was the last time any of us spent any amount of time with our father. He would go on to have five wives (I think), but we were his only biological offspring.

I lost track of my father for decades until he started dropping in for a one-cup-of-coffee visit several times a year. I lived in the Pink House in the same village we grew up in—the village he had left many years earlier—so I wasn't that difficult to find. I think he just asked at the post office where I lived. He would stay for one cup of coffee and talk nonstop about whatever big plans he had cooked up for the future. On one drive-by (which is what I called his visits), he handed me his cat Peepers and a large portrait of my fifth-great-grandfather. He was on his way to Nova Scotia to pick apples. My kids would thereafter refer to him as that man who gave us Peepers. During his visits, he didn't inquire about my family or me, which was fine. He didn't know the names of his grandchildren, which was fine. He was like a one-trick pony who could obsessively do one thing. His trick was talking about himself.

When his last wife, Pat, died, my father inherited $500,000, which was an enormous sum to a man who had been a dairy farmer, an itinerant apple picker, a beekeeper, and a steelworker. Over the next several drive-bys, he laid out his big plan: he was going to buy a place in Canada on Manitoulin Island in Lake Huron. I dissuaded him from purchasing a motel because, as far as I could tell, there was no need for a motel on an island that had little to no tourist trade. I tried to talk him out of the whole cockamamie idea of moving to a place where there was no hospital and few services. He was seduced by living in the middle of nowhere and planting an orchard and raising sheep. He was seventy-nine years old at the time and had had at least one stroke and his heart needed the support of a pacemaker.

He bought a place on Manitoulin that had a ranch house, a pole barn, and lots and lots of land. It was, I believe, thirty miles from the nearest gas station and grocery store. It was a twelve-hour drive and one border crossing from where he currently lived in Pennsylvania. He spent half his $500,000 on the place and the other half on huge pieces of farm equipment. He was then back to the familiar state of living hand-to-mouth and by his own wits. I had to figure that was how he liked to live.

The drive-bys were less frequent once he moved. Although he was traveling back and forth to Pennsylvania to doctor's appointments and to pick up six months' worth of medicine, Freeville was way out of the way. He was trying to establish permanent resident status in Canada so the government of the Province of Ontario would take care of him. Then, one night in the middle of winter, I got a call from either a hospital or the police near Buffalo (I don't remember which) saying he had been in a terrible one-car accident. His truck had plunged down a twenty-five-foot embankment on a snowy curve of the road, and if a nearby homeowner hadn't seen or heard the crash, he would surely have died. He had head injuries, broken ribs and assorted other broken bones, and some internal injuries. We did not expect him to live. That was two years earlier.

It was raining as Amy and I drove toward the nursing home, first heading southwest through the low hills of the Southern Tier of New York State, then driving south into north-central Pennsylvania, where the landscape felt closed in. We passed numerous broken-down old farmhouses with dilapidated barns and through villages with pathetic wet Christmas decorations tacked to telephone poles. This was country where you knew the locals were thinking, *everything would look so much better if we just got a little bit of snow to bury the ugliness.* The dreariness of the gray but snowless weather pushed down into the hollows and moved along narrow main streets, moving hopefulness out of its way.

We talked about the present—her life, my life—because although we live in the same town, we rarely spend this much time alone together. We ran through what each of the kids was doing. We dissected and solved many problems our offspring were having. We talked about Jack, and because it was two days before Christmas, I was wound up and wondering what the Jack-effect would bring this holiday season. At that point,

at home, I was just thinking, *get through the day, get through the day.*
I knew that if I ran across his stocking or any Jack reminder from Christmas past, I might take to my bed and never want to leave. Being with Amy was a reprieve.

Our father was sitting at a table in the cafeteria when we arrived at the nursing home in Bradford. Although Amy had called and said we would be coming, they had not yet passed that information on to him. He was sitting in a wheelchair and was wearing a green tee shirt with the Marine Corps insignia on it and some message about remembering the fallen troops. I had never seen my father, who had managed not to fight in any war, wear anything like that tee shirt. He also had on gray sweatpants, socks, and brown moccasins. He was a little old man with gray stubble on his face and a buzz cut on his head.

He looked up and, after a moment, recognized Amy, who had visited him several times in the past year. I had visited once. I said, "Hi, Dad, it's Rachel . . . your daughter." He clearly couldn't place me, so I started taking things out of the bag that I had brought him while Amy talked to a nurse out in the hall. When Amy and the nurse came back into the room, he said, "I see you've met my youngest daughter, Amy, and this is her friend," pointing to me.

The rest of the visit was a blur, and although I knew the visit was not supposed to be about me, it was. We stayed for only about half an hour and just before departing went back to Dad's room with him. (In classic Dad fashion, he said about his roommate, "He's a queer but he's nice, and once he found out I wasn't interested, we became friendly"—his arrogance and bigotry clearly in place.) Amy said, "Goodbye, old man," and he said he was so glad she came. I moved in for the hug and said, "Goodbye, Dad," and he looked confused. *Why is this person touching me?* was the thought I discerned on his face.

When we got to the car in the parking lot, I began to cry because I couldn't believe he didn't know who I was. For years I was the one he visited (because I was the only offspring he could find). I was the one who took his cat. I was the one who tried to steer him toward a less destructive path when he inherited that money. I was the oldest daughter. I had sent him cards almost weekly for two years while he was in the nursing home. I sent him books. Me. Me. Me. I was getting some kind of karmic comeuppance, but I didn't know why.

I took two Valium so these thoughts wouldn't be in the front of my brain for the four-hour drive back to Freeville. Amy tried, half-heartedly, to tell me that he did recognize me but I gave her a withering look and she quit. She then said, as we were backtracking through the sad, rain-drenched villages of northern Pennsylvania, "You know, you were his favorite." And I don't remember if I said this aloud or merely thought it loudly: *Who would want to be in that role?* Then she said that once, several years ago, when Dad had found out where she lived, he did a drive-by, and as he was getting ready to go, he told her that he was leaving everything to me. She told me she was silent then told him she didn't want anything but that he did have other offspring.

I looked at her and said, "Who would want that? He's got nothing but debt and has left a trail of bad decisions and angry people wherever he's lived."

I looked at my sister, and even in my Valium-fogged state I knew that it was all about parental love and approval. I had paid attention to the old man for many years when the rest of my siblings were hiding from him. Now, at the end of his life, Amy had stepped up, and I had lost even the status of a memory.

I have no desire to write about my children—this is not their story—yet they are so embedded in my story that it's hard to omit them. Each time a crisis with the children rears up, I can't help but make it about me. *Why me? Why me?* I repeat over and over in my head. They are likely doing the same thing but my *why me?* is really *why them?* They are my children. I will never see them as independent from me. They, however, assert free will and see their actions as having nothing to do with me. This is the generational trap that ensnares mothers and binds them to their children.

This is another Christmas without Jack. I give rage-crafts for presents—framed bits of needlework that I do only when my world is spinning. As I framed each piece, I remembered how I felt when I made it. *Can my sisters or daughters see what I was thinking,* I wonder? *Do they see the craziness in the little stitches and designs?*

Jack wanders as a ghost through the Pink House. He stops to look at my handiwork—my rage-crafts—and I imagine his approval. Drawing was his rage-craft. He admires the tree, a tall Fraser fir that emits a piney smell when you walk past, though he must wonder where all the grade school ornaments he made are. You know the ones, where the kid uses his school picture and creates a popsicle stick frame around it. They are not on the tree, Jack. I can't look at your boy face and be happy, and I want to be a little bit happy, although I'm not sure I know what happiness is.

Maybe happiness is out of reach for me. I can dull my senses with Valium, antidepressants, and wine, but that doesn't make me happy. I can't seem to find any new movies or television shows that make me happy. Books don't make me happy. The family doesn't make me happy. I am alone on my journey, accompanied only by the flawed television detectives I seem to gravitate toward. Maybe my focus should shift from a search for happiness to a search for thoughtfulness, but that sounds like a tough thing to do for someone as self-absorbed as I've become.

The other day, I think it was the same day that I escaped from my father's memory, Tim told me about his upcoming trip to go searching for the ivory-billed woodpecker in Cuba. This would be an important discovery if he located the bird. For much of his adult life Tim has been searching for the ivory-billed woodpecker—the largest woodpecker in the United States, which has been rarely seen and thought extinct by many since the 1940s. Tim and his friend Bobby Harrison were the ones who rediscovered the bird in an Arkansas swamp in 2004. Since then, Tim has published a book about the search and rediscovery, coauthored a scientific paper, appeared on numerous radio shows and *60 Minutes* and *CBS Sunday Morning*, and was interviewed by journalists around the world.

As he was planning the trip a week earlier, I told him to be sure to be back for the anniversary of the day Jack died. When he told me his return date, and it was the day after Jack's death, I was stunned and said, "How could you do that?" He looked puzzled. "Jack died on February sixth, and you're coming back on the seventh. How could you do that?" Tim said, "No, Jack died on the eighth, and anyway, why do you want to commemorate that day?" I looked at him and said in a low voice, "You are wrong, it is February sixth, and you know it, and we mark that day because it's the day our family changed forever."

If I'm feeling kind, I believe Tim's psyche was telling him to move on and to forget about the terrible thing Jack did to the family. But I feel unkind most of the time, and I find his unwillingness to be with what's left of his family on February 6 almost unforgivable. We don't talk about it because he will never bring it up, and I feel too stunned by what Tim did to open my mouth and begin the conversation.

I dissect and pull apart my feelings and I realize it all comes down to abandonment. First, my mother. Then, Jack. Then, my father (a two-part abandonment separated by four decades, so maybe his abandonment was technically first). And finally, Tim. Father, mother, son, father, husband. Tim's abandonment is of family history, and not specifically of me, but I can't help but see it as personal.

Merry effing Christmas.

Learning to Travel

I don't know when I first became conscious of wanting to travel. As kids, we didn't do much traveling. We lived in central New York on the edge of a village on a poor-as-dirt dairy farm that my mother inherited when her mother died in the late 1960s. It had been a tenant farm for many years, and when we moved to the old house with the asbestos shingles and the front porch that was falling down on one side, we found some of the rooms were painted hideous colors like dark purple and Pepto-Bismol pink. And there we stayed, tethered to a twice-a-day milking schedule, as tied to the routine as the twenty or so black-and-white Holstein cows (all of whom we named). They ambled into the barn morning and night and walked right to their own places, ready to eat their own stacks of hay that we pulled from bales (which reminded me more of big shredded wheat biscuits).

Although my father came from people who traveled—ancestors who had made their way across the country and back in the almost four centuries they had been in America—he didn't or couldn't really leave home because of the cows. It was my mother, who came from people who didn't travel (people who had moved just three hundred miles west since they landed in Connecticut in 1637), who would get to a point in the summer when she'd turn to us kids and say, "Get in the car. We're going to Washington." My father, at least back then, stayed put with the cows.

She grew up in Washington, DC, in the 1930s and 1940s because her father worked for the government. But she, her sisters, and their mother spent all of their summers in Freeville, where my grandfather had grown up. When we'd pile into the car, it was to visit aunts and cousins who had stayed in the Washington area long after my mother headed back to the ancestral homeland of her people.

My memories of travel begin as a child, when I was always climbing into cars that were on the verge of breaking down: cars with holes in the floorboards (once I lost my sneaker somewhere in Pennsylvania through a hole in the floor); cars with faulty brakes and leaky radiators; cars that overheated as we swung around Baltimore on the beltway on our way south. We traveled with worn-out spare tires and learned odd automotive fixes like hitting the top of the carburetor with a wrench when the car refused to start. Those old cars were fueled by sheer desperation and managed, eventually, to get us where we were going.

My mother and her traveling ways were a mystery to me. An intrepid traveler and a naïve traveler rolled into one person. Foolhardy might describe her actions, but she didn't have the brash disposition of a foolhardy person. We would leave for DC—my mother with $20 gas money and no credit card. She had no sense of direction. Once, we went over the same bridge crossing the wide Susquehanna River outside Harrisburg, Pennsylvania, seven times. She could read a map only if it was oriented in the direction in which she was traveling, which meant whoever rode shotgun had to keep turning the map as the road veered left or right. But none of that stopped my mother from getting us into that car to head 250 miles south and as far away from what I now suspect was her unbearably sad life back on the farm.

My mother took us to see things. She believed in the moment and knew the value of grabbing that moment before it disappeared. My contemporaries traveled to visit relatives and, as they got older, spent time in malls, water parks, and theme parks. Maybe they'd take a camping trip with the family to the Adirondacks or—if they had some money—spend some time at a family cottage on the shores of one of the Finger Lakes.

My mother had a different idea about how we should spend spare time. She took us to see President Eisenhower speak at Cornell University when I was four years old because it was a moment. She took us to see Senator Bobby Kennedy standing on the roof of a car in a park in Ithaca when he was running for president because it was a moment. She drove us through sections of Washington, DC, where buildings were smoldering and some had plywood-covered windows on intact storefronts reading "Black Owned Business" during the race riots of 1968, because it was a moment. We stood in a three-hour line to see a moon rock brought back to Earth in 1969 by astronauts who walked on the moon because, at that time, it seemed like a miracle that anyone could get to the moon and back, much less walk on it. She drove us past the White House on the night of the Saturday Night Massacre, when Nixon fired Watergate special prosecutor Archibald Cox, because it was a moment. We were dragged to Cornell's campus to hear writers like Joyce Carol Oates, Richard Price, Tobias Wolff, and Eudora Welty read from their work. Moments all.

On our trips to Washington, we learned to love the National Mall with the Capitol building on one end and the Lincoln Memorial on the other. There was something about those monumental buildings flanking the mall that held the nation's relics and secrets that awakened in me a lifelong love of public buildings and spaces. We really loved the National Gallery of Art—in particular the rooms filled with dreamy nineteenth-century impressionist paintings, where we'd sit on the padded benches, look at the paintings, and pretend we were in those boats floating among lily pads or were strolling with the families at the seashore. We all appreciated beautifully captured moments.

My mother also traveled to find remnants of her childhood in DC. Remnants that included memories of her father taking her and her sisters to bear witness to events that wouldn't be repeated. They saw Marian Anderson singing on the steps of the Lincoln Memorial when she was barred from singing in Constitution Hall by the Daughters of the American Revolution, and to the inauguration parades of Franklin D. Roosevelt. My grandfather was a bigot, and he hated FDR, but he loved history, and when he saw it being made, he made sure his daughters were there as well.

This was my introduction to travel. Moving through space and time with a woman who periodically had to take a hiatus from the sadness of a broken-down old farm and from a man who by then may or may not have loved her. When she was on the road—when we were on the road—the farm first disappeared from sight and then fell out of mind, and in a way, that was all that mattered. She knew we'd somehow make it to DC and family because strangers helped us fix flat tires and would often slip my mother gas money after taking in the condition of the cars we drove and of the woman who stood with several small kids in weedy patches on the shoulder of the road. Her desperation to leave trumped her common sense in many ways.

My mother taught me to look for the moment and to be there fully, for, according to her (and what I later identified as the laws of physics), we will never see that moment again. Look hard and take it all in. Surround yourself with your past and take aim at your future, but do not forget to acknowledge the moment. She also taught me, I think, that it was okay to run away from pain, even if only for a day, because it would still be there when you pulled back into the driveway.

Give Up the Ghost

Give up the ghost. This phrase came to me in a nap this afternoon. I never sleep in the afternoon because it's often so unsettling when I wake up or come out of whatever odd almost-sleep state I've been in. Today I lay in the bed and watched the sky with the big gray-and-white cumulus clouds bumping and moving into one another turn into a sky of all clouds. The bits of blue disappeared under layers of gray upon gray that looked like dirty cotton batting. The early December trees looked cold, and not a leaf was left dangling—not even on the oaks—after yesterday's wind. The only spots of color in the overall grayness were the dark red apples clinging to the old, gnarly tree. They were rotting in place. The remaining fruit was high in the tree because, I assume, the deer had eaten the ones from the lower branches.

Give up the ghost. Let winter pour through the shreds of autumn that cling stubbornly to the landscape the way the apples cling to the cold, dark branches. Give it up, autumn. Let it go. Let winter envelop the trees, the air, the weakening sun. Your exit can be graceful if winter doesn't bully its way in.

Give up the ghost. It's time to free up some space in my brain for thoughts other than of you, Jack. Being depressed is exhausting and, at times, unbearable. There are glimmers—just slivers of glimmers, really—that enter the edges of my thoughts, and I want to feel like I have the energy to reach for these shimmering tokens of hopefulness.

Give up the ghost. Is it time to abandon the comforting upholstered arms of the Green Chair and cautiously move about the Pink House? I have let you roam the Pink House, Jack, for years now. I sense you moving just outside my sightline and although it never frightens me, it, in effect, paralyzes me. I'm trapped. If I pay too much attention to your absence, I become vaguely aware of your outside-this-world presence. So, if I let your absence go—if I give up the ghost—I'm afraid you will also disappear like a whisper immediately after it's uttered. The atoms that have been bumping and rubbing against one another and creating friction that I think has created the form of you will slow down and dissipate. You will begin to obey the laws of physics.

Give up the ghost. There are other interpretations that are too fearful to contemplate, so I won't. I will let my sleep-addled brain embrace the absence/presence of you, Jack. I can't say that it brings me comfort, but it is familiar at this point, and it is that very familiarity that keeps me somewhat settled.

Birding on Bleaker Island

Often, I bird to travel, and I travel to bird. It works both ways. Although I'm not what you might call a keen birder—I can't hear a snatch of a bird's song and tell you what species it's coming from—I am observant and can usually figure out which end of the binoculars to look through. I love looking at birds, noting their colors and markings, and watching their behavior. On my trip to the Falkland Islands right after Jack died, however, this bird-love was put to the test.

I was keen to see some of the birds of the Falklands while I was there. If I was lucky, I'd be able to see birds that were new to me, including black-browed albatross, five species of penguin, and flightless steamer ducks. On my first island-hopping trip, I grabbed the little red plane to Bleaker Island, which would get me at least two penguin species, the steamer duck, and, maybe, a black-necked swan.

The owners of Bleaker—Mike and Phyl Rendell—met me at the grassy airstrip and drove me the length of the island (three miles) to the settlement (their home, two guesthouses, and the house of the farm manager). There are no roads on Bleaker—there are no roads on most of Falkland's islands—so Mike headed overland on a vaguely defined two-track path. As he drove he pointed out where the penguin colonies were and the freshwater pond where I might see a black-necked swan. We drove through patches of heather-like diddle-dee, and through close-cropped grass on a headland that overlooked a blue-and-gray sea dotted with distant islands. There are no trees on Bleaker—which is true throughout most of the Falklands—and a large rocky hill covers about half of the small island. Because I come from a land of trees in central New York State, the sheer openness of the landscape was raw and I felt exposed.

I had just come from Stanley, the capital city (population 2,500) where I spent two days being guided through battlefields by two veterans of the 1982 war. These men could recount every single moment of these battles and spoke with an intensity reserved for the battle-scarred. No battles had taken place on Bleaker, so being there was a respite from the intensity of visiting sites associated with the war. This island was where I was going to relax and take a long walk. After getting settled at the Rendells' compound I put on my boots and rain jacket (weather in the Falklands is synonymous with changeable), slung my binoculars around my neck, grabbed my camera, and headed out to find some birds.

Have I mentioned the brown skuas? These are huge predatory birds that look like *uber-gulls*. They are the islands' bird bullies—harassing other birds to get them to drop their food, attacking and devouring young birds, and swooping and diving on anything they don't like, including people. I first met their northern cousin, the great skua, on Fair Isle in the Outer Hebrides, where I was hit on the head from behind by a skua as I walked along a road. When you're hit, you see stars, and you don't forget the incident. Now, while walking away from my guesthouse on

Bleaker, I saw that there were brown skuas everywhere. Why hadn't I seen them on the drive across the island?

Mike had earlier pointed out a striated caracara (which the locals called a Johnny rook), a big raptor that reminded me somewhat of a Harris's hawk, and said that they were very curious about people and not to be surprised if they came near. But he never mentioned the skuas that were patrolling the island. Figuring I needed some kind of strategy to steer clear of the big birds, I walked along the fence line, hoping the skuas might take me for a moving fence post. They eyed me, trying to decide whether I was worth harassing, as I struck out on my own.

I climbed through the fence, entering an area of amazing tussac grass—huge five-foot-tall clumps of grass growing out of foot-high root clumps that you had to wedge your feet between to move through. I headed toward the sea. The strong smell of ammonia and a sound that was a cross between braying and honking hit me as I approached the headland. Rockhopper penguins! These foot-and-a-half-tall penguins have long, droopy yellow eyebrow feathers, orange beaks, and red eyes, and when they walk, they waddle and hop (hence the name). They also have extremely sharp claws, giving them purchase on cliff faces. I stood and looked at the messy, loud, smelly penguin colony filled with half-grown birds and molting adults. Some of the rockhoppers looked to be in a serious state of undress as new feathers grew in to replace molted ones.

I knew I ultimately wanted to reach the sandy beach, where the gentoo penguins come in after a day of fishing. I moved back through the tussac grass, aware of how easy it would be to break an ankle among the root clumps. I wondered how long it would take my hosts to find me if that happened. Would rockhopper penguins surround me in the tussac grass? Would they peck me with their sharp orange beaks? I shook those thoughts from my head, climbed back through the fence, and walked on grass close-cropped by both sheep and upland geese. I saw big patches of diddle-dee, and it reminded me of Scotland, where I had lived for a year. I stooped to look at the tiny pink diddle-dee flowers, and I was transported back thirty years to the Highlands and a day of walking on heather-covered hills. Suddenly, just six feet away, a skua rose out of the diddle-dee and came right at me. I ducked and then started to run toward the beach, flailing my arms, knowing I was channeling Suzanne Pleshette in the schoolyard scene in Hitchcock's film *The Birds*. For some reason, the skua stopped buzzing me when I got to the beach—perhaps it knew it would have another chance to harass me when I headed back to the guesthouse.

I sat panting on the beach from my skua-induced run and watched penguins emerge from the blue-green surf, stand up, then waddle-run toward shore with flippers akimbo. Gentoos are medium-sized penguins, and everything they do seems adorable. They are the *Happy Feet* penguins. And they were curious about me—coming closer and closer as I sat still. The sun came out from behind a bank of clouds, and looking at the Caribbean-colored water, the reflecting white sand, and watching the antics of the bright white-and-black penguins put me in a relaxed, trancelike state. I knew, however, that I had to leave the safety of the beach and walk back.

I stuck to the beach for as long as I could, searching for a piece of driftwood in an island group not known for trees. I found a three-foot-long piece of wood—what might have been a two-by-four a hundred years ago—and picked it up to use as my skua protection. My plan was to hold it up over my head so the skua would go after the driftwood instead of me. I headed inland, trying to stay clear of the diddle-dee, spying plovers and dotterels in the grass on the way to the freshwater pond to look at the black-necked swans. But I lost sight of the pond and wandered off course. Then I saw them. Several skuas flying low, looking for something to harass, menace, or eat. I started running, waving the two-by-four above my head while yelling, "Get out of here! Leave me alone!" Two of them double-teamed me, coming straight at me and then striking the stick.

At that point, I lost all interest in birds except for the ones that I was convinced were trying to kill me and feed me piece by bloody piece to their young. The faint two-track road running down the middle of the island lay ahead, and I ran for it. The skuas got bored—they had me right where they wanted me—and left. I held my driftwood high, ready for combat, knowing there could be a sneak attack from the rear.

I passed the tussac grass and the rockhopper colony—spying a pretty little tussac wren flitting through the waving grasses. I paused to watch as thousands of large black-and-white imperial cormorants flew toward the island, bringing food to their young. As they passed over me like a squadron of planes, I felt like I could reach up and touch them because they were flying so low. They landed about two hundred yards away in

a colony on the crest of a hill. There were tens of thousands of cormorants gathered—many of them young birds just leaving the messy ground
nests—and the calls and caws and mewling sounds were deafening as
parents sought out their chicks. Several dozen skuas glided low over the
crowd of cormorants, hoping to nab a young bird or a bit of fish dropped
by an adult.

I swung wide of the colony, again hugging the fence line, and was
thrilled when I saw the tiny settlement up ahead. As I walked between
the Rendells' home and the guesthouse where I was staying, I stopped and
knelt down to take a photo. Two skuas rose from a patch of diddle-dee
about three yards away and hovered right in front of me like they were
curious. I dropped my camera and started waving my stick. They looked
puzzled, then settled back down in the low shrub, watching me as I ran
to my guesthouse.

Later, over a wonderful dinner of lamb, broccoli, new potatoes, apple
crumble, and a bottle of merlot, Phyl and Mike told me that Elaine, one
of the farm managers, feeds the two skuas near the house, so they associate people with food. "Why would she feed them?" I asked, and the
Rendells told me that it was something she started doing when they were
young birds, and now they just hang around. They wouldn't hurt you,
said Phyl. I didn't mention what a coward I was. We talked about people,
politics, and the 1982 war. Neither of them was in the Falklands when the
Argentines occupied the islands thirty years earlier—Phyl, who grew up
in the Falklands, was in Britain at school, and Mike, who was originally
from Britain, came to the Falklands as a serviceman right after the war.
In a way, I was relieved because it meant I didn't have to talk about the
war that left those who lived in the occupied Falklands with a kind of
community-wide PTSD. The war stories I had chased down while in Stanley were intense. So the Rendells and I relaxed and talked about birds,
birds, birds, and then local politics and books and movies as we listened
to the braying and fussing of the Magellanic penguins in the colony right
behind their house. We talked long into the evening and watched as the
sun set on Bleaker Island and was replaced by a billion stars.

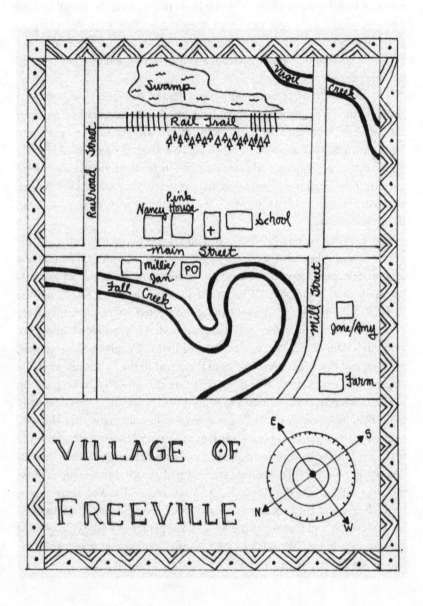

VILLAGE OF

FREEVILLE

SPECULATION

Fictional World

Growing up, I always imagined myself walking behind a wagon pulled by two heavy-footed oxen. We are moving through a prairie of swaying grasses taller than my head. Sometimes I close my eyes while I'm walking and am able to move forward by listening for the rattle of the furniture, the bumping of food barrels that aren't properly tied down to the sides of the wagon, or the sounds of the tired oxen's great exhalations. I hear the rhythmic squeak of the left rear wheel as the metal axle grates against the metal wheel hub. I hear the low murmur of Pa talking to Ma while he walks beside the oxen, and she sits on the bench seat in the front of the wagon. Occasionally they laugh, and I wonder what the joke is. When I open my eyes, I see nothing except the back of the wagon and the immense sky that spreads like an overturned bowl to encompass the landscape. If I turn my head, I see only prairie grasses—grasses so tall I can't reach their tops when standing on tiptoe and stretching my arms as high as I can. I am walking in a green chute capped by a sky so wide and blue and endless I know I'll faint if I think too much about the nothingness of my existence in the midst of such vastness.

As an adult, I realize I cribbed my imagined childhood from books by Laura Ingalls Wilder. I devoured her *Little House on the Prairie* series as a child, beginning with *Little House in the Big Woods* and ending with *The First Four Years*. Although Wilder's series is out of favor today because of her sometimes anti-Native and anti-Black sentiments—her name was stripped from an American Library Association medal in July 2018—I don't want to condemn the series even though I would criticize it. But that's the adult me writing. The child me was too entranced by the action in the story—plowing and planting and moving from place to place over rutted trails—to take note of much outside the action. Then there was the family—Ma, Pa, Mary, Laura, Carrie, and eventually Grace. The invisible bonds that held them together stretched but never snapped. I was in thrall to their domestic fidelity.

While I was growing up on a dirt-poor subsistence dairy farm, my child mind needed immersion in another world—one I could dip in and out of at will. A world I could return to when I was trying to make sense of what lay around me. A source of comfort even for all its exotic qualities, the *Little House* series provided a story that was both familiar and not. The experience of the Ingalls family was in some ways a corollary to how my own family operated. In the books, Pa was restless, always wanting to move, forever searching for a new stretch of land with few neighbors. Ma just wanted to stay put. Pa speculated on both land and newfangled ideas, only to lose his land and his shirt over and over again. And sometimes the Ingalls family was just struck by the kind of bad luck that befalls all farmers, like the year the locusts swarmed over the wheat fields and ate every single plant down to the ground.

Like Pa, my father loved the idea of being land-rich and engaging in what amounted to get-rich-quick schemes. His schemes always involved working hard but were entirely speculative in nature. (The thing with agricultural land is that success, if it ever comes, is never swift.) Like the year my father planted fields of sugar beets—plants not grown in any quantity in New York State before or since. As the sugar beets grew, we were sent into the fields to yank and pull long bindweed tendrils that were the evil twins of the lovely blue and purple morning glories covering the trellis against our house. We were just four little kids under the age of ten fighting acres of weeds that seemed to grow and slither across the ground before our eyes, all for a crop that—had it thrived—would have ended up rotting in the fields.

It was the early 1960s, and Pepsi had just built a sugar beet factory in Auburn, thirty miles up the road, an irresistible draw to my father, but the summer he grew sugar beets, the factory closed on account of a world-wide drop in sugar prices. The crop was doomed anyway; that summer we endured a drought. Every day we woke up sweaty, our bodies giving in to the white heat that seeped just after dawn through our bedroom windows in the stifling upstairs of the house. When we went to the fields, we could almost see the tender sugar beet plants wilting before us. It turns out that sugar beets need water to thrive, and our fields were not irrigated. I can almost hear my father say, *Why the hell would I invest in a system to irrigate a crop when water falls from the sky?*—dismissing the vagaries of nature.

With some regularity, Pa Ingalls would tell the family to get in the wagon and bring only the essentials. This was not unlike my father saying, *Get in the car—we're moving.* When Pa Ingalls packed up the wagon, it meant traveling hundreds of miles over a bumpy trail and cooking over a campfire, then sleeping under the stars. He'd hitch up Pet and Patty—mules more used to pulling a plow than a wagon—and Ma and the girls would climb in and settle themselves around the family's belongings. Jack, the bulldog, would take his place in the shadow of the wagon, and as the wagon began to move, he'd trot alongside. Oh, the romance of heading into the prairie in search of more openness.

It was in direct contrast to watching a pickup truck pull out of the driveway with our belongings haphazardly piled up high in the back. My mother, my siblings, and I—plus a cat or two—would squeeze into whatever old car we owned and follow the truck to our new home. Our moves were always to houses within a thirty-mile radius of the village where I was born. We traveled along back roads dotted with tired dairy farms. I never felt like we were heading toward anything; there was nothing romantic about swapping a house in Tompkins County for one in Chemung County. I'm not quite sure why we moved so often when I was very young, but I suspect it had to do with not being able to pay the rent. We were running away.

By the time I was in grade school, the moving stopped. My father's parents moved out of their beautiful nineteenth-century Federal-style home with a thirty-foot waterfall out beyond the backyard. They sold this house to my parents, although I later heard that my father made only one payment.

While we lived there, my father was gone a lot, working as a steelworker on buildings around the state. As little kids, my siblings and I spent many unchaperoned hours playing on top of the falls, walking in the six-inch-deep channels cut into the limestone by the eroding power of water rushing for thousands of years toward the thirty-foot drop. My mother seemed happy in this house. I remember her sitting at a table with a book, a cup of coffee, and a lit cigarette held loosely between her first and second fingers, wisps of smoke curling toward the ceiling. When I was an adult, I should have asked my mother two questions: Why were we allowed to run amok around the waterfalls? And was my memory of her being happy a real memory? Only I never did ask her.

Our final move as a family came five years later when my grandmother died, and my mother inherited a farm on the outskirts of the village. I was ten when we moved into the farmhouse, which had been occupied by tenants for years, and I remember rooms painted purple and no heat in the upstairs bedrooms where my sisters and I slept. My father bought a small herd of dairy cows and seemed content as he used his excess energy to rip and tear at the landscape, all while trying to keep those cows and us alive.

Like Ma Ingalls, every time we moved, my mother had to create a home. She became adept at wallpapering because that was the cheapest way to hold crumbling plaster walls together, and she developed an eye for cheap faux-oriental rugs from Woolworth's that covered a multitude of flooring sins. Every time the Ingallses moved, Ma would place the china shepherdess on a shelf to signal that the setting up of the home was complete. My mother, however, was never done with papering and patching and painting. Our homes were always in the process of becoming, and there was no point in designating a symbol for the state of completion that would not arrive.

It was this last house, this last move, when I first felt afraid that something awful would happen to my parents. If they left the house together, I worried they might never return. In a recurring dream, they were killed in a car accident, and my sisters, brother, and I were left alone on the farm with the cows mooing in distress waiting to be milked in the barn. We would then be split up and sent to live with various aunts and uncles. When I awoke, for a moment I would wonder if that had happened. I don't know why I started having these dreams—perhaps I sensed that there was trouble in the marriage. I had no doubt that our father was capable of abandoning us because he seemed to randomly slip in and out of our lives already. I was panicky at the idea that my mother could leave as well.

Five years later, when I was fifteen, my father made one more move—this time to the North Country and out of our lives. He had met a waitress at a diner, and he left us to be with her. My father sold the cows and pocketed the money, and my mother was stuck with a forty-year mortgage from his borrowing money on a fully paid-off farm she had inherited and a huge nineteenth-century barn that was destined to fall in on itself because he never got around to fixing the roof. There we were—four teenagers and a single mother—plunged into automatic poverty by a man who refused to pay child support and a mother who wouldn't pursue it.

My mother sank into a two-year-long depression. She managed to hold a job as a typist in the dean's office in the College of Engineering at Cornell, but when she came home in the evening, she'd often go into her bedroom and lie down on her bed with her coat and shoes still on, clutching her purse, and say to us as we shyly gathered in her doorway, "I just need a few minutes." We might or might not see her over the next few hours as we did our homework and then, if left on our own, ate Rice Krispies for dinner. I didn't know then and don't know now if she hated her job or was worried about money or missed my father. Maybe it was all three. The *Little House* books provided no model for how I should behave or feel or think about this. Pa never left the family high and dry; all the Ingallses shared in Pa's dreams and failures.

At about the same time my father left, a new show, *The Waltons*, began to air on television. The narrator and principal character, John-Boy (played by Richard Thomas), and I were both sixteen. And, like him, I think I often displayed the petulance of a teenager who wanted to leave home and see the world and then write about it. I felt like I had to move beyond the pluckiness of *Little House* and into the Waltons' world of more complicated relationships. Based on Earl Hamner Jr.'s book *Spencer's Mountain*, *The Waltons* was set during the 1930s in the Virginia

Piedmont as it rises to the Blue Ridge Mountains. The Walton family—mother, father, seven kids, and one set of grandparents—lived on a farm on Walton's Mountain, land that had been in the family for generations. Of the seven kids, John-Boy was the oldest and the most conflicted. He loved his family but wanted to bust out of the constraints of home. Unlike the Ingallses in my beloved *Little House* stories, the Walton family bickered as they pulled together to keep their heads above water. When the father, John (who operated a home-based sawmill), had to move to a large town to take a job, Olivia, the mother, was despondent, unlike my mother, who, when still married, seemed content when my father was away.

My fictional world, populated by the Ingalls and Walton families, made everything in my real world less cheerless. I could lie on the Sears Roebuck couch with nineteenth-century hunting scenes printed on the fabric and think about how hard it must have been for the Ingallses to build a log cabin, but, by golly, it got done. Or about the mounds of food—stacks of light pancakes dripping in butter and maple syrup, sides of ham, sausage, and bacon—depicted in the *Little House* book *Farmer Boy*. Or about the barefoot squabbling Walton kids walking to Ike Godsey's general store to pick up the mail and stare at the candy. I still smile when I think about these fictional friends, with their fictional troubles, and fictional solutions and successes.

It struck me then, and it strikes me now, that as a kid I frequently had no desire to live in the time period I was occupying. I knew enough to realize that the 1870s of *Little House* and the 1930s of *The Waltons* were tough times in American history, and that the portrayals of children in calico dresses and sunbonnets or kids wearing patched jeans with rope belts were completely idealized. But I didn't care. I wanted to live in a world where people rode horses for transportation, and the prairie was still a place of waving grasses.

Or maybe that wasn't it at all. Maybe I was drawn to those stories because they were depictions of what I saw as whole families with fathers and mothers and children who were entwined and basically happy. The Ingalls girls and the Walton children never behaved as if the family structure was imperiled—no one lay awake at night wondering if their father was gone for good or if their mother would be able to get out of bed in the morning. When the locusts ate the Ingallses' wheat crop, and when John

Walton couldn't afford to have the sawmill fixed, rather than explode from the stress of poverty, the fictional families rallied.

I believe it was the intimacy between family members shown in both *Little House* and *The Waltons* that was the irresistible draw. Laura felt particularly close to Pa, who behaved as I imagined a good, kind, fictional nineteenth-century father would behave. Pa played the fiddle when he was both happy and sad, and later in life, when Laura wrote the *Little House* stories, she even peppered the text with lyrics of the songs Pa played. The Waltons gathered around the radio to listen to shows, music, and President Roosevelt's fireside chats. We didn't gather, as a family, around a television set or a radio or someone making music. We gathered around my father, not because he was kind and affectionate, but because he demanded it. He had the charisma of a two-bit con man and when he was home, he was the sun, and we were planets orbiting around him.

Now I realize that when he was in the family, my mother and my siblings and I often behaved as a group because he kept us off-kilter. We were never sure what he would bring to the table (bankruptcy? moving? some cockamamie scheme—like planting sugar beets—hoping for quick money?). By pulling together, we could offset some of the chaos my father created. We possessed some of the cohesion that I admired in the Ingallses and Waltons, but we came by it from fear and not out of love.

My mother made do by wallpapering and painting, and we did well at school and were basically good-natured and helped out around the farm when asked. But it was us versus him. We never considered ourselves farm kids, and my mother never considered herself a farm wife. None of us wanted to live on a farm except my father. He made and controlled the money, so we were dependent on this farm that none of us cared about. When he left for good, our connection to one another weakened. The person who wielded approval and disapproval like a machete was gone, and we no longer had to band together for mutual protection. There was no farm to keep running. The effect was a realignment of the familial universe that knocked us from our trajectories and left us to wander, separately, through space. This didn't happen in the *Little House* books or *The Waltons*. The Ingallses and the Waltons faced adversity as family units. Neither Pa nor John Walton left. The families did not break into a million shards.

About a year after my father left, my need for the Ingalls and Walton families diminished. It was time to search for more complicated models. To this day, however, I can easily put myself back into the fictional worlds of my youth. I can imagine walking up Walton's Mountain with John-Boy and Grandpa and seeing the doe with her fawn at the edge of the meadow and the red-tailed hawk perched on a snag. I listened as Grandpa told his grandchildren of the Waltons who had occupied that land for a hundred years. I rode to town with the Ingallses in the buckboard, heading across the prairie—Pa being ever mindful of the slough that could mire the wagon in mud. And I remembered how we laughed and sang songs as the wagon moved along the rutted road through the swaying grasses.

What Would I Take If My House Was on Fire?

Our house is filled with things. I feel like I have a responsibility for these things because most of them have come from someone else's house. The Pink House has become the repository for family relics that somehow magically transform from the worthless and unwanted to objects of value and desire once they cross the threshold. I should quantify this principle, if it's not already quantified, and then write about this transformative property for a pseudoscientific journal dedicated to advances in alchemy. It applies to chests, bookshelves, desks, chairs, photographs, paintings, books, old boots, the collection of ceramic dogs, lamps, a zinc-topped oak something-or-other, the cherry drop-leaf table, a painted birdhouse, pottery, falcon hoods, a bronze statue, more books, and bookends featuring busts of Washington and Robert Burns. And that's just in the front room within eye's reach of the Green Chair (another discard).

What is it about these things? And what is it about me that allows them to come through the front door? My behavioral theory—which is paired with the alchemical principles—is that my house is on the way to the dump and that my sisters stop in my driveway with massive pieces of furniture jammed into their SUVs and say, "I'll help you carry it up the front stairs if you want this," and I'll look at the whatever-it-is and remember that it came from the family house in Troy, New York, in the 1840s or that my father bought it at an auction in 1960. I can't stand to see it go to the landfill and so I'm stuck with it. My sisters sit in their cars and wait for it. It's all about timing. They watch my facial expression morph from determined resolve to recognition of the piece, and they then get out of their cars and open the back and begin to haul the now treasured family piece toward my front porch. It's as if there's a sign next to the front door, visible only to family members, that reads *Family Dumping Ground: Play Up the Family Connection.*

The weight of the obligation to keep and then protect the family stories as written through objects is heavy. I have large portraits of not one but two great-great-great-great-great-grandfathers from different sides of the family. I often stop and look into their oil-painted eyes—one set greenish-blue (like mine) and the other velvety brown (like my sisters')—and I'll ask them, sometimes aloud, *Why are you hanging around my house?* At some point, I'll place them in the same room so they can see each other in hopes that will ignite a spark that will lead to a conversation between the two, maybe about the wonders of the twenty-first century—like flat-screens and computers—that they see around them. I imagine their nineteenth-century eyes will light up at the recognition of the other, and questions they've each held close to their waistcoats for the past two hundred years will spill out at night in feverish whispers.

I often wonder what I would take if my house was on fire. This is a useful exercise, especially when you're burdened with the family trash/treasures. Would it be the broken Windsor chair in the attic that I remember my father sitting in every morning when he was still hanging around the family? (I sobbed when my daughter Clara, then ten, stood on the back stretcher and snapped it neatly in two.) Or maybe I would gather up paintings, prints, and photographs and stack them on the porch. Or maybe I would fill a garbage bag with all of my dead son's clothes from drawers in the cross-sawn oak Stickley highboy I haven't opened in years.

I have a friend who is not sentimental about things and does not play the house-is-on-fire game, and I view her with awe. Her parents came from poorer-than-poor dirt-floor farms in Ireland in the 1950s, and Marian, along with her four siblings and parents, crowded into a small house in a suburb of Boston, where her father was a bricklayer and her mother stayed at home. Marian is now entrenched in the upper-middle class as the wife of a longtime college professor. The other day when I was visiting, I asked her if she had objects from her family. She pulled a photograph from a drawer in the sideboard in the dining room and one handkerchief. The photo was of a young couple in the late 1940s—her parents—standing awkwardly with each other and looking at the photographer as if to say, *Now what?* The handkerchief was small and white, and edged with a different-colored thread. It reminded me of something I'd buy in a collectible shop. These are her family things. Then I looked around her house, which was filled with beautiful paintings, rugs, china, and silver, and she said, "None of my kids are going to want this stuff," and I told her that she should not make that decision for them; that it was up to her children to decide what was important from their childhood. She may well let them decide, but she has made up her mind.

I am envious of people who can walk away from the tangible objects. I can't make myself go into the attic and drag my broken chair collection down and put it out on the curb. I'm the only one who knows where each of those chairs came from, and when my dementia sets in, their meaning and power will be gone—the pseudoscientific principle that converted them from trash to treasure will reverse—and in the end, they will be a pile of broken chairs. I carry my family's tangible goods like Marley carried his chains in *A Christmas Carol*—as a cautionary tale to others who might fall prey to sentimentality and nostalgia. Only dementia or a good house fire will free me from these ancestral burdens.

The Time Tim Went to Cuba

Saturday. After you left, I stayed in bed for a while and worked on trying not to be so very angry with you. Who leaves on a long grueling trip without first spending some tender time with their wife? That made no sense to me. I was hurt by the fact that it didn't even occur to you. Why am I no-where in your universe?

I dreamt I was a moon orbiting around you, my planet. You turned and turned, exhibiting your splendor from all sides, while I watched your revo-lutions from afar, never able to come nearer; never able to reach out and brush my fingers across your spinning beauty. Sometimes I couldn't stand it and wished to retreat into the vast blackness that is space, but you wouldn't defy the laws of physics and release me. If I were free of your gravity, I knew I'd spin slowly to see how it felt to be so self-contained, so self-assured. I imagined I'd grow powerful and attract cast-off moons, and we'd move languidly through the universe saying *see you later* to our former planets.

I made a lot of chocolate chip cookies for Gwen's roller derby bake sale. I was home alone tonight and tried to knock myself out with wine and a sleeping pill, so I didn't have to think about you.

Sunday. I went to Walmart to get ink for the printer. Walking into that store is such a clear reminder of where we live. I walked past people with carts full of crap to eat and crap to wear—food with no nutritional value and cheap clothes from Southeast Asia made in some steamy sweatshop.

My cousin came over for a glass of wine and stayed until midnight. Her husband is suffering from severe malnutrition and no one can seem to stop whatever is going on in his body. My cousin is a wreck.

Monday. Got up and made pancakes for Gwen and me. There was a lovely sunrise—the kind that lights up the whole eastern sky with a deep pink glow. I haven't walked along the trail behind the house in well over a week. I'm again anchored to my chair. I think exercise would make me feel better, but I can't muster the energy to get out. My cousin's husband went to an oncologist today, and they're waiting on the results of lab tests.

I discovered the back door doesn't stay locked and decided I'll have to put a hasp on the outside. I called a handyman because I don't want to make a real mess of it.

I don't want to miss you because if I even think about you, it makes me want to cry. I am having a hard time forgiving you for not being here on the anniversary of Jack's death. I feel like your supposedly forgetting the date was convenient and coincided with getting the best airline prices.

I feel like you fucking abandoned me. Found the Bombay Sapphire bottle on the enclosed back porch with the inch of gin in the bottom. It must have ended up there after Christmas. Drank that and went to bed.

Tuesday. We were supposed to have freezing rain this morning, but the sun was peeking out through mostly gray clouds. The snow is melting rapidly, and the roads are bare. Gwen was asked to go to the semiformal dance by a boy named Dalton. The dance is on the anniversary of Jack's death. I asked if she wanted to go—she said she knew it was a weird day but that she did want to go. You'll miss seeing her get dressed up.

I took a walk through the swamp—it's slushy with icy spots left on the tracks. It felt like spring. I took Gwen to roller derby, and they scrimmaged most of the time. Gwen is tentative as a jammer, but has a grasp of what's happening on the track—and there's a lot going on out there. Opened a bottle of wine. My cousin came over, and we stayed up until 1:30 a.m.

Wednesday. Winter is back with snow showers on and off and temperatures in the upper twenties. Managed to get up and walk this morning at 8:30. Heard and then saw a pileated woodpecker in the swamp, which is always a thrill. The handyman came over and took a look at the door lock and found things out of alignment. I wonder if this is a metaphor for anything. I've thought a lot about why I am so angry with you, and I know that at the center of that anger is Jack. We never talk about Jack. I feel like I was the parent who paid the most attention to him, and, in some ways, I feel like I now bear some responsibility for his death. This horrible burden has almost done me in. When you chose not to be here this year on the anniversary, it felt like you were saying *I wash my hands of this.* Whereas I need unconditional support on that one day of the year. We clearly need to get some things out on the table, but I don't know if I will ever have the energy to do this. We need to have a conversation about Jack and guilt and responsibility. I am like Mrs. Bridge from the Evan Connell book. Like her, I am unable to confront anything or anyone, including, or maybe especially, you.

Tonight I made a chocolate cake from a recipe I found on the side of a box of cocoa. Gwen and I had a dinner of chicken, goulash, and cooked carrots, and we sat in front of the fire and watched several episodes of *Parks and Recreation*.

Thursday. It's a raw day, in the twenties with a slight breeze. It snowed during the night, and there's a new dusting covering all the architectural sins in the village. Gwen is home for the day because it's exam week, and she doesn't have a test, so I left her sleeping while I headed to Dryden to Dunkin' Donuts to get a cup of coffee. After being so angry with you, I am exhausted from the energy that took. Now I'm just tired and wonder what lies ahead. I envision you coming home and settling into the pattern of you not asking me about my day and me staying up late and you going to bed early. And we won't be able to figure out how to have a conversation about anything of substance.

Friday. Hardly slept a wink. Got up to walk on a slippery sidewalk—was so afraid I'd fall and hit my head and then wouldn't be able to yell at you when you came home. Railey, Gwen, and I drove to Syracuse and picked up Clara at the train station (the train was only twenty minutes late) and, when we got home, we sat around the living room. The girls entertained themselves by making fun of me. It was so nice to hear them laughing and goofing around, even if it was at my expense. Does it mean anything that I am the butt of every joke? It's night, and the temperature hovers around freezing, and there's a dusting of snow on the ground as I stumble up to bed.

Saturday. Woke up early to get chores done before the girls stirred. It's an overcast day—gray on gray—and the front room is quiet except for the thrum of an occasional early riser driving past on Main Street. It's interesting how a new crisis will push previous crises to somewhere in the middle of your brain. I imagine all of my crises looking like lawyers lined up with briefcases in hand waiting for their day in court. When it's their turn, one by one, they come to a podium in the front of my brain and begin to argue the case. Bored lawyers representing faux lawsuits, the book I'm not writing, the impending February sixth, and finally what to think about you, mill about the antechamber in the middle of my brain opening briefcases, shuffling papers, then snapping them shut. Some murmur their arguments, and those are the ones that periodically disturb my sleep, and I wake thinking *What to do? What to do?* That's when I borrow a line from Scarlett O'Hara and whisper, *Oh, fiddle-dee-dee, I can't think about that right now*. I don't know what we're doing today. Maybe the girls will head off somewhere, which will be nice for them.

It was an afternoon and evening of washing clothes and drinking wine.

Sunday. It's a warm morning—in the forties. I don't want to chronicle this anymore. My cousin's husband is going to die any day now, and I know I'll have to be with her when it happens.

Dreamworld

In the past week, I've had two dreams about Jack. In the first, he was everywhere I happened to be, and the weird part was that he was always laughing or smiling. I wanted to be with him in that dream, and when I woke, I had the idea it was a premonition of my death: Jack was beckoning me to come to the other side to be with him. I felt unsettled and nervous all day because of this dream. But I wasn't frightened.

In the other dream, I went to a polo arena to watch a match, and Jack's girlfriend Isabel is there. She has gained weight, has curled her hair, and is wearing glasses. She hands me a floral arrangement of chrysanthemums and lilies that is half-dead from riding a long way in a car. Many of Jack's and Clara's friends are milling around, waiting for the match to begin. Then I see Jack. He looks older, and as if he too has put on weight, and he is smiling. *How can you be here?* I ask. *There are ways,* he answers and then wraps his arms around me and gives me a big hug. *Don't tell anyone I'm here,* he says as we watch the horses begin to enter the arena.

Going to the Spiritualist Camp

My whole life, I've lived in a village with a spiritualist camp on the outskirts of town. When you're a child, you think nothing of this. You ride your bike along the cracked sidewalks and take in all the familiar sites—Methodist church, little school, Park-It Market, Bob Whyte's gas station, the little lumberyard, and the spiritualist camp. The camp sits back from the road, and you get to it by taking the gravel drive that passes between two columns made of cobblestones and cement. When I got older, I realized the columns resembled cairns I'd seen in Scotland and Iceland. Around the gravel circle are small cottages built among towering elms (which have been devastated by Dutch elm disease) and old maples. Each summer, the camp residents—mostly mediums—swelled the village's population of four hundred by several dozen.

As kids, some bike-riding friends and I would sneak into the back of the tiny auditorium where the mediums gave messages from the dead on Thursday evenings. In my memory, these messages were mundane and consisted of things like "Aunt Maude says to go back home because the stove is on." The messages seemed prescriptive, like they were meant to prevent the recipient from lurking household danger. *What's the big deal?* I thought.

Nobody really talked about the spiritualist camp, and when it was referred to, it was called the spook camp. Eventually, some of the cottages were winterized and people began to live there year-round. The mediums attended Sunday service at the little Temple of Truth church on the campgrounds. After the Christian service, mediums would give messages to members of the congregation. As an adult, I attended the church several times and sat on a hard, narrow wooden pew hoping for a message from the other side. I didn't prove to be very receptive. It's also possible that my people—at that point it was only my grandparents who had died decades earlier—had nothing to say.

My fascination with spiritualism grew despite those early frustrations. I couldn't understand why people in the village weren't flocking to the spiritualist camp on Sunday mornings. We had this amazing portal or conduit to whatever it was that lay beyond death right in our backyard, and yet there seemed to be no interest.

Our spiritualist camp was founded in 1895. One of my great-great-grandfathers was a builder in the village—his solid wooden houses adorned with simple architectural doodads, as was the late Victorian fashion, cover one end of the village. He also brought the spiritualists in. I don't know if he had a premonition that his daughter and four-year-old grandson would drown in a steamboat incident on Cayuga Lake just a few years later, but I like to think his subconscious had already made that connection and knew he would be seeking their services when he laid the foundations for the cottages. The heyday for the Freeville spiritualist camp was around World War I, when thousands of people flocked to town in the summers to try to reconnect with lost husbands and sons.

About twenty years ago, I wanted to learn more about spiritualism, so I made a four-hour drive to the western New York community of Lily Dale—one of the largest spiritualist camps in the world. Lily Dale is a village of brightly painted Victorian houses occupied by mediums who offered a full summer program of workshops and daily message services. Houses were built cheek by jowl on snug lots, and front yards were a riot of colors between the flower gardens and the lawn ornaments. The houses were crowded on narrow paved roads running perpendicular to Cassadaga Lake. Lily Dale had several guesthouses and the nineteenth-century Maplewood Hotel to accommodate visitors who wanted to stay on the grounds. You paid an entrance fee at the gate to the village, parked your car, then had access to as many message services and private medium visits (these were for a fee) you could squeeze in.

I registered for a three-day workshop on discovering your mediumship. Our instructor, Janet, had been a Catholic nun for decades but decided to split with the church when it became impatient with her over her gifts. A small woman wearing a plain skirt and blouse, her dark hair cut in a bob with bangs, greeted our group of about twenty people who had traveled to Lily Dale from all over the States and Canada. She explained that a medium's message was all about proof of existence. The medium could be seeing colors, shapes, visions of people, or hearing words or voices, but for all of that, if they could not prove to the recipient that their loved one was there in spirit form, they weren't doing their job. "Names, dates, the way they died, or specific incidents that only the recipient could know," she said. "These are examples of proof of existence beyond the grave."

The medium is like a telephone, Janet explained. Just an object through which communication flowed. Mediums don't have to make sense of what they're saying because they aren't really doing the talking. "It's almost like watching and then narrating a movie," she said. According to Janet, a spirit is a form of energy vibrating at a very high frequency. Matter and spirit are co-related, but we have to be open to receiving messages from the spirit world. We have to be open to watching that movie.

Over the next couple of days, I discovered that, at that time, I had no talent for mediumship. Actually, it was as if I existed behind some kind of force field that repelled the spirit world. Janet had us working with partners and cards, each person trying to intuit what the other was holding. We had cards with symbols, colors, and numbers on them. I felt sorry for all of my partners because as much as I relaxed, meditated, concentrated, and even guessed, I failed in this basic, ground-floor communication skill. "Don't think," admonished Janet. "Feel. Try to tune in to the right radio channel." She told us that the harder you work, the more you tense up, and the likelihood of failure skyrockets.

I was the class failure. At the other end of the scale was John Paul, a young man from Washington, DC, who could have been a Pre-Raphaelite model with his long dark curls, fine features, and porcelain skin. Janet was clearly very taken with him and his abilities. John Paul told us he had always felt intuitive and that he suspected he had a gift. During our last workshop session, Janet called him to the little raised stage at the front of the room and asked him to do a demonstration. He was to give a message, but the recipient was not to identify himself or herself until it was over.

John Paul moved to the front of the room, closed his eyes, then began to speak in a soft voice. He told of a woman standing behind him, and from his description, all I could see was Auntie Em from *The Wizard of Oz*. Then he followed the woman, in his mind, on a tour of the farmhouse where she had lived. With his eyes squeezed shut and his head down, John Paul described the patterns on the wallpaper and objects in the various rooms. Finally, he said that he had a message for a granddaughter who was in the room. "She's telling you to always make tea the right way," he said, and with his hands began demonstrating putting tea in a tea ball, then opening the lid of a teapot and placing the tea ball inside. I nearly fainted, it was so extraordinary. John Paul opened his eyes, looked a little confused and embarrassed, and left the stage. Janet asked if anyone could identify the spirit. The young woman sitting next to me said it was clearly her grandmother, who always made tea with a tea ball. She said the details about the farmhouse were astonishingly accurate.

Between sessions, we were encouraged to visit as many message services as we could to watch the mediums work. There were at least three services a day at Inspiration Stump, which was in a clearing in the woods at the edge of the village, a couple of services at the Forest Temple, and one large service in the auditorium. Each service was crowded with people searching for messages from the other side. I began to recognize people who were also staying at the Maplewood Hotel ($25 per night with the bonus of a spirit painting hanging in most of the rooms) and from the café where most people ate (breakfast with coffee for $1.99). We were a motley-looking group—a lot of overweight white people who shopped for clothes at Walmart, smoked cigarettes, and drank lots of coffee. As we started to recognize one another, we became invested in one another's story and quest for recognition from a special spirit. We silently cheered the others on when a medium would look their way at a message service and say, "May I come to you?" the standard opening for a medium about to deliver a message.

Not only was I terrible at developing the skills of my mediumship, but also I don't remember receiving a single message over the four days I was at Lily Dale, although it was not for lack of trying. I became a regular message junkie racing from service to service. I began to recognize who I thought were the best mediums and tried to will them to look my way. I was like the kid in third grade who always knew the answer and had her hand perpetually raised and whispered, *pick me, pick me, pick me*. As I drove away from Lily Dale, all I could think was that my ancestors were a cold lot.

Lately, I've been thinking a lot about Lily Dale and spiritualism. I don't know what's going on with our spiritualist camp. The sign that said it was part of the Central New York Spiritualists Association is no longer affixed to one of the cobblestone columns, so I don't know if the mediums are still active. Lily Dale, I knew, was thriving. So, a couple of years ago, I decided to make another trip to the world of the spiritualists. This time I signed up for a course—Developing the Psychic Self.

It was August, and the sultry summer weather was oppressive for the four days I spent in the hamlet. The whole vibe had changed since my visit two decades earlier. The visitors were younger and skewed more middle class. I saw groups of women who were visiting the camp together and also young couples. On my first afternoon there, I saw a group of Tibetan monks moving across the lawn in front of the café—saffron and maroon robes flowing in the slight breeze caused by their brisk strides.

I stayed in a guesthouse where every room above the first floor had been turned into a bedroom. I was on the third floor, and it was like walking into my own private fussy Victorian oven. I found that if I lay absolutely still, I could almost trick my mind into believing there might be a breath of air coming through the open window. Wi-Fi was spotty throughout Lily Dale (maybe all that spirit work interfered with it?), and it was no exception at the guesthouse. Most guesthouses at Lily Dale advertise a coffee porch where residents can hang out and chitchat. For some reason, this reminded me of porches on cure cottages in Saranac, New York, for the tuberculosis patients who came for healing air and waters in the nineteenth and early twentieth centuries. Those of us in the guesthouse did get to know one another and chatted in the morning and evening before people went off to their readings or classes.

Several groups of women were staying in my guesthouse—it almost felt like a girlfriends' getaway destination. Sally and Annie were one pair, both a little older than me and infinitely cooler. Sally had a shoulder-length head of curly white hair, wore green-framed glasses, and was slim with an affinity for black linen dresses. Annie was petite, had a spray of curly gray hair, and wore linen pants and sleeveless tops. She'd brought a kayak with her to paddle in the lake. Sally was a documentary filmmaker, and Annie was a sculptor. Annie and I got into a little tiff about weight—she blamed the heavy for being heavy, and I took her to task for this. She also dismissed the ivory-billed woodpecker sighting in Arkansas in 2004. "You don't believe that, do you?" she asked me in an incredulous way even after I told her that my husband, Tim, was the one who saw the bird. I later discovered that she had created a group of sculptures of extinct species and that the ivory-billed woodpecker was one of them, so I suppose she felt she had some skin in the extinction game. Only she didn't tell me that when we were arguing on the porch.

On the last day of my visit, when we were sitting in a café, I told them about Jack when it came up in an organic way. I cried and was angry with myself for crying. *Why must I always cry?* It brings me unwanted attention. Sally was very kind. Annie was cool.

Message from Inspiration Stump from a medium named Margaret: "May I come to you? I have someone coming in from the spirit side of life. There is a woman who is very close and all around you. She wants to tell you she likes the gravestone you chose, and when you come to the grave, she is always there. Are there flowers? Do you tend the grave? It looks like a family plot. I see people eating at the family plot. Like a picnic? She likes that and says the food looks good. She is always with you. She wants you to know."

Message from Forest Temple from a medium named Ron: "I like your brooch. Did someone give that to you? I see the color green, but not in a bad way. You are searching for something and having a hard time finding it. Reverse engineer this—figure out what you don't want, then it may become clear."

Message from medium Drew Cali during our workshop: "I have to stop because I keep seeing someone behind you, and he's really trying to get my attention. I see an older man, below average height, and something happened to his head. He's watching over you. He was a—and I hope you don't mind me saying this—a real pisser. I also see the letter J . . . a gifted musician." Drew looked puzzled. "The message I'm getting is for you to stop observing and be willing to participate. There's also B–T—Betty or Beatrice—well, keep thinking about that."

When I didn't have any particular place to be, I found myself wandering the grounds of Lily Dale taking pictures of flowers and houses and headstones in the pet cemetery. Cassadaga Lake, which is more a large muddy pond, was behind the guesthouse. There was a small dock with a little covered area at the end, providing shade for two picnic tables and benches. I sat at one of the tables, and within minutes, a couple—Kathleen and Breighton—sat down at the other. She was a thin, very tan woman wearing an emerald-green tank top and flowing pants. She had a full head of white hair that spread like a mane from her head. Her husband/partner had a kind, open face and a very long, skinny braid draped over one shoulder. He wore billowing trousers gathered at the ankle. They had just arrived at Lily Dale to teach the geomancy course that evening, having traveled from West Virginia, not far from Harpers Ferry.

I asked what they did, and they began telling me about clearing Civil War battlefields of the ghosts of soldiers who didn't want to leave. They told of going to South Mountain dressed in period clothing (it creates resonance, said Breighton) on a beautifully clear night. Breighton was taking still photos using infrared, and a friend was shooting infrared video. They were there with Kathleen's teacher, who had already successfully cleared ghosts from several other Civil War sites. Kathleen said she stepped off the path and into the grass and felt her feet sink like she was walking through hay. She took a couple of steps when a man in a Confederate uniform suddenly sat up in front of her and screamed in a terrified way, "Are you real?" and she screamed, "I'm real but you're not!" and then Kathleen's teacher screamed, "Get out of there!" Breighton said that Kathleen had broken between the two worlds, and there were two realities happening at the same time. Kathleen got back on the path and began to "sing the spirits away." Breighton and the videographer got images of horses and men with slouch hats riding past. Apparently, Confederate soldiers were told to stay and hold South Mountain in the three days leading up to the battle at Antietam. They were all killed. "You need to tell them they no longer have to hold the line and that they're okay to go to spirit world," Kathleen's teacher told her. So that's what Kathleen did. Kathleen told me that her teacher also believes that soldiers who are missing limbs won't leave to go to spirit world because they are not whole, so she brings prosthetics to the fields and tells them to take what they need. I wasn't quite sure how this worked and if any ghost soldiers actually took a limb with them.

Then Breighton told a story about trying to clear an old dirt basement of ghosts in Harpers Ferry right on the Potomac Water Gap. This involved moving a cranky Confederate general and two little kids who'd hidden in the basement during a battle. Breighton also said he had to move a "two-dimensional golem who got stuck on this side of the gap when the rocks shifted twenty thousand years ago, and he found himself on the other side from his home and was unable to cross back over the gap." According to Breighton, moving the golem involved programming crystals and providing a path for it to cross the fault line and enter its cave. "We had to program the crystals because we couldn't stay much longer," he said.

What was this place I had brought myself to? I feel like I am open to just about any kind of experience, but these stories were wilder than most I'd heard. A big part of me loves listening to people who are passionate and involved. I don't think Kathleen's and Breighton's stories were beyond the pale, but they had certainly come up to the line and danced on it before retreating.

Before my last visit to Lily Dale, I tried to imagine what it would be like if Jack tried to contact me through a medium. Would Jack say he's fine and that I shouldn't worry about him? Would he tell me not to feel guilty? Would I be like one of the weeping women who comfort each other and say, *Well, now that there's some kind of closure, the healing can begin*? I'm still not sure I really want to hear from Jack. I'm afraid he'll say he wanders through the house looking for songs he can no longer sing or that he sits by Gwennie's bed at night when she's home from college and watches her breathe. Or that he's in the attic rummaging through all of his belongings Tim put under a blue tarp—running his ghostly finger along the spines of the books in the green bookcase or riffling through calculus papers that are piled in a heap on his red nightstand. I thought a Lily Dale medium would look at me with sad eyes because she'd know Jack was my son and that he committed suicide. And I thought she'd say what any mother would want to hear—*It's not your fault.*

It wasn't until I got home—and it was pointed out to me—that Drew Cali was talking about Jack when he said he saw the letter J and added "a gifted musician." I threw him off the track by mentioning my mother, Jane, and my father's other wives with names that begin with the letter J. The odd look Drew gave me stuck with me.

He had seen Jack.
He was talking about Jack.
Jack wanted to give me a message.
I didn't acknowledge Jack.
Why had I failed to recognize him?

SEARCHING

The Dude Ranch

It's November, and this morning it's dark and dreary and rainy, and the clouds have pulled right down to the hills and are spilling over ridges and down into the valley. A constant barrage of gunfire comes from the valley as deer hunting season is in full swing, and it's a Saturday morning. No work obligations are keeping the hunters out of their tree stands. I worry about a stray bullet hitting me as I walk in the backyard, but really, what are the chances of that?

I spend my days reading and writing. I haven't read or listened to the news, I haven't talked on the phone. I've cut myself off from my already tiny world to concentrate on trying to feel better. My family understands my need to do this. For decades they've seen me travel around the world—never with them—and they know that if I couldn't do this, if I were somehow trapped in the Pink House, I would go mad. Jack's suicide has exacerbated this need to go to places where I won't be known, where I can be anonymous and alone.

Since Jack died, I've been to the Falklands, Italy, and Arizona without my family. This last trip was the toughest because I attended a conference where, because I was a regular attendee, everyone knew my story. I wore my dark glasses and slunk around for a day or two until people got comfortable with the fact that I was there. Before attending the conference in Scottsdale, I spent several days at the Tanque Verde guest ranch outside Tucson.

I've always wanted to go to a dude ranch—my fascination probably stems from the first time I saw *The Women* as a ten-year-old. Set on the edge of miles and miles of federal land and within the Sonoran Desert, Tanque Verde was everything I had hoped for—low-slung pink adobe buildings, a large dining room, slouching wranglers with cigarettes dangling from their lips and spurs on their boots, and a focus on relaxation. I knew I was too heavy and arthritic to ride. My disappointment, especially when I saw the corral with the dozens and dozens of horses milling about waiting to be saddled up, was enormous despite my knowledge that riding would be painful and likely harmful.

I grew up with a quarter horse—Stormy—and, for years, rode along back roads and through fields with another girl from Freeville. Then, when Railey was young, I took her to riding lessons at a local farm because she was also one of those horse-crazy girls. As a little girl, she had a collection of Breyer horses, My Little Ponies, and dime store plastic horses that she kept in a huge plastic bag that she'd lug to the neighbor's house or to the place beneath the huge pine tree in the backyard. She and her friend Anna would then spend hours playing horses. As far as I could tell, those two little girls spent all of their time on the setup. I'd overhear them saying things like *your girl will say this, and then my boy will say that* as they held the plastic horses—many of which had broken legs that were mended with popsicle stick splints and Band-Aids. I think their form of playing was all about creating and controlling the narrative and leaving nothing to chance.

Railey remained chronically horse crazy, and so she and I went to Iceland for ten days when she was sixteen, and I was forty-five. We stayed at a farm in the northern part of the country—not far from the Arctic Circle—and slept in bunk beds in a tiny room. There were six of us there for a week of riding Icelandic horses. After a day of getting used to saddles with the long stirrups and the stocky little horses with an extra gait that had developed over a millennium of making their way in rocky landscapes, we set off on a journey that involved riding across wind-swept glacial plains, up and along the sides of mountains, and through icy-cold streams. One night we stayed in a mountain hut where we slept on wide shelves that ran along one side of the room. In the middle of the night, a road crew came in and climbed up onto the sleeping shelves as well.

As I stood at the edge of the Tanque Verde corral and watched the horses mill about, softly nickering and licking the salt blocks wired to the fences, I remembered that trip to Iceland and how much I loved riding. I loved the thrill of leaning forward while on the back of my horse and just letting him run like the wind. And I yearned to recapture that feeling of weightlessness, where your burdens fly into the air behind you, and it's just you and the horse and the moment.

Instead of riding, ceding to the reality of my infirm body, I spent my time at Tanque Verde walking around with binoculars slung around my neck and a bird guidebook and camera in my backpack. That first after-noon I took a nature walk with the staff naturalist—an older man—who led me along a trail and told me about the plants of the desert: saguaro, cholla, prickly pear, mesquite, creosote, and barrel cactus. We looked at these plants closely—touching their spines, running our hands along the bark of trees, and crushing leaves between our fingers to release the scent. Then we came upon what looked like a warehouse and a little corral with a metal water tank in one corner, and the guide told me that this was the set for the Nickelodeon series *Hey Dude*, a show filmed in the early 1990s that Railey used to watch when she was little. We walked over to the warehouse to look for some barn owls the guide thought might be roosting in there, but I really wanted to see if there were any remnants of the set left. We looked through the opening where the door used to be and saw lumber piled on the floor and several wooden chairs, a table, and then lots of wires and air ducts and insulation hanging from the high metal ceiling.

I texted Railey that I was looking at the place where *Hey Dude* was filmed, and she immediately texted back the words to the theme song, which she also sang aloud in the office, much to the puzzlement of her boss.

Most of my time at the ranch was spent watching birds, and after that initial excursion with the naturalist, I ventured alone. The ranch had built a little covered pavilion—a ramada, they called it—with a couple of benches facing several feeders. Someone at the ranch had figured out that there might be somebody like me coming along, and this was how they could provide an easy birding experience. While others rode, I spent hours watching birds come to the feeders and then gather and fuss around in the scrubby trees and cactus nearby. I watched a cactus wren—a large, flashy fellow with black and white stripes and speckles—dismantle a nest in one thorn tree and start to build a new nest in a neighboring one. A curve-billed thrasher—a sleek-looking brown bird with a striking yellow eye and a long curved bill—hung out in a mesquite bush near the feeders, sometimes hopping to the ground to check out what was there. About a dozen California quail came to investigate, running beneath the feeding stations calling *ka-KAA-ka*, making me feel like I was in the jungle rather than the desert. They looked like plush wind-up toys darting here and there. Then there were the sparrows—white-crowned, song, house, rufous-winged—and the finches, mainly house finch, and the cardinal and the pyrrhuloxia, an Anna's hummingbird, and a Gila woodpecker that posed on top of a nearby saguaro cactus. At one point, all the birds scattered as a Cooper's hawk blew in, then casually landed in a mesquite, acting as if he didn't mean to catch one of those birds anyway.

Sitting and watching these birds made me happy. Maybe it was because I decided I was going to figure out which species all of the birds were. Most of them weren't my birds or birds I'd see in upstate New York, so I had to spend time looking at them and figuring out their identifying marks. (Did the bird have a ring around or a line through the eye? What colors were on the bird, and how was the color distributed? How big was it? Did it have streaks or speckles on its breast? What did the bill look like?) Then I'd try to pick out the bird in the guidebook. Although I've been looking at birds for years and know how to use binoculars, I'm usually with a birder who is so much better than I am that I do the lazy thing and let him or her point out the distinguishing features to me. Now I was on my own.

I marveled at the redness of the cardinal—it seemed much redder than our eastern cardinal—and the sharp crest of the pyrrhuloxia; the sleekness of the curve-billed thrasher; the antics of the quail. And every now and then I thought to myself, *I am happy*, a feeling so unfamiliar over the past year that it was as if I had to pinch myself to check if I was awake. I wanted to stretch those hours at the bird feeders into days or even weeks. I wanted to figure out what it meant to be happy and determine how I could replicate the feeling. Could I make this feeling permanent, or was happiness destined to be ephemeral, always slipping away almost as soon as it was felt?

When I really thought about it, I realized my happiness while at the ranch boiled down to three things. I was alone. I wasn't home. And I was engaging all of my senses to solve a problem. This realization horrifies me because I don't know how to reconcile this with being in a family.

Visitation

Gwen's Girl Scout leader called me one morning not long after Jack died, and after tiptoeing around, asked if I would be open to hearing some messages that had come through when she was doing her deep meditation. She told me she was a Reiki master, which I didn't know. She said that Jack was coming to her in her meditations. The first image she got was of a waterfall, and then she asked if there was an important date that week for our family. She then said she thought he was trying to get messages to me through Gwen, and she wondered if Gwen had seen him in her room or in her dreams.

I didn't tell her that I had seen a Facebook message Gwen, then age twelve, had sent to Jack about a month earlier saying that he should let her know if he got this message but that he should remember that she got scared easily.

The scout leader then said that in her vision she'd seen an old wooden door with stained glass somewhere nearby and told me that the door was locked and needed a skeleton key to open it. Then she saw Tim carrying groceries. She asked me if someone had called the police right before Jack shot himself, and I said *yes* (kids who read a message he'd posted on

Facebook). She said Jack didn't intend to shoot himself but then panicked. She said he wanted to hurt himself but that it was not meant to be this way. He was trying to get the help he needed. She then said that she'd seen him a few times in her meditations and that his energy started out weak but now was strong and that he wanted me to know that he was okay.

I listened quietly as she talked and didn't tell her that the door to Jack's room was an old wooden door that required a skeleton key to lock it and that there was a decorative leaded glass window next to the door that couldn't be seen from the street. Jack's door wasn't locked but was shut tight because I couldn't bear to even get a glimpse of that room. I also didn't tell her that not only was Tim getting groceries but also he was taking care of all of us because the rest of the family was having a terrible time just functioning. I thanked her for the messages, then ended the call and tried not to think about Jack trying to reach me through the Girl Scout leader. I didn't really need her to tell me he was here—I knew he was just outside my field of vision wherever I was in the house or the yard.

Searching for Home in Italy

A few months after Jack died, I forced myself to pack a bag and head to the airport in Syracuse to grab a plane to New York and then on to Italy. I just threw things in my bag. This was going to be a quick trip—less than a week—and I didn't care what I looked like. I was going on a tour with some other travel writers. We'd be based in Bologna then take day trips. Inertia wanted to keep me in the Green Chair, but the pull of leaving was even stronger.

Right before I left for Italy, I visited Dryden Lake and noticed that the low-slung hills on the far shore looked like nubby brown-and-green fabric as the buds of leaves began to cover the trees. Dryden Lake is less a lake than a big irregularly shaped pond—a kind of widening of the stream.

People fish there during all four seasons: fishing from the tiny pier, casting out into the water, or from kayaks, or by cutting holes in the ice and dropping lines straight down into the dark waters.

I've been visiting the little lake for at least forty years. It serves as a kind of anchor to the world I inhabit when I'm not traveling. The geography of the lake includes me, my mother, and my children—shimmering half-present corporeal bodies sitting at picnic tables, playing on the wooden play structure, and throwing pebbles into the water from the pier. Over the decades, I've watched the big creek willow on the water's edge grow old. It eventually split. Half of the tree now lies submerged, providing places for fish to hide and linger in the shadows of the dead branches when the midsummer sun beats down upon the water.

It's a place I go during the day to escape the noise of traffic on Main Street and focus on the sounds of the wind in the trees and the birds calling, chirping, and singing. I clearly associate Dryden Lake with my mother, and since her death—which happened just a year before Jack died—whenever I visit, I still hear a whisper of her voice in the air.

I came home from the lake and took a rare nap, dreaming this, which I wrote down in a note to otherworldly Jack so I'd remember the details.

> *Jack, this afternoon you came into my room. You were wearing your soft blue-and-red flannel shirt, sleeves rolled neatly to just below the elbow, unbuttoned, showing a very faded lavender tee shirt underneath. You were so tall and thin, and you always wore clothes that accentuated that. Faded skinny gray jeans. Aqua low-rise Keds. Your hair was like it was before you had it all cut off in January—short on the sides with bangs you cut yourself. You crept into the bedroom while I was taking a nap and stood by the edge of the bed. I didn't really hear you, but I knew you were there. Then you sat on the edge of the bed—I was aware of your weight on the bed—and you said, "Mom?" in your low voice. I asked if you were a zombie, and you said no.*

I didn't know what it meant but that's what dreams are like for me. It was sweet and unsettling and made me feel off-kilter for days.

On the trip to Italy I didn't take good notes. I didn't really care and spent a lot of my time in a daze as we were shuttled here and there in a van. I kept looking for something familiar. I kept looking for Dryden Lake in a foreign land.

I did love the city of Bologna with its wide piazza at the city center sporting a fountain of Neptune. Stone buildings spanning a thousand years of architecture surrounded the piazza. Bologna is home to the oldest university in the world, founded in 1088, and when I walked through the university's oldest building and its courtyard, I felt almost faint as the ghosts of thousands of scholars milled around me. The walls surrounding the courtyard are covered with coats of arms painted on the stones. Some were elaborate, while others looked hastily painted. All there, I suppose, as a way to say, *I was here.* Even at a storied university people are forgotten and families fade away.

On one side of the city's Piazza Maggiore is a large redbrick building where Enzo, a son of Frederick II—the thirteenth-century Holy Roman emperor—was held prisoner for over twenty years. Across the piazza is the massive Basilica of San Petronio, the fifteenth-largest church in the world. When I walked into the basilica, its huge proportions dwarfed everything within it. The vaulted ceiling rose 147 feet in the air. I yearned to take photos in there to try to capture some of the airiness that the space evoked. I tried to be sneaky about it and was admonished by a guard.

As I stood near the Neptune fountain, I saw people going about their business: old women on bicycles with baskets attached to the handlebars heading to the markets; people sitting at café tables drinking coffee and reading newspapers; students strolling under the covered walkway near the university; impeccably dressed government workers bustling around city hall.

A group of students—clearly on their way to being very drunk—approached the fountain and asked me to take a picture of them. A young man with a laurel wreath resting on his curly black hair stood in the middle of the group; his friends told me he had just graduated with a medical degree, and this was part of the traditional celebration—a picture in front of Neptune. The graduate clutched a new MacBook that his friends had just given him. I took the photo. They all looked so happy at the prospect of the world spooling out in front of them.

They can't imagine themselves growing old and becoming me. I push thoughts of Jack from my mind as I realize he will never graduate from anything.

I wandered through the streets of Bologna, and under the covered walkways for which the city is famous. Many of the buildings are painted ochre and rose, and when the angle of sunlight is just right their walls light up during certain times of the day. On tiny side streets radiating from the piazza are cafés and shops. Early one morning I headed toward the university from my little hotel just in time for the morning market. Several of the narrow cobblestone streets were made even narrower by vegetable vendors who had dragged boxes and baskets filled with fruits and vegetables into the streets. I followed two nuns in habits as they pinched and poked and prodded the produce.

For some reason, the nuns poking the produce—or maybe it was the rows of dead fish at the market—made me think of taking my mother to Dryden Lake. Sometimes we'd stop at Dick Clark's Sure Save store in Dryden and order a couple of subs and get a bag of Wise potato chips. When we arrived at the lake, we'd get out of the car and walk up the small rise to the picnic table that sits under the old apple trees which drop a meager harvest of tiny green, wormy apples in autumn.

We'd unwrap the subs, smoothing the butcher paper for our tablecloth. We'd often sit in silence and eat our subs—periodically reaching into the bag of chips—and look at the lake. I'd point out any of the birds I knew like mallards, green herons, great blue herons, Canada geese, and the wonderfully chatty belted kingfisher. Every now and then, we'd see an osprey flying over the water's surface then watch as it suddenly dove straight down to grab a fish. Up it'd come with a wriggling fish in its talons—often largemouth bass but once it was a bright orange carp—then it'd flap its powerful wings to get altitude and take its dinner to a nearby stick nest.

Another time, while wandering through Bologna, I stepped into the shop of a violin maker who was sanding the back of a violin. The walls were covered with violins and violas. Several cellos were propped in a corner. The violin maker stood behind a wooden counter where he slowly and methodically sanded what had to be the world's most beautiful piece of wood—it had alternating bands of yellow and brown spreading like a flower from one end.

I think I was drawn into the shop because when he was in third grade, Jack played the violin. We then bought him one for Christmas when he was a teenager. I realize I don't know what happened to it.

I kept asking the violin maker questions and clung to each carefully formed word that came out of his mouth. He showed me his patterns that he used to cut the pieces that would eventually form an instrument. Behind him were vertical slots holding blocks and slabs of wood. He pulled one out and said he bought it for $10,000. I squinted my eyes trying to imagine all the violin backs that would be cut from this unremarkable-looking hunk of wood. In front of him on the workbench was a little dish of corks with oddly shaped chunks cut out from one end. I asked what these were for, and he showed me how they held pieces of wood together—or apart—as he was working on them.

All of his violins are commissioned and are not finished until the violinist comes to the shop. At that point the violin maker places the sound post inside the instrument and moves it a millimeter this way or that to adjust the tone the violinist is looking for. It takes him a month to make a violin for which he charges $30,000.

I wanted to stroke every instrument in the shop. The gorgeous velvety finishes pulled my fingers to places they should not be. Maybe some part of Jack was enveloped deep within the recesses of one of these beautiful instruments, I thought. Maybe I would be able to pull that suggestion of Jack from the violin's body and put it in my pocket to carry with me through the streets of Bologna.

Reluctantly, I left the shop and tried not to cry as I made my way along the narrow lane where the angle of the sun was casting long bruised-purple shadows across the cobblestones.

Even though I was traveling with several other people, I was lonely. We visited the Ducati, Ferrari, and Lamborghini factories and even got to drive Lamborghinis for about an hour on the rural roads surrounding the factory. I know this was something special, but the principal legacy of my time in a Lamborghini was a hip that ached terribly from trying to get out of a car that sat almost on the ground. *I am that middle-aged woman*, I thought, as a bolt of pain ripped down my leg as I tried to hoist myself out of the bright-green car that costs a quarter of a million dollars.

This was not the countryside I yearned for and not even the distraction I needed. We drove through flat agricultural fields in a region known for its cheese, ham, and balsamic vinegar. I wanted fewer people, more wildlife, some hills, and more desolation. If the landscape wasn't spectacular in some way, I at least wanted it to be familiar. I wished for a little lake surrounded by nubs of hills.

At one point, after touring Ravenna, four of us sat at a café on the edge of the Piazza del Popolo and ordered drinks. My three companions pulled out phones and began checking messages, Facebook, and who knows what else. I told them they were rude. They all looked up at me, kind of laughed, then went back to looking at their phones. "Put them away," I said. "You're being rude." At which point they put them on the table, and we then tried to have a conversation made awkward by my insistence that we interact.

After finishing my drink, I excused myself and walked across the piazza to look at Dante's tomb. They stayed at the table and picked up their phones.

Because I had spent so much time alone, I didn't know how to behave around people anymore. I began to think that I hated people most of the time. But that's not it. I was not making room for conversation or any human interactions in my crowded mind. I had become antisocial.

Several years ago, I drove to Dryden Lake on a snowy February afternoon and sat in my car and watched snow swirls like little tornadoes on the lake's frozen surface. Every now and then, a gust of wind would lift snow from the ice, which would rise in big clouds of swirling whiteness that met the falling snow at a midpoint between earth and sky. During a break in the squall, a muted sun broke through, and I could see open water near the far shore. There, a couple of hundred yards from where I sat, were half a dozen swans, unusual visitors to the lake. I didn't know if they were real or if I just wanted them to be real—layers of whiteness dissolving into a fairy-tale world. The swans disappeared several minutes later in gentle swirls of snow, and I found myself alone once again, sitting in the car at the edge of the lake.

Our last night in Italy was spent at a villa outside the city of Siena in Tuscany. Instead of traveling into the little city, I went up into my corner room and lay down on my bed. I opened the windows and listened to the swallows come and go—they were building nests right beneath the eaves above my windows. They'd swoop up to land on the nest then leave seconds later. Arriving and leaving. Arriving and leaving. And I started thinking that I am aware of their absence only because they made their presence known.

Oh, Jack. Why did you choose to leave? For the first time on the trip with the swallows stirring the air outside my window, I buried my head into my pillow and sobbed. You have created such a hole in my heart. I fell into a deep sleep, and when I awoke, the sun was starting to set.

I pulled myself together, putting enough water on my red-rimmed eyes to take away the sting of the tears and running my hand through my hair which had grown tangled during my nap.

I walked into the garden outside the villa with my camera. Streaks of orange and red crossed the western sky, where the sun was setting behind the Tuscan hills. I took several photos of a marble angel in the garden with the darkening sky behind him. At first the statue seemed warm and approachable in the glow of the sky—like maybe we could have a conversation about heaven and earth and all that lay in between—but within minutes, as the sun dipped behind the hills, he turned cold and severe.

A couple of days after I got home from Italy, I drove to Dryden Lake and sat in my car parked at the edge of the water. Things had greened up nicely in the week I had been away. The leaves were out, and I watched as a belted kingfisher sat out on a limb of the split willow tree, waiting for something interesting to show up in the water beneath him. A great blue heron walked through the brown reeds just across the way, also looking for something to eat. Eat or be eaten, I thought. You're either alive or you're not. Through the windshield of my car, as I watched the heron, that message was clear. But I could not sort out the lessons of nature, accept the future, and live.

I looked at the table beneath the apple trees which had just leafed out and wished I could call my mother on the phone to ask her to have a spring picnic with me. We'd order subs and buy potato chips. I looked at the tire swing where Jack would sit and twirl until he felt sick. In my phone contacts, Jack's phone number is right before my mother's number. Jack. Jane. I wondered what would happen if I dialed them.

Later that day I called my doctor, asking her to up my dosage of antidepressants. At first I thought it was just a reentry problem—coming back to the village and the Pink House—but I think it was deeper than that. I fell back into the Green Chair with the red quilt and had a hard time moving. Coming back from Italy was even more difficult than coming back from the Falklands. Was it because spring was really upon us? Crocuses and daffodils were forcing their way through the soggy leaves in the front garden I never bothered to clean up before winter. I couldn't seem to bear moving into another season, such a definite marking of time. Renewal. Rebirth. Who cares? I wanted to turn back the seasonal clock to the depths of winter. My depression felt more appropriate amidst snow squalls and dimly lit days.

That night I looked in the mirror and was startled to see that my hair was almost entirely gray. I didn't know when that had happened.

The Pull of Water

There's a spot in Lisle about twenty miles from my house where people pull off to the side of the road to get springwater. When I was little, there was a pipe that came out of the alternating layers of shale and limestone on the side of the hill, and a steady current of water spilled from its mouth into a small stream. Each time we drove past, I would snatch glimpses of people holding jugs, pots, and pails under the water flowing from the pipe, catching the water before it could feed the stream that spilled into Dudley Creek. I would sit in the back seat of the Buick and wonder where the water came from. How does it come out of the side of a hill? Once I asked my mother this question. She distractedly answered, "I don't know," as she tried to maneuver on roads that were slightly outside her comfort zone of ten miles from our farmhouse.

This was before I knew about artesian aquifers and flowing artesian wells. Our central New York land, it turns out, is lousy with water.

I grew up in a place that once had mile-high glaciers right over where our farmhouse sat. I first heard about the glaciers when I was very young. I tried to imagine this expanse of ice from the north being pushed over us, grinding and leveling everything that lay in its path. As a kid, I'd look up and squint at the clouds and wonder if the glacier was as high as they were. I'd also wonder if everyone from New York went down to Florida (like the snowbirds I'd heard about) as the glacier came bearing down on them. Did they have time to pack up all their things before the ice crushed them? I had little concept of time and was confused by the immensity of it all.

As the glaciers of the last ice age retreated about twelve thousand years ago, what I think of as my landscape emerged: rounded hills of glacial till; hills shaped like cigars; very low ridges snaking through the woods and pastures; ponds; deep gorges with plunging waterfalls; and long, skinny lakes. This is our reminder of ice ages past.

And there is water, water everywhere. In lakes, ponds, streams, creeks, swamps, and just beneath the surface of the land in abundant aquifers. The glaciers carved, elongated, and created waterways that we see today, but much of the water itself comes from the earth. Long before the glaciers, a shallow sea covered this part of the world, leaving behind layers upon layers of silt and mud and sand filled with shells of tiny sea creatures. Some were exotic—like trilobites and horn coral—and some were clam-like and common. All of their fossilized remains can be found trapped in the hundreds of feet of limestone and shale exposed by the ceaseless flow of aboveground streams in my region. These layers, particularly the more porous ones, also provide underground paths for the groundwater. Sometimes when a well is drilled and taps into one of these layers and if the conditions are right, the water is forced to the surface by the pressure of the rocks above. This creates an artesian well, or a well where the water flows without the use of a pump. This explains the water flowing from the pipe coming out of the side of the hill in the town of Lisle.

When I was in elementary school, we lived in a large house in the middle of the tiny hamlet of Ludlowville, tucked down between some hills. Our backyard abutted Salmon Creek. A hundred feet downstream, the water plunged over a thirty-foot waterfall. This was our playground. We walked on the rim of the falls, our feet fitting in the little channels worn away in the limestone by the force of the water. We would sidle up to the edge and look at the plunge pool below, ringed by large jagged rocks. Then we'd solemnly recount the story of the boy who had jumped off the falls and died. Every kid knew this story. No one ever questioned its authenticity because each one of us could imagine its truth. We were mesmerized by the water moving, moving, moving toward the edge, then disappearing. We all felt its pull. The impulse to join the water was so strong I had to stand back lest I found myself giving in to its power. Never has an impulse felt so strong; it was as if I was being pulled on a molecular level to join the water.

Join us, join us, join us, whispered the water droplets that banded together and formed the creek that plunged over the falls. It was almost impossible to block their whispered cries as I picked my way across the creek, careful not to slip on the slick surface of the rocks. I never knew if my siblings heard these voices from the rushing water—it wasn't something we talked about—but I know we all felt the pull of the creek.

CHANGE

Minefields

I visited the Falkland Islands five weeks after my teenage son Jack killed himself—a trip that had been planned for a year (and, admittedly, one I went on to escape my home). I looked out at the vast minefields left by Argentine forces in 1982 near the little city of Stanley, a lethal reminder of a war fought thirty years earlier, and wondered what it would be like to live with the possibility of an explosion always lurking beneath one's feet or car wheels. Each of the minefields is surrounded by barbed wire, with skull and crossbones signs nailed to the fence posts. There are now two generations of Falkland Islanders who have grown up with the minefields, and to them, they're part of the landscape. To the older generation, they're a constant reminder of fear and boredom and food shortages and bombings that came with the Argentine occupation of their country. Little by little, the Falkland Islanders are locating and clearing away the mines, but removing them remains a painstakingly slow and dangerous process.

When I returned home, I sobbed when I saw that my husband, Tim, had taken everything out of Jack's bedroom and placed it under a blue tarp in the attic. He also had painted the blood-spattered bedroom walls a bright yellow. To this day, I can't go into the attic because I might see that blue tarp, and beneath that tarp is everything from the Before Time—the years Jack was alive. The blue tarp and the yellow-painted room have not become part of my domestic landscape. My memories are embedded in physical space, creating potential minefields within the very rooms of my house.

I have wanted to move from our house since Jack shot himself in his bedroom in 2012, but some mysterious formula of Landscape + Sadness + Ancestral Homeland = Inertia. I've spent those years trying to blot out all memories of that evening. Of course I can't. What I sometimes try to remember—and never can—is how I ever managed to walk up the old oak stairs, turn left at the landing, and then walk past Jack's room and into our bedroom that first night. I think, *That's okay, you managed to do it*, but also, *You couldn't possibly have slept in the house where your son just killed himself.*

It was just past 8:00 p.m., and I do remember policemen and EMTs rushing up the porch steps and into the house, and having to talk to a detective from the sheriff's department and then a cop in a patrol car that sat idling in our driveway with its lights flashing. While the cop questioned me, I watched as a few snowflakes fell in the cold February night, landing on his windshield and melting. And then I walked inside, got a beer from the refrigerator, and tried to drink it while sitting at the dining room table. The Methodist minister sat across from me. All I heard was *blah blah blah*. Then I remember the local funeral director—a man who has buried generations of my family—coming to talk to me, and he cried while saying, *I tried to clean it up as best I could*, and I wondered if the upstairs hall would smell like Clorox.

Every room in the house is a minefield. The kitchen—I can never again prepare or eat cheese ravioli or pancakes because that was Jack food. The dining room—his chair at the table. The living room—the couch where he used to sit and stroke the old dog. The front room—an elaborate cut-paper snowflake taped to the front window (the last thing I remember him making). His Christmas stocking at the bottom of the bin holding Christmas ornaments is like a spent nuclear fuel rod. During warm weather,

I can sit on our wide wraparound front porch—a place where Jack didn't spend much time—and turn my back on the house. At some point, inevitably I'm driven back inside by mosquitoes or the cold into the house of the explosive objects.

Land mines were invented more than 150 years ago, during the American Civil War, by Confederate general Gabriel J. Rains and his brother Brigadier General George Washington Rains. They were known as the Bomb Brothers for their creation and strategic use of booby traps, torpedoes, and land mines. The Rainses' design of a mechanically fused high explosive land mine was refined by the Germans in the run-up to World War I. Since then, land mines have been used on battlefields throughout the world. Up to 110 million mines still lie just beneath the surface of the ground, salting the countryside of at least sixty nations. In 2015, more than 6,500 civilians—many of them children—were killed or injured by these mines.

In the Falklands, many mines were planted in peat bogs or in sand, and over the years, as the ground froze and thawed and froze and thawed and the dunes migrated, the mines shifted. Some buried themselves deeper or turned on edge or were sitting upside down. When they decided to begin clearing the mines, British government officials hired highly trained Zimbabwean de-miners to assist them. The government had been working at this task for years, and 70 percent of the mines in 130 minefields had been cleared by the time of my visit. Unfortunately, the last 30 percent would prove to be the most difficult to clear because they lay in peat bogs and below the beaches of delicate habitat occupied by penguins. Using metal detectors to locate the mines, de-miners then use scrapers and prodders to carefully excavate them. A metal detector can produce false positives for mines at a rate of a thousand to one because anything containing metal will set it off—ring tabs, coins, zipper pulls, even traces of metal in rocks. A good de-miner in the Falklands might find one mine a week.

Walking through my house means averting my eyes lest they spy the mines—photos of Happy Jack as a four-year-old standing in a playground wearing his favorite *101 Dalmatians* tee shirt; as a six-year-old towhead wearing a maroon soccer jersey and smiling at the camera; as a two-year-old standing with his three-year-old sister at an outdoor water fountain in a park and they're both laughing hysterically because water is squirting everywhere. I wander from the front room, through the living room, and then the dining room, and finally into the kitchen. Along the way, I've made it my habit not to look directly at any of these photographs because they return me to the scene of the flashing lights in the driveway. Like the British government, I've delayed dealing with my minefield, making the task more difficult since many of the Jack photos feel more embedded as over the years they've shifted and made themselves integral parts of the landscapes on the top of the sideboard, the bookshelves, and the fireplace mantel. Other family members have integrated these objects into our new lives without Jack. They are hard to dislike.

Neither Jack's sisters nor Tim nor I can manage to go into Jack's bedroom, though it's been painted a bright and sunny color, and all of his objects—the bed, his bureau, his bookshelves, his musical instruments—have been removed. I can't even touch the doorknob with its beautiful tarnished brass face made in a local wire factory over a hundred years ago and worn almost smooth from a thousand turns. For me, it would be like touching a hot iron.

I read more about clearing land mines and discover that in addition to people with metal detectors, Gambian giant pouch rats (native to East Africa), dogs, honeybees, bacteria, plants, and drones have been used to detect them. The animals, plants, and bacteria respond to the presence of the TNT used in the mines. Giant pouch rats are better at detecting mines than dogs, and honeybees are better than giant pouch rats. When bolted to the end of the metal detector, a ground-penetrating radar unit also proves a useful but expensive tool for locating mines.

I've wanted to move away from this house—have wanted to walk away from all of these physical reminders (my *memento mori*) of Jack—but my husband, Tim, can't seem to do it. Maybe he feels like he would come completely unmoored if we moved. Maybe what is my albatross is his anchor. I will probably never know because we can't seem to talk about it.

I've sent Tim Zillow listings of houses in Maine where the soothing sounds of the ocean might wash away the resounding blast of the shotgun. Tim doesn't acknowledge them, and I don't bring it up. I can tell, though, that he's afraid I will just take off one day and not look back, and for good reason. When I was feeling particularly low, I wallowed in this idea of walking away from the sad house and going to a place where no one knew me and my family's story. I thought I kept that desire hidden from Tim, but how can you hide such unhappiness?

I've only recently put some of the photographs of Jack and pieces of his artwork into drawers. For years I thought, mistakenly, that I could desensitize myself to the fact of Jack—could live like the Falkland Islanders and come to the point where I could pass by the skull and crossbones signs and not notice them. I thought I could do this by walking past photos of my boy and drawings he created (like the sweet four-panel drawing in colored pencils depicting facts about the Ojibwa that Jack drew in fourth grade). I've found, after almost a decade of trying, it's not possible to desensitize myself to the fact of Jack—his existence and his de-existence make me so sad. So I've been slowly and painstakingly trying to clear my personal minefield.

Many of the minefields that remained uncleared in the Falklands turned into beautiful natural areas of dunes and sea cabbage and tussac grass. It's an enticing, deadly beauty that's become home to several species of penguin—like the Magellanic and gentoo penguins—which are too small to trigger explosions. No human has been killed by a land mine in the Falklands since the end of the war in 1982, although several sheep wandered astray and met grisly ends. One problem Falkland Islanders had to struggle with was that in order to completely clear the last of the mines, they would have to essentially dig up these sensitive areas, which would then destroy the natural habitat and the penguin nesting colonies. I think about this and wonder if, as I clear more of my personal minefields, I have to destroy sensitive areas of my house in order to save myself.

I often think about memory—and what it is, and why it is—but I get flummoxed. Why do we have this faculty, and yet there are experiences so horrible and frightening that they should be forgotten? This seems antievolutionary although I know there are coping strategies for PTSD that focus on desensitization. Why is it that seeing a photograph or a drawing or a paper snowflake can trigger the very smell, taste, touch, sound, and feeling of an event that so negatively affected my life? Is it to remind me—as if I needed a reminder!—of the presence of danger and heartache? There are times when I want to reach into my skull and rip out the wiring that creates and then connects the parts of my brain that store memories.

What must it be like to live only in the present? I think. I read an account of a woman who suffered from this disease that goes by the prosaic name "severely deficient autobiographical memory syndrome." She could recall facts but couldn't conjure up any episodic memories. She knew she had a wedding but could not place herself back there to remember or relive the emotions of that day. She also couldn't speculate on her future. There are times when I yearn for this syndrome. Times when I wish to wipe the memory of that night from wherever it lies in my brain. I would be more comfortable with the memory of the fact of Jack's death than reliving the events of the night he died.

When I was in the Falkland Islands on the thirtieth anniversary of the war, I was surrounded by people with PTSD: the man who showed me every inch of the site of the war's bloodiest battle, the Welsh Guardsman who moved to the Falklands after the war to open a guesthouse in Stanley for visiting veterans of the war, the school superintendent who told me the story of a bomb hitting his house and killing three of his friends. When I looked into their eyes, I saw myself. I'm sure they would do almost anything to erase their memories. I know I would.

A while back, Tim proposed a house renovation project that we'd talked about years earlier. I suspect this was an attempt to temper my fury at not moving. Our house is built on the side of a small hill, and there is a large enclosed second-story back porch off the kitchen. This porch has banks of louvered windows on three sides. When you are on the back porch, you are surrounded by foliage because you are in the trees. You are eye to eye with the woodpeckers that hunt for insects in the huge sugar maple and the red and gray squirrels that fight for territory in the neighbor's Norway spruce trees. You can watch the crow family as they swoop around the line of Norway spruce standing in front of the swamp, and you can almost see the nest of the merlins—a species that a couple of decades ago had never been known to breed in New York State—which, like a miracle, have returned to the same spruce for the third year.

Tim's plan is to knock a wide opening between the kitchen and this back porch and replace all the louvered windows to make it weathertight, and then run baseboard heaters around the room. This will become new space within our previously closed circuit of a house. It is as far away from Jack's bedroom as a room can be and still be attached to the house.

Will this attempt to reorient the house exorcise the ghost of Jack? I do not remember Jack on this back porch. This will be new, never-occupied-by-Jack space, and therefore the ghost of Jack will not cross the threshold. We will have created an ultra-peripheral region and, in effect, will have placed virtual barbed wire around the part of the house where Jack lived. Perhaps, like with the last of the mines in the Falkland Islands, this will isolate and keep contained the reminders of Jack's life that throw me into a state of melancholia. Perhaps I can then treat the main part of the house like the delicate, sensitive habitat occupied by penguins in the Falklands.

This planned new room will be spare, housing only a chair or two and a desk. I might put a small single bed in one corner. There will be no personal land mines. I will sit in a chair or lie on the bed and watch the birds because this makes me feel better. I will watch the sky lighten as the sun pushes up from the swamp hidden behind the spruce trees. And in the fall, the maple leaves will turn blaze orange and fiery red and golden yellow and they will float to the ground. I will keep an eye on dark clouds which knit together into storms that swoop in from the east. In the winter, as the wind lifts and propels snowflakes into squalls that wend their way through and around the bare branches of the massive maple, I will be sitting alone in my own snow globe. And like the front porch, I can be in this room—this former porch—with my back to the house where Jack lived. If I'm lucky, I will be in reclaimed territory, and the memory of his death will not sit like an unexploded mine on my heart.

Soft Edges

It's a rainy October morning, and when I look across the newly mown field toward the far hedgerow, it makes me think about lines and edges. The farmer's John Deere tractor and mower have left distinct lines where each lengthy pass of the mower overlaps with the previously mown patch. The field is long and narrow, and ever so slightly hilly. The lines created by the mower are accordingly long and undulating. If you squint, the mower lines look like waves moving across water.

My eye follows a line to the far hedgerow and because it's raining, there's a blurry uncertainty about the landscape in the distance. Many deciduous trees still sport leaves of orange and yellow and fiery red, but these colors are muted on this leaden-sky day. I strain to see the very spot where the farmer has turned the mower around to mow another long stretch, but I cannot distinguish it from the beginning of the hedgerow. We would call this a soft edge in painting because the transition from one space to another is not well defined. You just know, as a viewer, that it has happened because your eye has left the field and is taking in the colors of the far trees.

When I first began painting several years ago, I could not achieve a soft edge. I still can't. The first medium I chose to use was watercolor, and I wanted precision. In a way, I was making my own coloring books by drawing images first in ink and then painting inside the lines. I concentrated on painting pictures of buildings—the more intricate, the better. I drew the details as best I could then struggled to replicate colors with my imperfect notions of how color worked. I learned by trial and error that if you mixed X with Y then you might get Z. I was self-taught and determined to do everything the hard way.

I started painting because I could not seem to write. I felt such internal pressure to write about Jack and what happened to our family, yet did not want to talk to any family members about how they felt. To me, it seemed like I would be crossing a boundary that had been erected around each person. In retrospect, I now know I would have been crossing a boundary, but it was a boundary I had erected around myself. I lived within an impenetrable bubble and was very careful to control the information within my sphere. No one could get inside my bubble unless they were invited in, and that didn't happen often.

Painting became my way to live in the world. Copying in watercolor buildings and then paintings of buildings by other people felt safe. It also provided me with structure. For example, I copied every single Edward Hopper painting that included a building. I went from New York cityscapes to Cape Cod, then to Maine with Hopper. I learned a bit about perspective and how to really study a painting in order to paint a somewhat reasonable facsimile. I switched from watercolor to gouache—also water-based paint—because I liked the latter's opaqueness and brilliant colors. Then I switched my medium to casein—which is also water-based but includes a milk protein. When casein dries, it will not reactivate (or run) if water gets on your painting surface. Casein is unlike the other water-based paints, and this unique property means you can paint over your mistakes without making a muddy mess. Casein colors can be brilliant but what I really like about this paint is that it dries with a matte—even chalky—finish. Casein has been used by painters for thousands of years (think cave paintings) but had not been popular with painters for about a century until recently.

Every day I scroll through Instagram and find images I like and take screenshots. I follow many artists on Instagram and marvel at the technical skill I see in their paintings. As I look through the images I've saved, I'm often startled by how many of them include fog and mist and rain. These are things I cannot replicate on paper, for to do so requires the ability to create a soft edge—to blend and wipe out the very definitions of place and space that I cling to. I like to think that I'm saving these pictures executed by other artists because they're aspirational. I'm starting to think, however, that when I stare at these examples, it's my mind telling me to soften my edge—open my border—let people in.

Called Back

It seemed like a great place to think about death. At the end of May 2018, I spent two weeks in a large one-room cottage in Maine as artist-in-residence at Hog Island Audubon Camp. A nature camp for adults interested in birding and other aspects of the natural world, the Audubon camp on Hog Island has been operating every summer for more than eighty years. My cottage—Bingham Cottage—was a half-mile walk through the forest from the main camp. My hope, while there, was to have time to think the big thoughts about life and death and tangled, messy, complicated family relationships.

I love Hog Island. I had visited this tiny outcropping—a mere 330 acres—in Muscongus Bay and the nature camp twice before. I always felt I was wandering through the rocky-coast landscape of central Maine as if in a watercolor dream. I had no responsibilities other than to walk through the pine forest, explore the rocky shore, and sit in an Adirondack chair to admire the bay. In midsummer the air was sometimes thick and salty, then in an instant it could freshen with a stiff breeze bringing whiffs of generations of pines and forest floors deep with needles and leaves. Both summers an osprey pair had chicks in a nest on a platform near the edge of camp. I loved hearing the food-begging calls of the chicks and the whistles between the parents as they traded off bringing fish to the nest.

One of my favorite places in camp is the Bridge, the big white wooden building that sits where the channel separating the mainland from Hog Island meets the rest of the bay. Upstairs are rooms for the volunteer staff and downstairs is the big open dining hall with its long tables for eight, and the kitchen with the pass-through windows. At dinner, the Bridge was the heart of the camp, as people gathered around tables and ate and talked about what they'd seen that day. I loved the mornings, after breakfast, when I'd sit at a table covered with a checked vinyl cloth, drinking coffee from a thick diner-like cup and saucer. I'd look out the windows through fluttering lace curtains and watch lobster boats cruise past.

A couple of weeks before I left for Hog Island for my stint as artist-in-residence I was at the hospital bedside of my father as he took his last breath. We didn't know each other well because he left the family when I was about fifteen and he didn't look back for many years. Then decades later he started doing drive-bys. I'd see a strange car pull into the driveway, and then he'd be quietly standing at the door. I'd invite him in and offer him a cup of coffee. He'd sit, legs crossed, coffee cup in one hand, and proceed to talk about himself. He didn't ask me any questions and I didn't offer any information. I'd passively listen to him yak about the next big scheme where he'd make his millions. (*Or lose his shirt*, I thought to myself.) He was on the edge of being a part of my life, but I was also aware that he was an unreflective blowhard who didn't know how to have a relationship with me so he remained on that edge and proceeded no further. As he got older, he'd send me items he'd ripped from a magazine or the newspaper—always articles about nature or the history of wherever he happened to be living. I knew he was trying to connect in his own clumsy way.

When he heard that Jack had committed suicide, he tried to call but I wouldn't answer. I didn't want to talk to anyone. And I really didn't want to listen to him talk. I couldn't hear anything except the voice in my head that said, on a loop, *Why did this happen?*

I didn't see my father for a couple of years after Jack's death. Then in 2014 he landed in a nursing home after a terrible one-car accident. I began sending him cards every few weeks and once made the three-hour drive to see him. He didn't really recognize me when I visited, which made me feel terrible. He had spent fifteen years popping in on my life, and I had spent those years trying to passively punish him for abandoning his family. Now he didn't even know we had done that dance.

My sister Amy and I drove to Buffalo, where my father lay dying in the hospital. I sat for days and watched the shrunken man in the hospital bed breathe—his mouth hanging open and his eyes tightly closed. I thought about the tenuous thread of family connections: it was a thread that in my case had been broken then retied several times, thereby weakening the overall strand. In . . . out . . . in . . . out. Waiting for each exhale to be his last, I considered the tiny man who was once at the center of our family. Staring at the man who, at the end, had nothing to offer other than genetics. (And even there my connection seems tenuous, as I didn't inherit brown eyes or thick brown hair.) As I get older, my nose is turning into a Dickinson nose—long and straight—but that's about it.

Since I was young, I've been told I'm distantly related to the poet Emily Dickinson. When the play *The Belle of Amherst* came out with Julie Harris as the housebound poet, my aunt Anne (my father's sister), who had seemed so certain of this family tie, began to waffle and equivocate on the exact details of the relationship to the Dickinsons of the Pioneer Valley.

"So, are we like first cousins four times removed?" I'd press.

She'd demur and say she'd have to check. As a teenager I desperately wanted to be related to the reclusive poet. She was exotic and wrote poems that spoke of a vast hidden life, which appealed to me. But when I thought about my father, being related to Emily seemed like a remote possibility because I saw in him none of the thoughtfulness so evident in her poetry. Getting no help from my aunt, I eventually took a page from my father's book of behavior and made up the sticky details. I finally settled on second cousin four times removed because that sounded plausibly distant enough to those unfamiliar with Dickinson genealogy.

I've grown accustomed to being Emily's shirttail relation—comfortable with the mere possibility of being related to the poet who lived in her head and created her fierce world on paper.

On the ten-hour drive to Hog Island, I thought a lot about my father, who was my tenuous connection to Emily. Unlike Emily, he lived a semi-nomadic life after leaving us, sometimes picking apples and working on farms in his search for the next big thing. I understood this restlessness because I suffer from the same thing. When my children were young, I was gone as much as I was at home. I had a compulsion to travel and acted on it, which shaped my life and the lives of my family members. My children lived in a two-parent household, so while I was gone, they were with their father. I was also aware of the times they needed their mother and I wasn't there.

Unlike my father I was not looking for the next big thing; I was search-ing for solitude and a stark landscape. During those years I made a living as a travel writer visiting the exotic and the familiar, often looking for stories that illustrated the experience of being a fragile human in a vast natural landscape. Two of my favorite places on earth are the Falkland Islands and the Outer Hebrides—places that are more than eight thousand miles apart but are remarkably similar, with few trees and fewer people and a common British culture. Places where the sheep far outnumber the humans. Where the sea pushes up to the land with a violence. Where birds wheel in the wind and create gigantic tornados of wings and deafening sounds that swirl around the cliff faces.

My father married five times—my mother was his first wife and my three siblings and I were his only children. Although I made no effort to get to really know him after he began to drop in on my life, I now wish I had. Maybe knowing him would have helped me understand the restless gene that we shared. We both wanted to run away from home and toward solitude but after that initial impulse we took different paths—like a man, he always wanted to tame nature and alter the landscape in some way, whereas, like a woman, I wanted to sit in the middle of it and comment on what happened around me. His leave-taking was permanent; mine was episodic. His first impulse was to change the landscape, whereas my desire was to write about it.

Having a relationship with my father, even a superficial one, was genu-inely difficult. On one of his drive-by visits, he said, apropos of nothing,

"I was a good father . . . I mean look at how all of you turned out." I looked at him and began to answer, "That's because of our mother," but before I could get those five words out, he had moved on to something else about his favorite subject—himself. Because he was hard of hearing, in addition to his natural obliviousness, it was difficult to have a real, much less a meaningful, conversation with him. But then he died, and his was the third death in five years to touch my life in a profound way—first my mother, then my son, now my father. Melancholy surrounded me as I traveled along the turnpike through Massachusetts on a dreary day in May. I felt like I was moving through a forest on a misty morning—I had to pay attention to where I was, else I'd fall.

Through sheer coincidence—the kind that when written down seems made up—the cottage I was staying in on Hog Island was built by Mabel Loomis Todd. Mabel was the lover of Austin Dickinson—Emily Dickinson's brother—for the last thirteen years of his life. I wondered if maybe her spirit would acknowledge me as a Dickinson descendant while I stayed in her cottage. You know: moved objects, the sound of a chair being dragged across the floor at night, a book falling from the shelf. Why couldn't that happen? Right before leaving for Hog Island I began reading a compilation of hundreds of extant letters between Mabel and Austin. Part of me hoped that reading the love letters would keep my thoughts of death at bay and would quell the grief that threatened to well up and overwhelm me.

My mother's death was expected, but when it happened, I almost couldn't bear the pain of the grief. That grief was obliterated the following year when my seventeen-year-old son Jack took his own life in his bedroom. For the next year I lived in a shadow world, moving from my bed to my chair then back to my bed. My husband spent that time trying to keep me and the children tethered to this world, which was not easy. Five years later, we'd mostly found ways to live with the crippling sadness of Jack's death. My response to the death of my father felt different from my grieving for my mother and Jack. His demise led me to grapple with what it means to be part of a family continuum. When dominoes are set on end they can easily stand alone, but when they topple, they fall back against one another. I imagined the generations of my father's family to be like those dominoes, and to understand more about who I was, I had to examine each domino in turn. I sought self- and family knowledge rather than collapsing into feeling and pain.

Austin Dickinson grew up in the heart of nineteenth-century Amherst, Massachusetts, with his younger sisters Lavinia and Emily. Emily attended Mount Holyoke Female Seminary in nearby South Hadley, came home after less than a year, then gradually became reclusive. At some point she began to dress all in white and did not leave the house, relying instead on Lavinia and Austin to bring the outside world to her. Austin attended Amherst College then trained as a lawyer. He married Susan Gilbert, a friend of Emily's, and moved into their new home, The Evergreens, next door to the Dickinsons' house, The Homestead. Austin eventually became treasurer of his alma mater, succeeding his father in that role, and thoroughly relished his status as a community leader. The Dickinson siblings were tight and the path between the two homes was well worn. Lavinia and Emily never married, but they adored Austin's three children.

In an early photograph Austin appears a handsome brooding figure— barely controlled dark hair springing from his head above intense eyes. In 1881, when Austin was fifty-one years old and comfortably settled into his role as husband, father, and respected community leader, David Peck Todd, age twenty-six, was hired to teach astronomy at Amherst College. Todd arrived in town with his young wife, Mabel, who was twenty-four at the time. Austin was the same age as Mabel's father. Like my father, Austin betrayed his family. Within a year Austin Dickinson and Mabel Loomis Todd began a thirteen-year affair. Unlike my father, Austin didn't physically leave his family, although I can't quite figure out which might have been the more devastating course. The affair ended only with the death of Austin in 1895.

Susan Dickinson and David Todd both knew about the affair. Susan was perpetually furious and froze Mabel out of much of the social life of the village, where she held great sway. The prospect of being a divorced woman in the mid-nineteenth century was horrifying, and Susan was determined to hold on to her marriage and her place in Amherst society. While Austin was conducting his affair, Susan was raising their children and running their household. She was trapped in a kind of hell that was not of her own making and from which there was no reasonable escape. The only thing she could do was to make Mabel as uncomfortable as possible, and to that end Susan made sure that Mabel would receive no invitations to social events. David, by contrast, gave Mabel his blessing, partly because he too engaged in affairs outside the marriage. He wrote at one point that he "loved Austin as well as he could love any man."

Decades ago, my mother and I took a car trip—I don't remember where we were headed—but at some point we ended up in Amherst. We found the Dickinson homes, The Homestead and The Evergreens. Both places were closed to the public that day, but it didn't stop us from walking around the houses, tiptoeing onto porches, and peering into windows. On the porch of The Evergreens, where the Austin Dickinsons lived, my mother talked about the Austin–Susan–Mabel triangle and how strange it was to see the proximity of the two houses. Anyone entering The Homestead could easily be seen by someone looking through the front window of The Evergreens. Austin and Mabel's trysts in The Homestead would have been apparent to Susan and the children, which contributed to Susan's impotent fury.

After leaving the Dickinson houses, I made my mother pull over so I could ask someone where Emily was buried. We drove through the gate of the cemetery and then along the gravel path until we saw a plot enclosed by a cast-iron fence. There they were—Austin, Lavinia, Emily, their parents. Emily's headstone was near the fence: *Emily Dickinson, Born Dec. 10, 1830, Called Back May 15, 1882.* I reached through the cast-iron bars and touched the cool face of the white marble headstone, stunned, really, by the symbolic enormousness of what lay beneath. Then my mother and I placed pebbles on top of the gravestone—adding them to the collection of leaves, pebbles, pennies, flowers, and at least one poem that was already there. I decided then that I wanted *Called Back* carved on my headstone when I die. That simple phrase, which sounded like the title of a nineteenth-century hymn, was sufficiently ambiguous in meaning—*Called back to where? Heaven, the universe, the earth?*—to hold me in thrall.

When I arrived at Bingham Cottage it was forty-seven degrees in the sun in the middle of the afternoon. Mabel's lovely cottage on Hog Island was one large room without insulation or heat. Fortunately, my husband lent me his down sleeping bag, which I stayed wrapped in most of the time I was there.

The outhouse stood about thirty feet away from the cottage and I found myself becoming overly possessive of it during my two-week stay—I threw hikers the evil eye if they used it. Running water was half a mile away through the forest.

On my first day, I left at four in the afternoon to walk to camp for a meeting, then dinner. An hour and a half later I stumbled back, having managed to walk over three-quarters of the island without finding the camp.

The island is covered with spruce and birch trees punctuated with the occasional huge white pine and a few massive oaks. Moss, lichen, and fungus grow up the cool sides of trees and cover most of the rocks and boulders that litter the forest floor. The trails are not well marked anyway, and as I was the first person to stay in the cottage that season, the trails were faint to nonexistent. I took solace in the fact that I was on an island and knew I would eventually find the camp or the cottage. At one point I had to balance-walk my way across a log. Then I found myself at the summit, which I knew was the summit because there was a sign that said so. Ninety-eight feet above sea level in the middle of the forest makes summiting unremarkable. I never did find the Audubon camp that night. I was so sweaty and exhausted from the impromptu hike that I fell asleep on my little bed and woke as the sun was setting.

As I lay wrapped in my shawl within my red sleeping bag, I dug the book of Mabel–Austin love letters from my pack, using my headlamp to read. The letters are poignant and chatty, passionate and sometimes scolding. They reveal the depth of feeling Mabel and Austin had for each other and the lengths to which the couple would go to be together. Over the years they met in Boston and Washington, DC, for trysts and took many lengthy carriage rides in the countryside around Amherst. Early in the affair, Lavinia and Emily allowed Austin and Mabel to meet at The Homestead. It was in the dining room of this house that the affair was finally consummated, one year after they pledged their love for each other. I try not to imagine the consummation because I can't picture the furniture in the dining room apart from a table. For several years the couple rendezvoused at least twelve times a month at The Homestead. We know this because they marked their love letters with symbols indicating sexual encounters. Austin gave Mabel his wedding ring, which she wore on her left hand after moving her wedding ring from her husband to her right.

About ten years into the affair, Austin provided the money for the Todds to build a house on Dickinson land across the meadow from The Evergreens. He supervised all aspects of the construction, including making sure there was an outside stairway allowing him direct access to the second floor of the house. There is some correspondence indicating that for a time Austin, Mabel, and David engaged in a *ménage a trois*.

Around dawn on day two, I watched as a red squirrel carrying a Kleenex ran across the rafter directly above my head. It disappeared behind a huge mural of a heron rookery painted in 1920 and I laughed as it slowly pulled the Kleenex into the hole. I had heard the squirrel during the night but thought, hoped really, it was on the outside of the building. It was not. I texted the camp manager, Eric, who brought two Havahart traps and set them on ledges above my bed. I imagined the squirrel being trapped in the middle of the night and scrabbling about in that trap until Eric came to fetch it.

I went out onto the porch to sit. Even though the temperature was in the upper forties, it was warmer outside than inside. It may, however, have been an illusion because the porch brightened with any available light, whereas the one-room cottage remained dark even on the sunniest days. As I sat and tried to write about the geology of the island with hands that got increasingly cold and less adept at holding a pen, I listened to what was happening around me. On such a cold and dreary day there was little activity—even the red squirrels (with what sounded to me like their incessant imitations of belted kingfishers) were quiet. Only the occasional cawing of a crow from the top of one of the big white pines near the shoreline broke the silence of the forest. Sitting in an Adirondack chair on the porch, wrapped in my gray shawl, I was unnerved by the quiet and noted a familiar melancholy take hold. Visions of Jack as a little boy seeped into my thoughts—Jack in his long *101 Dalmatians* tee shirt climbing on the wooden structure in the schoolyard; Jack sitting down in the outfield during Little League tee ball and looking for four-leaf clovers—but I refused to let them lodge in my consciousness, I tried to relegate them to the realm of my heart.

I picked up the Mabel–Austin letters. Reading about them meant pushing my thoughts about Jack to a dusty spot in my brain. It was the place that gave me permission to be a thinker and a writer. The place where I stored my increasingly rare insights about life and death. A place that needed to be cleared of cobwebs.

As a child, I often thought about life and death. When my parents would leave the house, I was convinced they had been killed on the road until they drove back through the spruce trees and up the drive. I spent hours sitting in a Morris chair, legs curled beneath me, reading through the onionskin manuscript my grandfather had prepared about our family history. I'd read the brief entries and wonder: *Is this it?* Is this all we will know about people after they die? And if we know only birth and death dates, does that somehow negate their time on earth? These youthful thoughts creep into and provide fuel for much of my writing today. As an adult I wonder why we, as a species, tend to ruminate on big questions like life, death, and the nature of existence. For me, these are areas of inquiry that outstrip my brain power. But the questions have lodged in my consciousness: the part that allows me to fret while trying to ferret out some understanding. There are days when I believe the answer may be as simple as trying to assess my impact on the living in hopes that the fact of my being will lodge in the memories of my descendants.

When Austin Dickinson died of congestive heart failure in 1895, it was clear that Mabel Loomis Todd had lost her soul mate. She dressed like a widow, much to the legal widow's dismay. Fortunately for Mabel, she had a project that kept her occupied and still within the Dickinson orbit. Emily had died almost a decade earlier, in 1886. At the time of Austin's death, Mabel was typing and editing six hundred poems that Lavinia found in Emily's room. One volume had already been published. Todd was working with the author, editor, and reformer Thomas Wentworth Higginson, a correspondent of Emily's, and they would go on to edit and publish two volumes of Dickinson's poems. Todd edited the poems for punctuation (Emily's beloved dashes!), diction, and rhyme to make them more palatable to the public, but Higginson undid many of the changes and managed to salvage much of Dickinson's original work before publication. On the third volume, however, Higginson withdrew his support and Todd worked alone. Those poems show Mabel's heavy touch as she edited Emily in order to hold on to Austin.

I thought about how Mabel, through access to Emily's poems, was in many ways supported by and connected to the Dickinsons for the rest of her life. If not for Mabel's efforts, we likely wouldn't know of Emily Dickinson today. In spite of her heavy editorial hand, Mabel introduced the world to Emily's work. Her entanglements with the Dickinsons, first when Austin was alive and then as editor of Emily's poems, expose two sides of Mabel. She was the selfish interloper wrecking both a family and the structure of Dickinson's poems. And she was also, in a more personal way, the star-crossed lover and savior of Dickinson's poems.

Mabel and Emily never met in person, but they did communicate via letter and through family members. Mabel, an accomplished pianist and soprano, came to The Homestead with Austin early in their relationship to play and sing for the Dickinson sisters and their ailing mother. Emily listened from the stairwell and after the recital purportedly sent Mabel a glass of sherry and a poem she wrote while listening to the music. Mabel was fascinated and awed by Emily. Over the years, the language in Emily's notes to Mabel became more abstruse and took on a sharp, almost snarky tone, which Mabel may or may not have been able to discern.

It's not difficult to see how the Mabel–Austin affair tore the Dickinsons apart, at least emotionally, causing the tiny close-knit family decades of heartache. Susan didn't want Austin to leave; she wanted him to end the relationship with Mabel, something he was unwilling to do. The affair was the worst-kept secret in Amherst. The Dickinson sisters felt pushed and pulled, convinced at times that they had to choose sides between Susan Dickinson and the children and Mabel and Austin. Although Emily kept to the house, creating her own intense world on paper, she was not at all oblivious to what was happening. It must have been exhausting for all of them.

When my father left the family, he never looked back, and we never talked about his absence. He did not tear our family apart so much as he broke apart from it. My sisters and I watched as our mother got into her old Chrysler and drove to Ithaca to get the first job she'd had in nineteen years. Fortunately, she had learned how to type in eighth grade and found employment as a typist at Cornell University. She made only $6,000 a year, and we descended into poverty. We also suffered through the humiliation of being part of a broken family in the early 1970s, when divorce was not common in rural upstate New York. Unlike Susan, however, my mother did not want my father back. He had abandoned us all so thoroughly that the thought of him walking back into our lives must have made her ill.

Nine years after Austin's death, Mabel visited Lily Dale, the spiritualist community in western New York, where she spent a couple of weeks among the Victorian cottages set chockablock on narrow streets. She visited mediums and attended séances, yearning for a message from Austin.

She walked to Inspiration Stump, where she sat with dozens of others on benches in the woods, all of whom hoped a medium would look at them and say, "May I come to you?" then give a message from their beloved. For someone seeking solace, Lily Dale was irresistible. According to Mabel, Austin did finally come to her through a medium who spoke in his voice and said things only she would know.

Like Mabel, I've also visited Lily Dale and have sat on a bench at Inspiration Stump waiting for a message. During my last visit, which occurred after my stay on Hog Island, I received messages from Jack, my mother, and my father.

One day most of the Audubon campers came to visit my cottage. The weather was miserable—spitting rain accompanied by sheer dreariness. Temperatures hovered around fifty degrees. I was so cold and damp and chilled to the bone after leaving camp earlier in the day that I huddled in Tim's red down sleeping bag with the blue blanket the camp provided pulled up over that and a knit hat pulled down over my head. I got out of the sleeping bag only when I heard voices outside.

One of my duties as the artist-in-residence was to tell people the history of the cottage and what it was like to stay there. I didn't mind the questions about daily life: *Don't you have a kitchen* (no kitchen—please see the cooler on the low wooden chest), *where's the bathroom* (outhouse is out back), *why don't you use the fireplace* (this is a historic wooden structure and the Audubon Society does not trust me with matches). I did mind those who clomped in with boots covered with mud and then proceeded to walk around the whole once-tidy place leaving me with a mud trail and the feeling that all my things had been soiled.

One of the visitors told me they had seen a turkey with one chick in the meadow on the southern part of the island. When the hen saw the walkers, she sat on the ground and was silent, as if trying to imitate a boulder. I made a mental note to look for the turkey next time I headed to camp.

The following morning a turkey hen—likely the same one—strode past the cottage, no poults in her wake. Every day on my hike to camp, I had seen a pair of Canada geese walking slowly with two goslings between them, and a hiker told me she'd seen four adult geese with one gosling a few days before. Crows, ravens, bald eagles, merlins, mink, and maybe even red squirrels make it so hard for the very young to survive.

I'd noticed during the couple of weeks I was on Hog Island that the forest took on an eerie silence after a flurry of early morning calls, chirps, and birdsong. For most of the day I might hear only an occasional osprey whistle as it hunted for fish. (One morning an osprey tried to land on a none-too-stable perch in the top of a delicate birch tree beside the cottage.) And I'd likely hear the sound of a crow cawing. But that was about it. *Maybe the red squirrel will chatter more now that it's warming up,* I thought. In late afternoon a phoebe pair flitted around one end of the cottage, catching insects just beneath the porch roof. It seemed an auspicious sign as they hovered and moved up and down and side to side, maneuvering with calibrated flutters of their outstretched wings and tail feathers. A deep silence settled into the Maine woods and I sat on the porch to enjoy the exuberance of the phoebes.

My days began with the sounds of the diesel engine of a boat out in the channel in front of the cottage checking lobster traps. Some mornings it was as early as 4:45 a.m. I'd wake and note the lightening sky through the eyebrow window above the front door before getting out of bed. Wrapping myself in my gray shawl, I went out onto the porch and on most mornings noted it was already warmer than the previous day. Although the sun rose out of sight through a mile of forested island behind the cottage, the sky above the channel was often pink and cast a lovely salmon hue on the still, early morning water. Every morning when I got to camp, I'd read the note about the weather on the bulletin board. Every cell of my body yearned for the sun and some warmth.

Throughout the years of the affair and later, Mabel's husband, David, professor of astronomy at Amherst, was experimenting with a new photographic technique he developed to record solar eclipses. He traveled around the world, perpetually chasing eclipses, and had remarkably bad luck because most of the eclipses he tried to photograph were obscured by clouds. Once, long after his death, Millicent—Mabel and David's only child—met a British astronomer who referred to her father as Professor Todd of the cloudy eclipses! This never stopped Todd from making elaborate plans, involving numerous assistants and masses of equipment, as he set off, team in tow, in search of the next eclipse. After Austin's death, Mabel often accompanied David, visiting such exotic locales as Peru, "Old Arabia," Libya, the Dutch East Indies, Russia, and Japan. She proved to be an intrepid traveler and, when she came back to the States, became well known on the lecture circuit for her travel tales.

Mabel and David Todd also spent time in Muscongus Bay in Maine early in the twentieth century, and had, at some point, seen Hog Island, noting that part of the 330-acre island had recently been logged with plans to eventually fell all the trees. Beginning in 1908, Mabel and David started buying portions of the island—saving it from the loggers—and they eventually owned the entire thing. They built the cottage mid-island along the eastern coast in 1915, and from then on Mabel stayed on the island from May until October. David, whose behavior was becoming erratic—the effects of advanced syphilis—spent little time on Hog Island and was confined to a sanatorium from 1917 until his death almost twenty years later.

Before coming to Hog Island and digging into her story, I knew only that Mabel wreaked havoc on a lonely branch of my shaky and perhaps fictional family tree. Now I was awash in Mabel Loomis Todd information and having difficulty reconciling the two parts of her—Mabel the soul mate of Austin Dickinson, and the post-Dickinson Mabel who traveled, wrote travel pieces, edited Emily Dickinson's poems, and lived in a one-room cottage on a tiny island for six months of the year. Mabel really did manage to make something of herself in spite of not being able to marry her true love. I believe, no matter her busy life and obvious success, she never did get over the loss of Austin.

I closed my eyes and dozed in the sun.

On my last full day on Hog Island, I decided to take closer note of the trail as I headed to camp. I had spent so much of my time concentrating on not tripping over rocks and roots, I felt like this morning I needed to slow down and take note of what was around me. It was already a warm morning—mid-sixties—and the sun was high in the sky and bright. I admired the lowbush blueberries with their bell-like flowers, and the leafy ferns whose fiddleheads were almost unfurled, which covered the forest floor where the tree canopy was sparse. Heading into the forest I noted the occasional huge white pine and a few massive white birch trunks (both standing and littering the ground). The trail bisected an old stone wall of moss-covered boulders that snaked through the woods, a vestige of a nineteenth-century farm on the cleared land the Todds bought in order to return it to forest.

At the halfway point, the trail turned. This was the turn I'd missed on the first day, so I'd stuck a pine branch into the soft forest loam to mark it. I walked onto a narrow open neck of land with the bay on one side and a long tidal cove, Long Cove, on the other. I stood and admired Long Cove, which at high tide was filled with still, milky bluish-green water reminiscent of glacial runoff. I tried to imprint the shape of the cove on my mind, with its soft-looking light-green grasses that rippled with the slightest breeze and its long stony ridge arms, topped by pine and spruce trees, that embraced and held the water in. I turned and looked in the other direction at the bay and watched as a white lobster boat motored across the choppy water.

The trail continued through a forest of spruce and pine trees of uniform size. This part of the island had been logged more than a hundred years ago then replanted so the trees were in rows. The trail widened and followed the tidal cove. The understory was sparse and the trail itself was deep with years' accumulation of pine needles. Was I seeing the same landscape Mabel saw? I wondered. Then I realized that of course I wasn't, because the trees had been growing for almost a hundred years. I tried to imagine a more open landscape where I could view the sea on one side of the path and the cove on the other. Where the sun wouldn't be filtered through a hundred years of pine boughs.

That evening at dinner in the camp I sat with people I didn't know and found myself talking about Mabel and Austin, Hog Island, and the Dickinsons. At one point I must have noticed something flicker across the face of the person I was talking to that made me wonder if I was dominating the conversation. I am always on the lookout for character traits in me that were my father's. Being self-absorbed and yakking too much are the two that worry me most because in some social situations, I am prone to both. Telling a story is a way to stave off my innate awkwardness with other people that comes from spending so much time alone.

On my last morning in the cottage, boats circled the channel, setting lobster pots. I heard the chugging of the engines before I saw them. I crawled out of bed and stood on the porch with my gray shawl wrapped tightly around me. It was 5:45 a.m. The sun was up and threw a golden light over the channel. One handsome boat had a painted white cabin and deck and forest-green sides. Dozens of stacked yellow wire lobster pots covered the deck. Pop music from an AM station blared from the cabin, the sound wafting up to the cottage each time the boat turned. Silence and solitude were gone on this beautiful morning.

I went into the cabin and took a wonderful photograph off the wall and brought it out to the porch. It shows Mabel, a substantial older woman wearing round black-framed eyeglasses beneath a mass of white hair piled atop her head. She's sitting at a table placed on the cottage porch with a typewriter in front of her and stacks of papers to one side. At the time of this photograph Mabel and her daughter Millicent had already spent a decade of summers at the cottage. As I sat in the Adirondack chair, books perched on the chair's wide wooden arm, I realized that Mabel was about the same age as me when the picture was taken. I scrutinized the photo to see if I recognized bits of myself in her image—we were both travel writers, loved a Dickinson, and, at times, were solitary women. I then thought about how she'd died of a cerebral hemorrhage at the age of seventy-five while sitting at her typewriter on this very porch in the early 1930s, about ten feet from where I now sat.

Although Mabel was to most people of her time the lover, the traveler, the writer, and the editor, to me she was Mabel of Hog Island, where the osprey and bald eagle nest. Where the turkeys and deer and sometimes porcupine live. Where the occasional coywolf will swim across the channel to hunt its prey. Where the starflower blooms and the ferns unfurl around the cottage in late May. Where the setting sun lights the channel red and orange and throws long shadows into the cottage.

As a shirttail relation (at best) of Austin and Emily Dickinson, I still yearned for a sign of acknowledgment from Mabel's spirit. A nod, a slight smile, even a glance. I felt like the Mabel I was coming to know was the true connection to these nineteenth-century ancestors, not my father. (The lineage was spiritual and not genetic.) While in the cottage—Mabel's beloved cottage—I felt that she was there. I could see her in the Japanese-influenced painting style of the massive murals—one of a heron rookery, and the other of an osprey nest—covering the gable ends of the one-room interior, and in the Japanese-inspired torii gate that looked like a giant wooden pi symbol set over the path to the water. I could feel her on the porch with me as I sat on the steps wrapped in my gray shawl looking for warmth in the oblique rays of the early morning sun. I could hear her in the cackling sound of the laughing gull and the whistle of the osprey.

I thought about how natural my father would look sitting on that porch—leaning back in an Adirondack chair, legs crossed and a hand-rolled cigarette in one hand, getting pleasure from watching the lobster boats in the channel as they stopped to check their traps. But then he'd get restless and the next thing you knew he'd be putting in some kind of dock and buying a run-down lobster boat that stank of diesel every time he'd fire the engine. He wouldn't bother to get a lobstering license, and he'd end up in court and our name would be mud in the town of Damariscotta. And then he'd eventually scuttle the boat and the cottage would become a wreck and he'd move on in search of the next big thing. (Others could clean up the mess.) I truly believe that he admired the natural world, but it was with an eye toward how it could benefit him.

That was my father. That was how he operated. He believed that he could have or take anything he wanted without regard to those around him. When he died, I was just figuring out that I was forever trying to re-invent him in my mind—to make him into the father I thought he should have been—but that he could no more change who he was than the sun could rise in the west. As long as I was trying to change him, I didn't have to accept him for who he was. Austin was the same way. He, too, did as he wanted without regard to those around him. He kept his wife and his mistress within shouting distance. Poor Susan. Poor Mabel. They both had to accept the situation that Austin created for his convenience.

Sitting on the porch and looking at the photograph, I knew my connection to Mabel was through a mutual love of what was around us. If I dragged a table onto the cottage porch and found an old typewriter, we could be out-of-time twins. I wasn't special; the place itself was. The key to our time-travel relationship was that we were both drawn to the same rocky island, a place of solitude where we could think about the Dickinsons in our life and accept them for who they were. In the end, though, this love of place became more important than the Dickinson connections. The Dickinsons who loved us, left us. This was our shared obsession, but it did not define who we became. Mabel's post-Austin life allowed her to flourish. Like Mabel, I won't ever be able to let the Dickinson connection go, nor would I want to. I am one of those dominoes standing alone, waiting for the cosmic push. But when I go—when I'm called back—I hope I've given my descendants enough information to begin to answer the question *Who was she?*

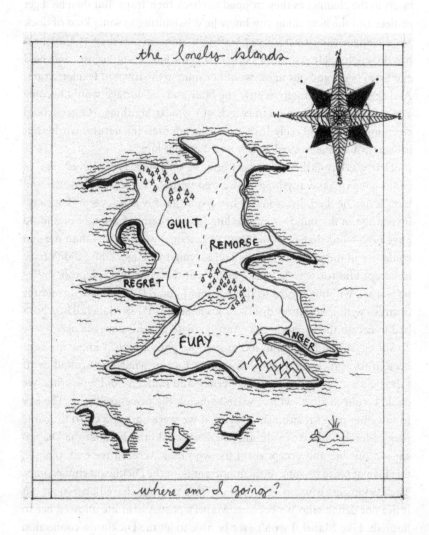

LONELY

Jane at the End

I was thinking about my mother as her birthday approached. She died a year before Jack, so my grieving for her was truncated by the loss of my son. A week before my mother died, she weighed eighty-seven pounds. That's almost fifty pounds less than the year before. One day when I went to visit her, I found her sitting in the wooden chair with a padded back, seat, and arms that sat at the foot of her bed in her room in her assisted living home. The television set was tuned to the movie *Brubaker*, and a young Robert Redford was engaged in conversation with M. Emmet Walsh and Wilford Brimley.

"You ever seen this?" my mother asked. Her voice was hardly louder than a whisper now, the result of years of drugs for rheumatoid arthritis. Or maybe it was because of the rheumatoid arthritis itself. "It's a good movie," she added.

Sophie, my mother's big Maine coon cat, was sprawled on the cream-colored bedspread, eyes closed as she soaked up the rays of sun coming through the window. I sat in the Victorian Morris chair by the bed and tried not to look alarmed at my mother's appearance. As she asked questions about my family and what I was up to, I noted that she didn't act tiny and frail, as her whispered questions and her comments conveyed the same sharp observations and dry humor she'd always had. And I knew if I said something she didn't like, she could still make me quake with one sharp glance. Her spirit was strong.

She'd been in assisted living for almost a year, and for the first several months, she was very depressed about having to leave her house in Freeville and would try to cajole one of us into taking her back there to look around. I never took her on a return trip because I thought it would be too hard on her. I realize now that I never took her back because it would have been too hard on me.

My mother's house sat locked up and empty of life at the other end of town. Even though it's on Mill Street—a road that is the back way to Ithaca—I tried to avoid driving past the old Greek Revival farmhouse because it made me so sad. This doesn't mean I didn't crane my neck to look down Mill Street as I passed it while driving out of town. I kept expecting to catch a glimpse of my mother's black Jetta parked in the driveway and a curl of smoke coming out of the chimney, but I never did.

That day, a week before her death, I looked around my mother's room and took note of the things she'd gradually added over the past year. She'd think of something she wanted from the house and then ask a neighbor friend to go fetch it for her. The little World War I–era oak campaign desk that always sat in her living room in the Freeville house now sat in the corner of her room, and a two-foot-tall nineteenth-century statue of William Shakespeare stood on the chest of drawers next to her television set. The walls were crowded with paintings and photographs from the house, including her two diplomas from Cornell and some early twentieth-century photos of Freeville. A large portrait of Samuel Crittenden, my fifth great-grandfather and an early settler to this part of central New York, hung on the wall behind her bed. A 1907 sepia photograph of my two great-grandfathers fishing on the banks of Fall Creek hung over the campaign desk. This was not your typical fishing photo because the men—who are sitting on the bank—stare directly at the camera with solemn expressions on their faces, and both are dressed in formal-looking coats, white shirts, and ties.

Taking in the objects my mother chose to surround herself with was both fascinating and deeply upsetting to me as I sat and chatted with her. It was all about family—her ancestral family—and the village her family had called home since the mid-nineteenth century. She left the photographs of her children and our children back in the old house where they sat on walls and on tabletops gathering dust. I guess my husband, Tim, was right when he said my family engages in ancestor worship. My mother's room presented a stark visual reminder of just that.

She missed the howling winter in Freeville in her last year, which was good because I couldn't imagine having to make my way down to her house on some of those mornings so treacherous with blowing snow and ice on the roads. But she also missed seeing the daffodils come up next to her barn and did not see later in the season the amazing white flowers on the Japanese lilac. And she missed smelling the white and red peonies as they bloomed on the bushes that flank her driveway—a smell so overpowering that it would have made its way into her living room if her front door was open. She missed the full heat of a summer's day in Freeville when the cicadas started buzzing early in the morning, and the air was thick and still. And she missed sitting on the back porch with a glass of iced tea watching the families of Canada geese and mallards that made their summer home on the section of Fall Creek across from her house. Last autumn she missed the crimson leaves on the maple tree that is so large it kept her house cool during the summer months. And she missed those same leaves swirling to the ground as gusts of wind ripped them from branches until finally the tree was bare.

Maybe all of this doesn't matter because my mother had Freeville in her blood and in her bones. She saw what she wanted to see when she was there, which I imagine was a curious mixture of what was really there and what she saw in the part of her mind's eye that was fueled by memories. I know I'm a lot like my mother in this respect and that ultimately it doesn't matter where I am because I bring Freeville with me.

On the day my mother died, my sister Amy and I spent twelve hours with her—sitting in the beautiful little corner room in the Colonial Revival house in Ithaca that had been turned into an assisted living facility. She lay in the hospital bed, a cream-colored bedspread pulled up to her chin, and all she had to do was turn her head to look out the large window right next to her. The view from her second-story window on that first day of February was of the tops of inky black trees whose bare branches held a layer of snow.

My mother, who was in and out of her right mind that last day, seemed fascinated by whatever was happening outside that window. She watched the treetops sway in gusts of wind, sending little showers of snow down to the snow-covered ground. Her eyes were glassy and shiny—the result of morphine, I think—and it was like she couldn't grasp both the enormity and the simplicity of the landscape. I kept thinking she wanted to fly out the window—out of her body, which had been wrecked by decades of rheumatoid arthritis and now malnourishment—to be among those swaying treetops.

Her voice, which had been reduced over the past couple of months by disease and medicine, was oddly strong, and I kept wanting her to talk, just to hear that familiar timbre. Several times during the day, she looked at Amy and me and said, "Do you hear that?" When we asked her what she was hearing, she told us that for the past few days she had been hearing a male glee club singing almost nonstop. "And I think Nelson Eddy is singing the lead," she said. She looked disappointed when we said we couldn't hear the choir.

I looked at what sat on her nightstand and laughed when I saw four little framed photos of the cats she had loved over the years. Instead of Railey, Clara, Jack, and Gwen—her grandchildren—there were Gray Baby, Blackie, Sophie, and Emma.

As the sun went down and the treetops got darker and darker until they looked like line drawings against a charcoal-gray sky, my mother continued to look out the window. "I see Sophie," she said, referring to her cat which my sister had taken to her house the day before. "I see Sophie in the trees."

As night came on and the tree branches receded farther into the larger darkness, I found *Everybody Loves Raymond* on the TV, a show my mother really liked. I began watching because I had never seen the show before and was curious. My mother, who didn't want to take her eyes off the treetops, watched the wavy reflection of the show in the window.

Later, when I went over to say goodbye to my mother, I couldn't stop myself from crying. She turned her head and looked at me and said in a loud, clear voice, "Don't worry. Everything's going to be all right."

The Other Jack Gallagher

I was thinking about Jack's purple-and-pink wire-frame glasses he wore when he was three. With a jolt, I also remembered that when I took Jack to see the ophthalmologist who was going to do surgery to correct Jack's crossing eye, the doctor felt compelled to tell me a story. He said when he was younger, he went to college with a Jack Gallagher. His Jack Gallagher became a geologist, and he and the doctor remained friends for many years. One day his Jack Gallagher went to Cape Cod, walked into the sea, and was never heard from nor seen again.

It was a stunning and horrifying story to hear from the doctor who was gazing into the blue eyes of my son. I hadn't thought about that anecdote for twenty years, but about five years after Jack's death, while I was gazing at the Atlantic Ocean, the story returned as if I was supposed to recall it then. Its meaning lay hidden between the whitecaps that leap and then disappear like schools of tiny white dolphins. And in the seabirds that struggle against the wind—shooting like rockets in one direction and then when they turn, hanging stalled in the air like kites held by a string. I can't see the wind. We only know it's there because of its effect on physical objects like leaves and sand and clouds and birds. I could feel the wind as I looked out at the vastness of the ocean, but like so much in my life, it was one more thing I could not control.

"When people die, they cannot be replaced," wrote the late neurologist Oliver Sacks. "They leave holes that cannot be filled, for it is the fate—the genetic and neural fate—of every human being to be a unique individual, to find his own path, to live his own life, to die his own death." This is how I wish to think about Jack in the present and in the future. The past is littered with guilt, regret, and memories. Physical objects under a tarp in the attic. Drawings and photographs perched on windowsills and bookshelves. A paper snowflake taped to a window.

In the past, the Green Chair next to the fire in the living room enfolded me in its upholstered arms and provided the comfort I could find no other way. The chair smelled of my dead son and my dead dog. It's where I mourned the death of my mother as I pulled the red quilt retrieved from her house tightly around me. It's where I numbly watched television while my mind tried to make sense of the horror of my life. It's where I landed after a terrible bout of vertigo knocked me flat on what would have been Jack's nineteenth birthday. It's the site of all the rage-crafting I've done over the past few years. It's the home of reading and my search for a way to make sense of a world that seemed to be spinning out of control around me. It's where I've tried to take responsibility for myself. It's where I realized that things take the time they take.

I can now see the Green Chair as my launchpad, my Cape Canaveral, my seat in the slingshot that will release me from the sad past and catapult me into the future.

I stood at the brink of the ocean years after Jack died, and there I felt the urge to take photos of the sunrise and sunset. The need to capture moments was so strong that I got up well before dawn each day. *Click click click*. Red, orange, yellow, gray, green, blue, pink, purple—I wanted to hold on to it all. Maybe the impulse was akin to my mother staring at the tops of the snowy trees on the day she died, saying she saw her cat in the treetops. I saw Jack in the colors of the sunrise and sunset. He was in the waves that coursed across the bay. He was in the laughing gull that caught the wind and the bufflehead that dove for a meal. I couldn't comprehend the extent of his world, which over the years has grown larger as his corporeal being fades.

I know only I can put Jack in his proper place. Only I can encourage him to release his hold on me. One morning I whisper *Let me be* to the air, to the water, to the birds overhead. I wanted to move forward, to live in the future. The answer came as the sky brightened from an inky blue and revealed a splash of pinks and purples. The sun's rays broke through the clouds and lit up the marsh grasses across the way, and they changed from a dull middle brown to golden. Suddenly I saw hundreds of snow geese flying over those golden grasses, a horizontal blizzard of white cutting through the pink-and-purple background. And then they were gone.

Staying in a Ghost Town

It's a rainy day in Crisfield, Maryland—the kind of day when the color of the sky and water are matchy-matchy like a sweater twin set. If I were poetic, it'd be heather-colored, but since I'm not, it's just fucking gray. Sky pulled down to water, water pulled up to sky with the hint of a roll of fog creating the seam.

Three small framed photos sit beside my computer on the table. All four of my kids are frozen at the ages of three and four. Railey, whose dramatic tendencies I encouraged by taking photos of her in outlandish poses, is standing against a cream-colored wall and is wearing black tights, black shoes, and a long black tee shirt; she is captured putting one arm through the neck hole along with her head. She is also wearing a sun hat and is cradling a baby doll wrapped in a little blanket my mother made for the dolly. She looks toward something past the camera, and her expression is solemn in a three-year-old Madonna (either Madonna will do) kind of way.

I remember taking this picture. Railey and I were living in a crummy upstairs apartment in Dryden. All the floors had that cheap indoor-outdoor carpet, and the hollow-core doors made that dispiriting scraping noise (nothing is well made here) when they were opened or shut. The ceilings were low, and the walls were dingy, and the windows—at least there were windows—looked out on the state road. I had to leave one place and move into another for just three months while all the paperwork for buying my first little house in Freeville went through. Railey and I lived among the boxes holding bits of our former life, and we were poor as dirt and ate a lot of macaroni and cheese. But it was in this apartment that Railey said her first truly funny thing. I had a box full of videotapes I'd bought for a dollar. Among them were four of five tapes of *Merrie Melodies*—early Disney cartoons where the flowers and animals sing, and Betty Boop makes her pursed lip noises. We played these tapes over and over. When one of the tapes was just beginning, the federal warning about not copying or distributing these tapes flashed on the screen with the big FBI seal. Railey sighed and said wistfully, "FBI makes the best movies."

I gave my mother that Madonna-esque picture of Railey, which she trimmed and put in a silver oval frame. Because it was my mother doing the trimming, Railey lost part of her right foot in the process.

Then there's the sweet little wallet-sized photo of Gwen. It was taken at the Dryden Elementary School and placed by me in the dollar metal frame. Her head is tilted and resting on her crossed arms, clad in a pink shirt. It's hard to figure out what's going on with her hair because the photo is a close-up, and a lot of the hair is out of the frame. It looks particularly curly, which means she probably went to kindergarten with her hair uncombed and in a snarl. What sets this photo apart from all other Gwen photos from when she was young is that she's smiling. Gwen is famous in the family for her dour expressions in the hundreds of photos taken of her when she was little. She'd see the camera, and her mouth became a straight line or turned down into a scowl. Yet she was not a scowly girl. Her disposition was so sweet, and she was like everyone's favorite pet—the youngest in a family with four kids where there was a fourteen-year difference in age between her and Railey, and seven and six years between her and Clara and Jack.

Finally, there's the photograph my cousin Nancy took of Clara and Jack when they were four and three. The two of them, in long tee shirts over bathing suits, are playing with a simple drinking fountain (a metal pipe coming up from the ground with a push-controlled spigot head on it). They both have their hands on the fountain's head, and water is squirting in the air and spraying them. They look like two blond peas in a pod and are laughing with delight—eyes closed, mouths open, water squirting. It must have been the Fourth of July at Stewart Park at the southern end of Cayuga Lake in Ithaca. Our extended family would bring a picnic to the lakeshore, then eat and hang around until dusk when everyone stuck flares in the rocky beach and lit them. This happened along the shoreline as far as the eye could see up both sides of the narrow lake, spots of glowing red in the darkened landscape.

The Clara and Jack snapshot is stuck in an old brass table frame. At some point in the last couple of years, Clara tucked a fortune from a fortune cookie in with the photo. It reads: *We are very happy together*.

I ghost Jack's friends on Facebook, seeing what they're doing and what they post on February sixth every year, the date of Jack's death. I don't want to friend them because they'd think that's weird, and I don't want them to feel uncomfortable in any way. This year one of his friends posted a photo taken at a cast party for one of the high school plays, and Jack is in the foreground holding a clear plastic cup half-filled with what looks like white wine. He's got that "I'm so lit" expression with half-closed eyes and a cryptic smile, then the subject line under the photo says, "It's juice." So Jack.

In the aftermath of suicide, everything that came before suddenly seems important and clear. It begins by searching for oblique clues to someone's nature. Is this one important? Or that? If you're a parent, you dread every bit of information you uncover, believing that if this one moment had been different, so would the outcome. You want to gather the bits that have washed up on your shores and place them carefully in a small woven basket like you would sea glass. For they are remnants of a questioned life, and it seems only appropriate that they can be taken out of the basket from time to time and held up to the window to see if the light flows through the object or if it is too scoured by the constant tumbling of the waves to reflect anything.

I've come to the Chesapeake Bay and the tiny town of Crisfield to examine those bits. I've brought my basket of Jack memories with me, ready to hold up to the bright but cold February sun. I think of the Emily Dickinson poem "Shame is the shawl of Pink":

> Shame is the shawl of Pink
> In which we wrap the Soul
> To keep it from infesting Eyes—
> The elemental Veil
> Which helpless Nature drops
> When pushed upon a scene
> Repugnant to her probity—
> Shame is the tint divine.

I love Emily Dickinson—her word choice and imagery are stunning—but I admit to not knowing what many of her poems mean. This poem, however, cuts to the quick—its meaning clear to me. Shame and its fraternal twin Guilt fill my days since Jack died. I fight against those feelings because I know I must in order to survive.

I arrived in Crisfield in mid-February, right before Valentine's Day. I walked into a condo that I'd rented for the month that's in one of three six-story condo buildings at the end of Main Street, mostly deserted this time of year. I mean, who wants to go to the Chesapeake Bay in February?

The apartment's layout was exactly like the beach apartment my family used to rent for a week each summer in Ocean City, Maryland, which is only fifty miles to the east. Starting around 1970—when Ocean City was a family beach—my mother, sisters, cousins, and aunts would drive to the same condo building for a week in late July or early August. This condo was right on the beach. There were three bedrooms, a couple of bathrooms, a kitchen that opened onto the living room which led to my favorite spot—the balcony. I slept on the balcony every year that I went. Sometimes in a lounge chair, other times in a sleeping bag on the concrete floor. The rhythmic sound of the waves rolling into the beach, and the stinging smell of the salt spray that covered your body and hair with a patina, is an embedded memory triggered by the briefest whiff of salt air.

We were glued to the television set the summer of 1973 during the Watergate hearings while the hot sun beat down on the white sand beach outside. I remember thinking that John Dean was cute—I was seventeen (forgive me)—with his horn-rimmed glasses and sandy-colored hair. I grasped the enormity of what was happening. Yet I was indeed seventeen and wanted to lie on a towel on the beach in the bikini I had made from maroon fabric. The American political system was faltering and I insisted on toasting my pasty upstate New York skin.

Almost a decade later, we were at the beach and were again glued to the television set when Diana and Prince Charles got married. We all, Freeville nobility, had much to say about the royal wedding—Diana's wedding dress and hair, the look on Queen Elizabeth's face, the royal smooch. As I recall, we woke at three in the morning to start watching the proceedings—the adults lounging on the couches with cups of coffee and all the kids lying on the floor with pillows and blankets. In the days before everyone had computers and video and replay, it felt miraculous to see something that was happening in England in real time.

Although a core of aunts and cousins continued the Ocean City gathering well into the twenty-first century, I dropped out in the early 1990s. I did take Jack and Gwen one year when Jack was maybe twelve and Gwen about six. We made the eight-hour drive to the Maryland shore and stayed in the Ocean City condo with the cousins for several days, then drove north along the shore to Rehoboth Beach in Delaware, where members of my father's side of the family had gathered for a week. Jack and Gwen got along well, and we could travel for long peaceful stretches in the car together (unlike Jack and Clara, who fought from the moment they sat down in the back seat). I remember renting a boogie board for Jack to use in the waves at Ocean City and being afraid that he would get hurt or swept away because the riptide was strong along that stretch of beach. He also had no experience swimming in the ocean and hadn't yet been thrown to the ocean floor by a wave and come up gasping, having swallowed a mouthful of salt water. While watching Gwennie play in the surf and dig in the sand with a shovel, I kept an eye on Jack, motioning him to come closer if he drifted out too far or if the waves looked rough.

I sit in this condo and look out the sliding glass door to the balcony and beyond to the quiet marina and then a narrow arm of the bay. There's a red kayak tied down to one of the docks and a smallish—maybe twenty-five-foot—sailboat sitting beyond that. No pleasure boater is foolish enough to be out in this weather. The boat rocks up and down as a twenty-mile-per-hour wind whips across the bay creating whitecaps and stirring the marina water into constant movement.

Where do the little ducks go when the marina is choppy like this?

I've been watching these waterfowl since I got here a few days ago. Fortunately, I brought binoculars with me. I see some little ducks braving the chop and I grab the binoculars and go out onto the balcony, where I steady myself against the railing because the gusts of wind are strong. I look through the binoculars and try to memorize the features so I can identify them later when I'm at the computer. I know I'm looking at a little group of grebes and a group of small diving ducks. I look at all the white patches—because I know that's important—the color of the bills, and overall shapes of the birds. Another grebe has joined my group—it's a stranger, and my grebes move away. It's also a different species. This, I know, is a pied-billed grebe.

The birds float around the pylons of the marina. They do their bird dives—plunk!—then pop up again. My grebes chase the pied-billed grebe back. *We don't want you*, their actions say. I imagine the pied-billed grebe is looking for his peeps, which he lost somewhere in the tumult of the bay. He stays back from the group but watches them as they dive down then pop back up. The compact diving ducks are buffleheads in their winter plumage—a broad white band across their cheeks and sleek black heads make them distinctive. They stay away from the grebes as well. I watch as the grebes and the buffleheads work their way through the relative shelter of the marina, disappearing and reappearing beneath the docks that mark the boat slips and wooden walkways.

Inside I can't decide if my grebes are horned grebes or eared grebes. I scroll through photos and check the allaboutbirds.org website. I read again about the differences. I still don't know for sure.

Every day while in Crisfield I take a long walk. The first day I couldn't get over what a ghost town this place is this time of year. Restaurants and cafés are closed. Businesses are closed. The buildings are two or three stories at most and made of concrete block or brick and painted bright summer colors like sky blue, orange, deep yellow, and Pepto-Bismol pink, but they're all buttoned up for the winter. The colors were shocking to me because I was expecting—I don't know what—but maybe colors that blended in with the blues, greens, and browns of the intertidal environment rather than this Miami Beach palette that stood in stark contrast to the natural surroundings. I made my way out of the little commercial district and walked past some houses. One of the older ones was a two-story Victorian that would not have looked out of place in an upstate New York village, this one painted bright purple. A huge modern three-bladed wind turbine stood in the middle of town, adding a constant *whir whir whir* to the other sounds created by the relentless wind.

On one corner, right beyond the dry dock where huge powerboats sit on cradles waiting for the next season, is a vacant lot with sparse patches of short brown grass poking out of the sandy soil. Parked behind a chain-link fence on one side of the lot is a tractor-trailer with a faded *Quality You Can Count On* sign painted along its broad white side. On the first day of my walk, I saw a rooster and a hen wandering the unfenced lot. I stopped to take a picture of them with the tractor-trailer behind them as a kind of narration or caption but had time to snap only one or two photos because that big black rooster started running toward me, red comb flopping left then right, with his dark brown hen right behind. I took that as a sign to keep walking.

The next day I walked on the other side of the street and, when I was across from the lot, I saw that the chickens had been joined by mallards, some domestic white ducks, a couple of Canada geese, two huge brownish domestic geese, and a whole flock of pigeons. I snapped the picture of the bird posse.

Today I saw the same crowd, but while I was standing there, on the corner of the lot, ready to take what was now going to be my daily *Quality You Can Count On* bird picture, a small blue car drove up and parked on the edge of the brown grass. The birds ran toward the car. All of them. A short middle-aged woman got out, pulling her hat lower as she bundled up against the wind. She walked to the back of her car, opened her trunk, then picked up a large white scoop and plunged it into a big yellow bag. She started walking into the field with the scoop, all the birds surrounding her, the pigeons creating a gray swirl of fluttering wings, and she scattered a trail of corn. She walked back to her trunk for more corn, and I approached and asked if she fed the birds every day. She said she'd been doing it for three years and that she always scatters the corn in this part of the lot in a big heart shape for the birds. I stood by her car and watched as she poured more corn and talked to the birds in a low voice as they followed her on her heart circuit. Then she stopped and knelt by a female mallard, which I then saw couldn't use one of her legs, and she let her eat out of the scoop. She shooed away a white duck who tried to horn in on the mallard's meal. When she came back to the car, I asked about the mallard. "She's been that way for three years," she said. "I try to make sure she gets some food every day because she can't compete with the others." She then added, "I'm always afraid she won't be here when I come back."

With an apology for having to leave, the bird lady got into her car and pulled away while the chickens, the ducks, the geese, and the pigeons gobbled up the corn. I gave a little wave and thought, *see you tomorrow*.

Feeding time for the *Quality You Can Count On* birds is something I could now look forward to. When I passed the lot a couple of hours later while on my way to the grocery store, all the birds were gone. This wasn't where they hung out all day long. Like them, I decided to coordinate my walks with her arrival.

I have a preference for ghost towns. Not the hokey ones you find in the West—towns that were once real towns but the people all left and then someone bought all the properties cheaply and prettied the place up to make a Hollywood-inspired ghost town populated with cowboys and outlaws. Not those towns. I like towns where there are far fewer people—for whatever reason—than there should be. Places where houses and businesses and buildings sit empty for part of the year but where people—workers—live in the midst of all that emptiness.

These places—like northern towns on the ocean during the winter or towns near depressed ski areas during summer—draw me to them. That half-empty feeling of the underpopulated lived-in ghost town matches my mood most of the time. Where others would find it depressing, I find a small degree of comfort.

The off-season town I'm staying in contains only townies. They don't walk along the beaches and stick a toe into the too cold water. They work as fishermen and cannery workers. They are cooks and waitresses in the few restaurants that stay open for the fishermen and the occasional date night. They work in the insurance office, the clinic, and the grocery store. They work for the telephone company, the gas company, and the highway department. They rebuild and refurbish the big, expensive boats in the dry dock boatyard. They're part-time policemen and 911 dispatchers. They're unemployed and stand in the lee sides of buildings in stocking caps and old Carhart jackets while smoking cigarettes.

During the summers—which they likely look forward to and dread at the same time—their town is overrun with tourists who jaywalk and drive crazy and are too loud. The townies create festivals and special weekends to make their Eastern Shore town even more crowded, operating on the principle that more people equals more money in their pockets.

These are the kinds of towns I love. I rent places that are cheap and where off-season I'm likely the only one in a building. I know that when I look out my window, I won't see another person. When I look at the water, there won't be colorful kayaks gliding through the bay or the sound of powerboats ripping through the soft summer air. When I visit, I'll see fishing boats heading out into the bay carrying watermen wearing ripped rain gear patched with duct tape over winter coats and stocking caps. There won't be the sound of children begging their parents for another ice cream cone or couples looking at menus posted on the outside of the restaurants that occupy every other commercial space.

During the off-season, the brick and concrete buildings painted bright blue and orange and ochre and shocking pink will throw bits of light along the wide main street that is otherwise dreary, gray, and deserted. Squalls and brutal winds blow the bay into a churning mass of dark blues, grays, and whites. Leaden winter skies cast their muted light into the waters creating shades of pewter. The marsh grasses and wind-whipped bushes and trees are hues of brown and gray. But the buildings in town remain brightly colored, reminding the townies of warmer days.

Trucks and beater cars drive the length of the main street—a four-lane road with a slim median strip of dormant grass—and whip around in a tight U-turn right at the town harbor before cruising back in the other direction. I don't know what they're doing or who they're looking for because the sidewalks are deserted when I take my daily walk. I can go a couple of days without seeing another person. Eventually I wind up at the grocery store, lingering a bit longer than I normally would, just to watch people interact with one another.

The off-season ghost town holds no ghosts for me. I don't see my dead son on these deserted streets. He's not lingering around the corner, waiting for me to catch a glimpse of him. He is nowhere in this landscape. I go to these towns to escape Jack, for he's still in familiar places.

I have to go away to save myself. I need a place where happy families or even squabbling families won't be walking down the sidewalk. Where I can sit in my room and look out at the water and watch the grebes and the buffleheads swim around the marina. And I can watch gulls wheel overhead and catch the wind and glide without flapping their long, bent wings. And I can cry and cry, and no one is here to witness my despair and feel sorry for me or worry about me or tell me I have to get over this pain.

In Crisfield I've been watching the series *Rectify* on Netflix. The premise is that a man is freed from death row on the basis of DNA evidence after serving nineteen years in prison for the brutal murder of his girlfriend. He was a teenager when he was convicted and is now nearing forty. In one episode, the main character, Daniel, has been at his parents' home for several days, and it's the first time he's been alone there. He wanders through the rooms, picking things up, trying to make electronics like an iPod work, and just wallowing in the mysteriousness of this new world he's been thrust into.

Daniel pulls down the ladder that leads to the attic, climbs it, and finds himself in a space that contains all his teenage possessions. He locates his little tape recorder and his box of tapes, puts in a tape, plugs in his headphones, then proceeds to rock out to the tune. He sees his camouflage duck hunting clothes, puts them on plus his blaze orange cap, and picks up his duck caller, and begins blowing *quack quack quack* while still moving to the music. He roots through boxes and touches clothes on hangers.

While I was watching this scene, it struck me that if Jack came back—was released from his purgatory—he'd have the same experience as Daniel. He would try to fire up his old computer to check Facebook and listen to songs. He'd root through the green bookcase I painted for his room when he was a boy, searching for books he'd loved and papers he'd kept. He'd search the red bureau, where I used to look for cough medicine and over-the-counter cold medications he took to get high. His bed frame is there—a Victorian headboard and footboard—which he might try to set up so he'd have a place to hang out. He would have to find a new box spring and mattress set. I don't know what happened to the old set because his bed is where he shot himself and they were taken away.

The wind comes from a different direction today—from the west—and blows across this arm of the bay, creating rolling white wrinkles in the gray-blue wooly water. The sound of the wind silences the fish crow, the red-winged blackbird, the song sparrow. Even the large herring gulls and dainty laughing gulls with their black-tipped wings glide silently through the air, riding the crests of the unseen wind. The wind is made manifest in the whitecaps, the soaring birds, and the still-brown marsh grasses that sway and quiver and make shimmery movements. The wind, however, cannot block the sound of a plane overhead or the rough chugging of a fishing boat going out for the day's catch. Noisy human endeavors continue in bleak Crisfield.

I am pulled toward the wind and move from behind a building to feel its full strength on my body. I'm hit with the smells coming from the oyster cannery. It's overwhelming as the conveyor is turned on, and the belt carries shells up and away from the brick building which then fall into the back of a waiting dump truck. Gulls, feathers ruffled, watch the action from where they stand on the cannery's pitched metal roof.

A man walks to the end of the dock in the marina and unfolds a canvas chair. I'm waiting to see if it blows into the water before he sits in it. It doesn't. He sits and watches the water.

Yesterday I cried when I came in from walking along the docks of a nearby marina. I've been walking with purpose—walking for health but also walking in places where I can have some closeness to nature. I've been exploring the backside of Crisfield, where the fishing boats are moored and there are many empty slips waiting for summer boats to come and fill the ghost town with people. I want to smell the water. The full, salty smell of the bay. I want to see and hear the birds. I want to wallow in the slightly unfamiliar. This is not my swamp walk where I know every tree and bramble. Here I am on wooden docks and concrete paths. Private property, some of it derelict, rings the water, keeping me at a distance from the brackish ebb and flow. I do not want to get into my car to drive to someplace to walk because that seems foolish but what I'm left with is man's giant hand on everything I see.

I cried because although I am trying so hard to make this place mine—to be happy to be where I can see and hear water—even in this ghost town there are too many other noisy distractions. I should be on a pond in the Adirondacks where I won't hear on the wind an underlying thrum of machinery. Where I won't hear trash bags placed in the metal garbage containers on the dock outside my apartment flapping and whipping around in the wind. The bags are empty and tethered only to the rim of the mesh can. They rise and fall balloon-like from their containers depending on the vagaries of the wind.

I cried because I don't know if I am being true to myself. Mary Oliver wrote: "I did not give to anyone the responsibility for my life. It is mine. I made it. And can do what I want to with it. Live it. Give it back, someday, without bitterness, to the wild and weedy dunes." I abrogated my responsibility for my life when I gave Jack the power to determine how I should proceed after his death.

I cried because I am selfish. All I can think about is me and how I feel. That's not the same as taking responsibility. I'm still holding that needle in my hand and periodically pricking my palm to see if it hurts. If it hurts—and of course it will—I give myself permission to feel sorry for myself.

I cried because I don't care that I'm selfish. If I cannot care about myself—and I'm not sure I can—then how can I be expected to care about others? I am interested in others, but I'm not sure I care about others.

I cried because that sounds harsh and true.

I sit and look out the sliding glass door to the balcony. What I see from my vantage point at the table is morning light shining on the dock and lighting up the bottom of the red kayak that lies flipped over and lashed to one of the side docks. Beyond is the dark gray-blue water of this little arm of the bay alive with movement as the wind pushes against the current, creating chop. The temperature has dropped twenty degrees from yesterday.

I've not seen nor heard fishing boats this morning. Do they not go out on Sunday?

The duck triad I first saw yesterday—a drake mallard, another drake mallard that at some point had domesticated duck in its lineage, and a female mallard—bob in the marina. A perfect triangle, the female in front, they appear and disappear, appear and disappear in the chop moving steadily toward the open water of the bay.

The low angle of the morning light makes the marsh grasses across the way golden, almost the color you might see in the vast wheat fields of Nebraska. I see flashes of white above the marsh—a black-backed gull and herring gulls ride low on the wind.

Last night's thunderstorms pulled this cool air in behind them. When the storms got close, terrific bolts of lightning forked through the sky, and the thunder that followed had a metallic ring. I've never heard thunder sound that way before. I stood on the balcony as the storm moved south and down the bay, willing the sky to deliver more—more flashes of light, more ringing thunder, more rain lashing the estuarial waters.

In spite of yesterday's crying jag, I feel it's almost time for me to go home. Maybe escaping to other landscapes and off-season ghost towns has done its job. I miss the landscape of home. The Pink House, the Green Chair, my husband and children all wait for my return.

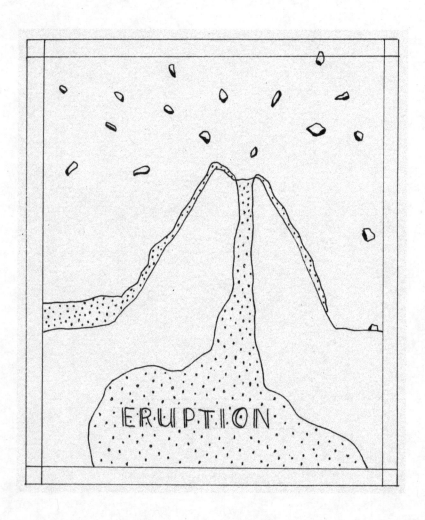

ANTICIPATION

Beside the Volcano

The volcano Hekla looms above the landscape about twenty-five miles as the raven flies from where I sit in Laugarvatn, Iceland. It has not been visible except during a brief respite in yesterday's weather when low gray clouds lifted to reveal the sun shining from some distant place reflected off Hekla's snow-covered surface. The volcano shimmered, golden, like a mirage. It reminded me of a fata morgana, a particular type of optical illusion experienced in Arctic waters, where mountains and ships are reflected above the horizon even though the real objects lie below. One night, many years ago, while on the Bering Sea, I saw what looked like a shimmering pink city in the sky when, in fact, it was multiple reflections of a container ship. The optical effects piled one on top of the other creating a magical city of containers. My glimpse of golden Hekla reminded me of that experience— a vision that couldn't be trusted.

The lake between me and the volcano, frozen and white when I arrived in Laugarvatn ten days earlier, was now ice free. The water was shades of dark blue alternating with slate-colored intrusions. Behind the lake stood Hekla, a cone-shaped vision seen in full from my cabin window when the weather was right. Hekla is shaped like a classic volcano, the kind of volcano a school kid would draw. It is magnificent. Unfortunately, I discovered, Hekla was visible only about a tenth of the time. So as I sat at my desk, I turned to look in the volcano's direction a hundred times a day, hoping for a glimpse. I was often disappointed. I read that the name Hekla comes, some scholars assert, from a Norse word meaning cloak.

I traveled to Iceland six years after Jack died to stay in a cabin in Laugarvatn, a town in south-central Iceland, for the month of March, hoping the trip and isolation would jar me into action. Once a prolific writer—the words tumbled from my brain onto the paper—I'd been unable to write a word for many months. I took up watercolor painting, hoping it would ignite the pilot light that had clearly gone out. It didn't. I kept painting, telling myself that doing anything creative was exercising the same area of the brain associated with writing.

Iceland, a spare and harsh landscape, appealed to me on a visceral level. Maybe being crowded among all the trees and houses and pinched hills of central New York was taking up too much space in my life and hemmed in my creativity. Maybe I needed to run away from my family and familiar surroundings to find the buried spark. Maybe I was haunted by the suicide of my teenage son. Beautifully bleak and bare Iceland promised a respite and seemed like freedom.

Decades earlier I was a geology student, and like all geology students, I learned that Iceland was a mecca for a certain kind of geologist. This small island in the North Atlantic, a touch smaller than the state of Kentucky, has a population of about 340,000. That's about the same number of people that live in medium-sized cities in the United States, cities like Tampa, or Anaheim. That demographic fact is beside the point. Geologists are drawn to Iceland like moths to a flame because the island is continuously in the process of becoming.

Iceland sits above a plume that comes from deep within the earth. There are about twenty such plumes around the world—places where magma or molten rock punches through the relatively thin continental or oceanic crust. Where these plumes exist, volcanoes rise above them.

Magma (once it hits the surface, this molten rock is called lava) from the plume spills onto the surface of the ocean floor or upon the land through fissures or cracks. A plume becomes known as a hotspot once it breaks through the Earth's crust.

The plume beneath Iceland has been active for 65 million years. In the 1960s, a new island—Surtsey—emerged dramatically off the southern coast of Iceland, the result of being directly over the plume. At the site of a plume geological time and human time intersect. All of the Hawaiian Islands were created this same way. The plume is stationary and does not drift with tectonic plates, so if you look at a map of Hawaii, you can see the direction the oceanic crust is moving by connecting the dots of the islands.

To add another layer of geologic excitement, Iceland sits at the tense junction of two tectonic plates—the North American and the Eurasian plates. As these plates move away from each other, a rift zone is created called the Mid-Atlantic Ridge. Think about the rate at which your fingernails grow; that's how fast these plates are moving apart. The Mid-Atlantic Ridge in Iceland also lies over the plume, making that region particularly active.

The possibilities of seeing the creation of new land made me feel dizzy. It was all about potential and becoming; a fresh start in a land that was constantly renewing itself. And it mirrored how I hoped to feel. Yet I believed the chaos of earth-building combined with the potential violence of earthquakes and volcanoes might also feel familiar. It was a place where I expected to confront my personal volcano—Jack.

When my mother died, people knew how to express their condolences. With Jack, it was different. When I was out and people noticed me, it took only a moment before they looked horrified and I could read in their faces that they couldn't figure out what to say. Then it was up to me to make them feel better. In the months after Jack killed himself, I spent most of my time avoiding people I knew. I didn't shop at local stores. I stopped going to the gym. I couldn't make myself go to things I used to like—readings, choral concerts, book signings. I didn't want to see that look in their eye. I didn't want to cry in public every single day.

When I look around the house at the photographs, the art projects, the furniture, the books, all I can see is my child. I think odd thoughts during the day—I look at the clock and realize it's 2:37 on a school day, and I'm waiting to hear the heavy front door open and then to hear Jack's signature whistle or humming. But at 2:38 it's not there. He's not here, and he will never be here again.

I pause outside his bedroom door as I make my way to the bathroom in the middle of the night, expecting to hear the sounds of Jack noodling on a keyboard or a guitar or a banjo. I strain to hear his soft singing—waiting for the lovely baritone voice that never comes.

I look at the spot at the table where Jack used to sit, and it's empty. I will never see him grab his fork in his left hand and begin digging into his pasta. I will never again have to cater to his weird food preferences—pasta, lite soy sauce, asiago cheese, waffles, and pancakes. I will never again have to fight about texting at the table. I will, however, have to look at the faces of his father and his sisters and see a deep, deep sadness that I know will always be with them.

One or another of Iceland's many volcanoes is always on the verge of erupting. Scientists have no way of predicting precisely when these blowouts will occur. They do know when the magma chambers beneath the volcano are filling with molten rock; monitors placed directly on the flanks of a volcano provide the data. Full magma chambers are often precursors to eruptions, but it's impossible to predict exactly when an eruption will occur. It could happen in a day or a dozen years after the chamber fills.

Geologists go back through the historic and the geologic record plotting eruptions to see if patterns emerge, but they discover what I already know—that nature is not always predictable and will not bow to a time schedule. The most reliable indicator of impending eruptions is earthquakes, measured by seismometers inserted into the bedrock. These instruments are so finely calibrated that they can pick up the rumble of traffic on nearby roads, and geologists have become so good at reading the seismometer's output that they can tell if a passing vehicle is a car or a bus. Often a swarm of little earthquakes will precede a volcanic eruption. If three or more seismometers placed in different locations record an earthquake swarm, the origin of the quake can be triangulated. This is the spot. This is where an upcoming eruption will likely occur.

But, alas, this too is an imperfect indicator because some volcanic eruptions occur with just minutes' warning or with no warning at all. It is a challenge to connect data to action, and Icelanders live with constant geological uncertainty.

I wasn't ready to acknowledge the part we played in Jack's death. Tim and I both had thought his over-the-counter drug abuse was occasional and not severe. We both had thought he was going through some teenage thing that he would grow out of. We both had thought that if we limited his access to a car and money, he wouldn't have the opportunity to buy cough syrup and whatever else he was taking. We both had thought that going to a therapist once a week would help Jack save himself by being able to say whatever he wanted to another adult. We both had thought that his insistence on visiting colleges and filling out applications and writing essays was a hopeful sign. We both had thought that having a close circle of friends—friends he had known since kindergarten and who were all headed to college in the fall—meant that everything was going to be okay. We both had thought that his singing and whistling and composing music—his irrepressible creativity—was ultimately hopeful. We both thought that self-preservation would trump any other feelings. We both had thought he would grow out of his adolescent brain and his hormones would come to equilibrium.

We both had thought wrong.

We didn't realize we were witnessing the human equivalent of an earthquake swarm and we failed to triangulate using the abundant data.

While in Iceland, I dreamt about volcanoes, which I assumed was a natural outgrowth of spending my days wallowing in volcano information. There are websites devoted to Icelandic volcanoes, some scientific and others maintained by amateur volcanologists who range from fascinated to obsessed. There are photos of Iceland's volcanoes when they're dormant and photos of them when they're erupting. I examined opinions and conclusions about predicting volcanic eruptions on the basis of speculation, conjecture, wishful thinking, historical research, and scientific data. I respected scientific expertise and I recognized that expertise did not provide Icelanders with any certainty.

One morning I woke at dawn, perhaps pulled out of sleep by the hint of pink coming from beneath my blind. I stumbled from bed—eyes half-open—pulled on a sweater, brushed my teeth, grabbed my iPhone, and walked onto the front porch of the cabin. It was biting cold, and I quickly learned there was a skim of ice on the wooden porch floor. I didn't care about any of that though, because, for a split second, I thought Hekla was erupting. Very dark gray clouds, imitating the ash plumes of an eruption, appeared to be coming from Hekla, which was remarkably visible as a perfect cone on the horizon. These clouds spread quickly across the morning sky, coming toward me like billows of smoke and ash. Within minutes the bottoms of these clouds were lit by the rising sun, and it then looked as if the gray clouds were resting on a pink net. I watched and took picture after picture. My fingers lost feeling at about the same time my phone battery lost its charge.

The clouds turned into a light-gray blanket covering the sky and obscuring Hekla. Within half an hour, I couldn't see across the lake. Big snowflakes began falling, covering the ground. Hekla—my fata morgana. I went back inside the cabin and read a book about volcanoes.

The snow turned to rain, and it rained steadily for several days. When I looked out the cabin's window, I could barely see across the lake. One day, as morning faded into afternoon, fog crawled down the sides of the mountain ridge next to the cabin and slid across the lake. There was no hope of seeing Hekla. Earlier, a dozen starlings had landed on a rafter under the porch roof. They preened their sodden feathers and shook their wings to dry off. They stood on spindly pink legs watching the rain. *Come here, come here*, they seemed to call to their friends as they puffed up their feathers and sidled down the rafter to make room for newcomers. I unintentionally scared them when I stood up from my reading chair, and they flew off to join the flock bounding through the neighboring field of rain-pocked snow.

In the summer of 1977, I went to the Bitterroot Mountains in Montana for a geology field camp, but before and after the camp I lived in Missoula with my boyfriend at the time. We worked for a landscaper—I can't remember how we knew him—digging trenches to lay underground sprinkler systems and raking rocks on what would eventually be lawns in the new subdivision that was crawling up the side of Mount Sentinel.

One night we went to a bar and ordered big slabs of meat and pitchers of beer because that's what you did when you lived in Montana. Where

I sat, I faced the end of the room that had a wall-sized poster of Mount St. Helens plastered on it—the iconic volcano of the Cascade Range a couple of states to the west. It was the classic depiction of the volcano— the photographer shooting across Spirit Lake toward the perfectly shaped snow-capped mountain in front of a bright blue sky. Three years later, everything in that scene was altered—what was left of the mountain was covered in gray ash, and once massive trees were reduced to burnt skeletons. I often wondered if, after Mount St. Helens erupted, someone thought to tack a post-blowout black-and-white photograph beside the poster with the idyllic scene.

An explosive blast came out of the side of Mount St. Helens. It, too, was a stratovolcano like Hekla, but St. Helens developed a weird bump on one side that filled with magma. The bulge grew by five feet a day until it jutted three hundred feet from the mountain. Then, in one explosive burst, the side of the mountain blew off.

Some geologists (particularly Barry Voight, actor Jon Voight's brother, a well-regarded volcanologist) had considered the possibility of a lateral blast, but that hadn't made enough of an impression to persuade Governor Dixy Lee Ray of Washington State to create a proper exclusionary zone around the volcano. As a result, fifty-seven people died in the violent eruption—including a geologist and a newspaper photographer who were near the peak and people who were camping and hiking among the enormous trees of the old-growth forest on Mount St. Helens' flank. The victim most people remember was Harry Truman, a man in his eighties, who ran a lodge on Spirit Lake. Truman refused to leave. He gave lots of interviews during the period when the chamber swelled with magma and scientists recommended evacuation—I remember them well. Some say Truman was anxious to leave as the bulge started to grow but wouldn't do so out of pride. Truman had painted himself into a corner by being so ornery and braggadocious to reporters. Suicide by volcano.

In the sixth century, a couple of centuries before the Norse arrived in Iceland, the Irish monk known as Saint Brendan the Navigator sailed past the southern coast of Iceland in a small leather boat. We know this from surviving medieval works written about his voyages. What fascinated me was Brendan's description of passing what he called the Island of Smiths. As they neared the island, which was "very rough, rocky and full of slag, without trees or grass, full of smiths' forges," Brendan could hear the sound of "bellows blowing like thunder, and the thud of hammers on iron and anvil." He described lumps of slag of "great size and heat" being hurled at the little boat, and where they fell, the sea began to "boil as if a volcano was burning, and smoke rose from the sea as from a fiery furnace." As the men rowed away, "it looked as if the whole island was on fire like a huge furnace, and the sea boiled as a cauldron of meat boils when it is thoroughly heated up. All day long they heard a great clamor from that island. And when they could no longer see it, the howls of the inhabitants still reached their ears, and a stench came to their nostrils."

There could not be a more perfect description of an enormous volcanic eruption—perhaps from Hekla. Or maybe the holy men witnessed the submarine birth of a new island, much like what southern Iceland residents saw when Surtsey emerged. The smoke rising as if from many blacksmiths' forges, the flying lumps of slag, the boiling water, the stench of sulfur, the appearance of the whole island being on fire—these are what I imagined I would see, hear, smell, and feel if Hekla were to erupt. This is what I yearned to experience—the violence of nature as big as the violence of my memories.

What does it mean that I am obsessed with the volcano I can see outside my window? I take the temperature of my psyche, trying to figure out if I am the volcano ready to blow, or was Jack the volcano? It's likely both of us.

Iceland was settled by Vikings and their Celtic Irish slaves in the ninth century. There were no indigenous peoples on the island to displace. For almost a millennium, the chieftains of Iceland's clans gathered annually at Thingvellir to hear a reading of the laws by the Law Speaker and to settle grievances among themselves. Thingvellir sits directly on the Mid-Atlantic Rift, and the Law Speaker would stand with his back to the cliff, which is part of the North American continent, and address the crowd who stood before him on the Eurasian continent. Of course, this was not known to them, but I can't help thinking about the strangeness of this fact.

Christian missionaries started visiting Iceland in the last decades of the tenth century, and in 999 or 1000 CE, the Law Speaker announced his decision that all Icelanders had to be baptized, although heathens would be allowed to worship other Norse gods in secret. With that decision, Icelanders were welcoming, among other things, a theological concept of Hell. Hekla stands almost within sight of Thingvellir, and it wasn't long before Hekla was viewed as the entrance to Hell.

In 1104 CE, Hekla erupted, blasting rock fragments across much of the northern part of the country; it is considered to be the second-biggest eruption in Iceland's recorded history. Nearby farms were showered with ash, rock, and lava bombs weighing up to a ton. But that was just the beginning. Carbon dioxide from eruptions swept down the sides of the volcano and collected in low spots, smothering livestock until farmers realized they could dig ditches to drain away the deadly gas. Farther from the mountain, fluorine-laden ash settled onto fields. Sheep grazing on the poisoned grass died from the toxins they ingested. They literally rotted from the inside out in a torturous death. Through it all, the pragmatic Icelanders continued to regard Hekla as a troublesome neighbor, whose occasional outbursts were to be understood and worked around rather than feared. Visitors to Iceland were not so sanguine about sharing the island with the volcano.

The Protestant Reformation swept through Iceland in the mid-sixteenth century, and within a decade, Catholicism was abolished in the entire country. Bishops were kicked out (or worse), and church lands were confiscated. Lutheranism, however, did not change visitors' impressions of Hekla. The sixteenth-century German physician and traveler Caspar Peucer wrote: "Out of the bottomless abyss of Heklafell, or rather out of Hell itself, rise melancholy cries and loud wailings, so that these lamentations may be heard for many miles around . . . Whenever great battles are fought or there is bloody carnage somewhere on the globe, then there may be heard in the mountain fearful howlings, weeping, and gnashing of teeth." A seventeenth-century travel book described how the devil would pull souls out of Hekla and throw them onto the sea ice to temporarily cool them off so as to exacerbate their torture when they were tossed back into the inferno.

The English poet William Blake banished the specter of winter to Hekla in his "Seasons" poems:

He takes his seat upon the cliffs, the mariner
Cries in vain. Poor little wretch! that deal'st

With storms; till heaven smiles, and the monster
Is driv'n yelling to his caves beneath mount Hecla.

Hekla has erupted at least twenty times since the island was settled, most recently in 2000. But the volcano had done even worse things in prehistoric times, such as about three thousand years ago, burying nearly the entire island with almost 207 billion bushels of ash. Geologists have been able to work out a detailed chronology of when Hekla has blown, and for how long, by studying the layers of ash and tephra that collect over time. Working with paleoclimatologists who study changes in diatoms in lake sediments and gas bubbles trapped in ice, and paleobotanists who note changes in and the presence and absence of plants, and, finally, dendrochronologists who interpret what tree rings can tell us about weather patterns, scientists can describe a complete picture of what was happening at the time of an ancient volcanic eruption. With an explosive eruption like that of three thousand years ago, the world would have felt the impact of volcanic ash blown high into the stratosphere and then carried around the earth on a stratospheric wind. The entire earth would have experienced a drastic change in climate as the gases belched out by the volcano created a dry fog of global proportions that dimmed the sun. This would have meant nonexistent growing seasons and extremely cold weather that could have lasted for years. Catastrophic events like this led to worldwide crop die-offs, famines, mysterious diseases, uncounted deaths, and even extinctions.

A chronicle of the mountain's eruption in 1300 CE describes people being unable to make their way across the countryside or to put to sea in boats because of the "sand" that blackened the skies and covered the ground. Much later, in 1845, Hekla sent a finger of lava down a gully toward its northwest flank, cutting off the water supply to a farm that had stood closest to the volcano for almost as long as there had been settlers on the island. Rather than panic, the pragmatic Icelandic farmer tore down his barn and house and rebuilt them on the other side of the lava flow.

After a long pause, Hekla came to life again in the early morning of March 29, 1947. Local farmers felt their bedrooms shake and saw a brown cloud rising from the cloud-covered summit. Within hours, a plane full of volcanologists left from Reykjavík to scout out the eruption. "No words can describe the awful grandeur of the sight which there met our eyes," wrote the University of Reykjavik's Sigurdur Thorarinsson in his book *Hekla on Fire*: "From the northeastern part of the ridge there rushed forth dark, greyish-brown eruption columns, monstrously big around and so closely set that they formed a solid wall. In swirling puffs resembling gigantic heads of cauliflower, these columns rose to a height of 10,000 meters. In the upper reaches, their color turned a lighter grey, and at the top, they showed almost white against the blue sky. From time to time, the fiery glow of the fissure showed through, and occasionally lightning flashed inside the cloud."

The 1947 eruption spewed a cubic kilometer of ash and lava bombs and rock particles across the landscape. Had Hekla erupted at this rate once a century since Iceland was born, it would have built the island six times over by itself. More recently, Hekla's eruption in 2000 lasted only eleven days and did little damage. Icelanders know Hekla will erupt again.

I began to look for my volcano-obsessed tribe online. Likely those who recognize their addiction early and are good at science become geologists and volcanologists. Others create wish lists of volcanoes they'd like to visit before they die, including Mount Etna, Stromboli, Hekla, Agung, Kilauea, and any of the many new volcanoes emerging in volcanic hotspots like the Pacific Ring of Fire. I discovered that a person can go around the world on guided volcano adventure tours. But I desired to find more than the geology tourist who learns facts and figures and can spout them with rapturous glee. My people were the poets, writers, artists, and the general wackos who become hooked on volcanoes. I wondered if my tribe came to volcanoes as a way to understand cataclysmic personal events; if they needed sensory confirmation that there were forces in nature more catastrophic than their own experiences.

On another gray, cloudy, rainy, not-rainy, not as cloudy, foggy Icelandic day, I thought about how much this changeable climate resembled that of central New York during springtime, except when I'm home, there is no chance of seeing a volcanic eruption. The temperature hovered around freezing, which made whatever form of precipitation falling from the sky at any moment a guessing game. It became difficult for me to get up early because I knew there would be an indistinct sunrise. Also, there was no hope of seeing Hekla on the horizon if the clouds were low.

But there's a saying in my part of New York State—if you don't like the weather, wait five minutes. I think we must have gotten the saying from Iceland because this morning the clouds lifted from the hills across the lake, and snow on the sides of the far mountains began lighting up in the early sunlight.

I know the parting of the clouds means nothing for what to expect ten minutes from now. The weather in Iceland is not stable. It's like a suggestive striptease involving clouds and mountains and volcanoes.

I started thinking about other aspects of volcanoes and realized I would really like to see a lava lake. I know I can look up lava lakes on YouTube and be captivated by their hypnotic qualities, but that can't be the same as withstanding the almost unbearable heat on your body or the noxious smell of sulfur from gases belched by the volcano. I wanted the feeling that happens only if you see a lava lake in person. Would my shoes melt as I stood on the rim of a caldera and peered into its fiery abyss? Would I be tempted to lean forward and pitch headfirst into the caldera? In some ways, I didn't trust myself to find out.

This morning after the clouds parted and the sky brightened, there was Hekla. I hadn't seen it for more than a week. As the day wore on, the clouds settled in. At 6:45 p.m., I saw Hekla's faint outline across the lake, the top completely obscured by clouds. For some reason, it looked bigger that way, I thought, perhaps because I could imagine the volcano's peak reaching up until it touched the stratosphere.

The following morning when I looked toward Hekla, it stood in silhouette against a yellow backdrop. Not far above the volcano, a solid blanket of gray clouds spread across the sky.

I have two windows open on my computer. One is a map of Iceland with red, blue, and yellow dots on it, designating the earthquakes that have happened within the last forty-eight hours. Black triangles show where the seismographs are stationed. You can focus on a particular region, so I have the page open to southern Iceland, where Laugarvatn and Hekla are located. The other open window is a running tally of the country's earthquakes that gives the time, magnitude, GPS coordinates, and place-name of the epicenter of the quake. I think both are interesting and very helpful to anyone obsessed with earthquakes and volcanoes. I could see where earthquakes occurred and note the intensities. I also scan the *Iceland*

Monitor, the English-language online paper, for any earthquake or volcano news. Amateur volcanologist that I am, I was doing my own triangulation work.

One day there were many little earthquakes at Torfajökull volcano, which is just a bit southeast of Hekla. This volcano last erupted in 1422, so the activity struck me as surprising.

I sit there and wait. The wind howls and whistles around the house. The far ridge is draped in snow, looking like a cake frosted with royal icing—the snow is smooth and glistening white as it fills in the tops of the numerous gullies cut down the sides of the ridge. I compulsively check my earthquake websites. There I find the map of Iceland, and I look at the graph to see if any quakes are over 3.0 on the Richter scale. These are marked on the map with a green star. Whereas most visitors would be relieved, I fear I will be leaving this island in a couple of days without having experienced a seismic or volcanic event.

I came to Iceland to jog my writing memory; to pick up the pen again after an uncomfortably long hiatus. When I saw Hekla from the cabin window it sparked something in me. It reminded me that decades ago I loved studying geology. Hekla's presence gave me something to research, something to obsess over that didn't involve anyone in the family. The volcano beyond my window gave me something exotic to write about.

At the cabin, there was an old clunker of a car I could use. One day I drove about fifty miles to the little town of Hvolsvöllur, home of LAVA Centre. I skipped the high-tech exhibition about Iceland's volcanoes and headed to the village's Saga Centre instead. I was looking for the people who were working on the Njáls Saga tapestry.

Scholars believe that this saga was composed in the late thirteenth century; it describes events at the turn of the eleventh century. Like other Icelandic sagas, it is based on stories passed down by oral tradition. What's fascinating about the sagas written down during medieval times is that they are the stories of the hardscrabble life of families who settled the land, and they are extremely site-specific. Today you can visit the farm where Gunnar—the eleventh-century warrior—lived and the farm of Njál and his family. The landscape of the Njáls Saga is dominated by the stratavolcano Thrihyrningur, which is often mentioned. Gunnar and Njál meet at Thingvellir, where Njál, a lawyer, ends up arguing cases for Gunnar.

What follows are sixty manuscripts filled with blood feuds, deceits, jealousies, and insults that result in brutal battles. Omens and prophetic dreams haunt the characters and foreshadow how things are going to turn out. The Njáls Saga is the longest and best known of the sagas and the only one set in southern Iceland.

I walked into the Saga Centre, and although the exhibits were closed, a door had been left open for the tapestry stitchers. One of the women who spearheaded the project, Christina Bengtsson, happened to be there. I entered a room with a long table running down the center. At one end of the table was a gigantic spool holding almost seventy feet of linen measuring thirty-one and a half inches wide. At the other end was another spool containing two-hundred and thirty feet of the finished tapestry. In between the spools, the linen ran down the middle of the table with chairs set on both sides so stitchers could work on the tapestry from either side. Images illustrating the saga were designed by an Icelandic artist and printed on the linen to guide the stitchwork on this contemporary adaptation of an ancient art form. Stitchers embroidered with wool made from Icelandic sheep and dyed with colors made from local plants and minerals. The stitchers used one stitch—the Bayeux stitch—found on the eleventh-century Bayeux Tapestry depicting the 1066 conquest of England by William the Conqueror, Duke of Normandy. At a projected length of 295 feet, the Njáls Saga Tapestry will be 66 feet longer than the Bayeux Tapestry. This is a community project writ large.

For about seven dollars, I could work on the tapestry and write my name in the book of stitchers. I sat down and was shown how to do the stitch and was then let loose to sew an axe. A battle scene with men in small boats attacking a ship was before me outlined on the linen. Heads were lost along with various limbs as both sides wielded axes. As I pulled my brown wool thread through the fabric, I thought about how many threads it would take to create the complete tapestry and that no one thread would be dominant. I tried to make this egalitarian notion personal, thinking it would help me find a kind of balance I lacked in my life but dismissed the prospect of equilibrium immediately because I knew I was not done exploring the emotions that kept me stuck. I had to play out the volcano–Jack connection. I knew I had to pull that thread until it either broke or held fast.

After stitching my axe, I left the table to talk to Christina. A small white-haired woman originally from Denmark, she taught in the local school for years. After retiring, she and a friend came up with the tapestry idea. They hired an artist to design the whole narrative pattern, got the pattern transferred to the linen, and in 2007 they began stitching.

Christina offered me coffee in a pretty bone china cup and saucer as we chatted. It was like drinking rocket fuel, but I drank it anyway. She told me that they were shocked by the number of people in the village who wanted to work on the tapestry. They have a solid corps of about fifteen stitchers who meet a couple of times a week to stitch and chitchat. It reminded me of a nineteenth-century American quilting bee, where farm women gathered to sew and exchange news. Only this would have been a really long quilting bee. When I visited in 2018, they had been working on the tapestry for eleven years.

As I drove back to the cabin, I thought about how a collapsing of time exists in Iceland. This tapestry sewn in the twenty-first century depicts events that took place a millennium earlier. These events feel as real to Icelanders today as when the sagas were created. As a people, they are pragmatic (e.g., rebuild your farm on the other side of the lava flow), yet they also carry a belief in elves and other mythical figures somewhere in their DNA. They telescope history and bring it close by reading the sagas and creating this tapestry. Their obituaries can span ten generations and read to an outsider like a genealogical data dump. They share a common religion because it's their historical religion, yet few of them attend church.

In so many ways, these are my people—living now but embracing the past. I need to get to the point where I can look at my past—both recent and generational—and not feel devastated. I need to adopt some of that Icelandic pragmatism. For that pragmatism allows them to live into the future and I could not see a future.

It is a winter wren morning. I woke early to several of them singing from the pines and low trees behind the cabin. I love their song—cheerful, hopeful, a bit chatty. It's my last morning in Iceland, so I want to make sure to catch the sunrise. It does not disappoint with its pastel splotches of pink and orange and shades of blue and gray. The dark fringy edge of a large cloud is lifting as light forces its way up from behind the far ridge. Hekla is a cold outline this morning. I am thrilled to see its massive shape above the hills across the lake. A squadron of whooper swans flies low in the distance, great white wings flapping, pink glinting off their bodies, braying like a pack of hounds as their massive wings row through the air.

Yesterday I took my last drive through the Icelandic countryside—it rained, the sun shone, then it rained again. The "check engine" indicator of the clunker car was perpetually lit. But the car ran all the same, and I figured it would be reliable until it wasn't. I thought how nice it was to have wheels. I passed field after fenced-in field where herds of small Icelandic horses ate from piles of hay left by the farmers. Occasionally I'd pass a farmhouse and barn—always painted white with a red roof. No matter how large the barns were, they seemed dwarfed by the vast landscape. I was acutely aware of the isolation and reflected on how these farm kids would have felt before the Internet. At the geyser field I joined dozens of people who stood and waited with iPhones readied. Strokkur, the big geyser, was about to spout and that primal release of pressure was to be recorded in MPEG files. I then drove up the long unpaved drive to the farm that sold homemade ice cream and stood outside eating my salted caramel cone while watching the brown-and-white milk cows chew their cud as they stood in the wet barnyard.

The next stop was a nineteenth-century Icelandic church painted dark brown perched on the side of a hill. These old churches are usually left open. I love their simplicity—straight-backed pews and plain glass windows. And I appreciate the way I feel when I walk inside. A preacher's vestments hung in a yellowed plastic garment bag near the altar, waiting to be used. I thumbed through the hymnals and prayer books stacked on the small half-pew next to the piano. The pulpit—the kind a preacher has to climb up into—was painted sage green with accents of earthy yellow and red. The ceiling was painted sky blue and as I sat in a pew and looked up, I imagined generations of Icelandic farm folk also lifting their heads and staring at the ceiling in hopeful recognition that there would always be another blue-sky day. They also knew that the volcano sitting on the horizon had the power, at any moment, to blot out the sun. I imagine they prayed that Hekla would not erupt in their lifetime or their children's lifetimes.

Jack was a volcano—he gathered strength and caused rumblings before the massive eruption. He blew up like Hekla. Jack and volcanoes. Random, but not. Jack's short life. Random, but not.

It's easier to write about volcanoes and suffering than it is for me to write about Jack. For a brief moment, reflecting in my Iceland cabin, I considered that I might be the volcano, ready to explode and self-destruct, but that would be wrong. I am always ready to implode, to fold in on myself. To cut myself off from everything that gives me pleasure. To crawl into my muddled brain.

While in Iceland, I asked Jack's best friend, Will, if he would write down some of his recollections of Jack and send them to me. He sent me a long letter and in it he wrote:

> Jack would consider deep unsolved questions about the universe, often involving the existence of God & meaning of life. Jack believed that God was made up by humanity to make the lonely individual feel better. Jack believed that the meaning of life was to explore . . . I was very proud of him, and proud to have him as my best friend. I was not angry with him when he died, and never got all that angry at him, though I was deeply angry with God for having allowed such a thing to happen, a war of which has long since been surrendered. The space he left allowed room for many, many friendships. To this day, my social circle is vast, as I can fit about ten close friends in the singular hole he left.

Will and Jack had known each other since they were babies. Will's mother, Marcia, and I were best friends and lived down the street from each other. Marcia and I both loved to sing, and we formed our own little group with a keyboard player and performed standards. Our voices meshed beautifully, and there were times when it was impossible to tell who was singing which parts. When I was the church choir director for the Freeville Methodist Church, Marcia was in the choir.

Will and Jack tumbled about with each other like puppies when they were little. They almost drove their kindergarten teacher into early retirement, and to control the disruptive behavior they were put into different classrooms after that exuberant year. Marcia's family moved to Trumansburg on the other side of the lake when the boys were about eight. I was heartbroken. Although we said we'd see each other all the time, we didn't. (These long, narrow lakes left behind by the glaciers also divide the land and people.) But our boys did. As soon as Jack and Will were old enough to take the public bus, they regularly visited each other. There were some tough times when Will went to Vermont to a private school, but the boys stayed in touch and saw each other on vacations. They were inseparable and involved in each other's friend group, which worked better when Jack was with Will's friends. They were intense boys who loved music and threw themselves into recording their own songs. Will wrote: "Jack had a creative mind that inspired those around him to discover their own creativity. He was a perfectionist, though when he was at his most perfect points, it was paired with effortlessness."

Will wrote about things I did know, but also about things I didn't know. "Jack would, many nights of the year, sneak out of his room and walk around for a majority of the night," Will wrote. "He would experiment with the abuse of prescription and over-the-counter medication and wait for months before telling his friends about his experiences, which were often vague at most. Jack would stay up late and wake early to compose some of the most beautiful songs I have heard to date. Jack struggled deeply with depression, and a now older version of myself wonders almost frantically if it could've been remedied by many adequate nights' sleep, although I almost don't want to know."

I wanted to stick a knife in my heart when I read that last line.

I cried only once while in Iceland, and that was when reading Will's letter. Maybe there's no real reason to cry anymore. There's a feeling of resignation at knowing that Jack is gone and that nothing will ever change that. At knowing that we will probably never move from our house—our own hotspot—because of my husband's reluctance to move away from our children and because of our own inertia. At knowing that Jack's three sisters will always struggle with what they've been through. At knowing that the hole in my heart—once so very wide and deep—is more like a wound that's healed over, leaving a smooth concave scar. At knowing my depression can be managed adequately with medication. At knowing I can take some control rather than always feeling like a cork bobbing in a wind-blown lake.

It's going to be okay, I think, remembering my mother's last words to me. A volcano will not erupt while I'm in Iceland, which, ironically, is a fitting end to my story. I always seem to look for an external drama to magnify my own feelings. I can do nothing except wish for an eruption that would allow me to neatly end a story about Jack and me. A non-erupting volcano means building pressure and momentary stasis. Even though I knew that chambers beneath Iceland's volcanoes were filling with magma as I sat there—that liquid rock was pushing and roiling and forcing its way into cracks in the earth on that geologically exciting island—I also knew that the volcanoes were going to blow on their own time.

We will never know the man Jack would have become and, in time, those who knew him in his short life will begin to forget him. It's inevitable. But our little family will always remember Jack—not because he killed himself, but because he was a fascinating and complicated presence in our lives. He was our son and our brother, our nephew and our cousin. And we all loved him.

on the edge

COMEUPPANCE

Feeling Isolated

Recently, as my husband and I were riding in the car, he told me he had been having trouble sleeping. I was totally unaware of this because I swear by CBD gummies that throw me into a stupor for a good solid six hours. I asked him what was keeping him up and, uncharacteristically, he told me about some of his worries. Tim is a stoic (at least by today's use of the word) and for him to open up about anything is both remarkable and startling.

He told me how difficult these months of COVID shutdown have been on him. Always reticent and reserved in the company of those he doesn't know, he now felt like he had so little contact with the outside world that he believed he'd lost his ability to be at all social. His only interactions had been at the post office or when he went to the large grocery store in Ithaca, and even there, he didn't talk to anyone because he was masked up and always did self-checkout. He had managed to avoid even the tiniest chitchat one has with the cashier while the groceries are being rung up and bagged. Tim's world has shrunk to us.

I mostly think of Tim as content. After retiring four years ago, Tim has enjoyed his post-working life; he's surrounded himself with creatures he has to take care of, including pigeons and falcons, the dog, and us. He thrives in the role of caretaker, and those responsibilities weigh heavily on him, but like a good stoic, he moves through his day making sure everybody and everything are all right. I believe he's always had this tendency. He was always rescuing animals as a boy and caring for them. Then, when he was a teenager, he felt he had to care for his mother and sisters, at least emotionally if not physically, after they left their family apartment in the middle of the night and moved across town to escape their abusive husband/father.

While growing up, our kids always had what they wanted and needed. Railey and I took a trip to Iceland when she was sixteen to ride Icelandic horses. Clara played soccer at an elite level in our part of New York State, which required driving to games and tournaments up and down the eastern seaboard. Jack sang in a nationally recognized children's choir. Gwen skied and was in roller derby.

After Jack died, things changed. Tim's focus went from making sure everyone got to do what they wanted to do to making sure everyone was safe. The sheer terror you feel for all of your children's well-being after one kills himself is staggering. When a kid calls or, more likely, texts, you try to read between the lines, searching for the hidden meaning or unwritten words that might indicate a crisis. Tim's work in the family was now 24/7 crisis prevention.

Recently Clara called and said that she and her girlfriend, Hannah, were getting engaged. They live outside Hudson, New York, in a house they bought not long ago and are having renovated. They're both in their twenties, have jobs, care for pets, and seem very happy. Hannah is from Ithaca, so this weekend her parents are hosting an impromptu engagement party for the girls where the two families can meet for the first time. Hannah's mother is a professor at Cornell, and her father is a medical doctor. The mother told me that they were both going to make little toasts to the girls, and invited us to do so too.

Oddly, this is what set off Tim's recent sleepless night. *What should I say?* he wondered aloud. *How long should the toast be? What should*

I wear? These questions seemed ridiculous on the face of it because he is a gifted nonfiction writer and speaker and always looks appropriate in every setting. But I knew the real problem was that he hadn't had a conversation in person with anyone but me for months. He was also reverting to the sixteen-year-old kid who had saved his lunch money for more than two years to rent an apartment for his mom and sisters and himself so they could slip away on a January night more than fifty years ago. There's a deep feeling of self-doubt in Tim when having to face those who have money. In his head, in spite of all of his accomplishments and successes, he will always be that poor kid scrambling to survive.

And he will always be the father of the boy who killed himself. How does one ever explain that to prospective in-laws or, well, to anybody? Do you invoke Jack's name or forget that he existed or is there some mash-up to revert to? Clara had three siblings but now has two siblings. I know that everything Tim and I write and say passes through that sieve. I believe that at the core of Tim's sleepless night is the anticipation of the awkwardness of talking to people he doesn't know, coupled with possibly having to allude to Clara's childhood which included a brother who no longer exists.

I wish he could believe me when I say that everything will be all right.

Tim Writes Me a Letter

As we all stumbled through the early days of COVID-19, and most of us learned how to live with lockdowns, wear masks, and socially distance, the biggest effect on me was not being able to travel. I couldn't get into my car and drive to Skaneateles to have lunch at the Sherwood Inn or drive to Cooperstown to visit the Fenimore Art Museum. I couldn't make plans to get on a plane to go to Iceland to look at volcanoes. I couldn't arrange to spend a week on a cove in Nova Scotia where the waves crash against the rocks and the sky portends the day's meteorological drama. I came to

see that these were my first-world problems. Also, my need to travel—my
need to run away—had lessened as the gap between Jack's death and the
present grew ever wider.

Getting emotionally better—being able to survive in my skin—has
come slowly. I can now walk into rooms that contain pictures of Jack and
not avert my eyes. The potency of my personal minefields is lessening.
Nevertheless, the one thing I still can't seem to do is talk about Jack either
with his sisters or with Tim. This horrifies me. I want to know what they
think and how they feel. I want to hear their stories of survival. But I can't
bring it up. I rack my brain to try to figure out why this is; why my reluctance is like a muzzle. With a start, I realize that this is how I was raised.

My mother, who was pulled through the knothole by my peripatetic father, was shut down for my entire childhood. She functioned but was terribly sad much of the time. We didn't discuss the sadness that surrounded
us. It just was. Because this became my learned response (a kind of don't
ask, don't tell), when Jack died, I withdrew and withheld my emotions.
It was the only thing I knew how to do. Unlike my mother, who got food
on the table and put money in the bank amid her depression, I withdrew
and stopped functioning. I felt like if I even had to hear or speak Jack's
name, I might explode into a million bitter pieces. This is the backdrop
to my asking Tim and the girls and some of Jack's friends via email how
Jack's death affected them. Several of Jack's friends wrote me heartbreak-
ing notes, but neither Tim nor the girls responded right away.

Then I received a letter from Tim.

As I read through the letter, I could feel my face burn. Tim wrote about
how Jack's death brought Railey, Clara, Gwen, and him closer together;
how they came to depend on one another in so many ways. They recognized that I had a different way of coping that revolved around a powerful
need to escape to faraway places where no one knew my backstory.

Tim wrote:

> The kids and I went through a very long healing process after Jack's death
> that you were not a part of. I think they still feel a sense of emptiness about
> that, though it has eased a lot. Gwen was sad that you missed so many of
> her school events. I realize you just couldn't bear to walk into the school
> that you and all of our children attended, but Gwen paid a price for that.

She told me she would often ditch classes in middle school and just sit alone hiding in the school bathroom or go to the nurse's office with made-up ailments. She told me I was almost like a single parent for a couple of years when you were traveling in faraway places or were emotionally absent when you were at home, sitting in the green chair. She was very happy when you started going to her roller derby practices and games.

As Railey noted, we are a tight-knit family—but like a pack of loners. When we lost Jack, it was devastating, but then we also lost you for two or three years. I remember doing a lot of family things—going to concerts; sitting through play rehearsals (the sad, lonely dad in the background); and various other school events. I look back on that with a twinge of sorrow.

I felt at times that I was pushing too hard to make things seem normal again. I strongly encouraged Clara to stay at Cornell and try to work through her grief. I met with the provost and with several professors, trying to make things work for her. And I told her to call me anytime night and day and I'd come and get her—and I did drive to her dorm a couple of times in the early morning darkness. I just didn't want our children to lose the momentum they'd built in their lives. It didn't seem fair. Clara told me she never felt pushed and wanted to keep going, too. I was so glad to hear that. The devastating trauma of Jack's death had a profound effect on her—being less than a year apart in age, they'd grown up like twins, constant companions—but she used the terrible experience to re-evaluate her entire life and to make changes, like transferring to Bard College, moving to the Hudson Valley, and pursuing a career in film. She believes she would not have done any of that otherwise. She probably would have completed her degree at Cornell and perhaps not known what to do afterwards.

Tim and I had exact opposite reactions to the loss of Jack. He felt the need to stay in the house and the village, close to the places Jack knew growing up and close to his grave. He knew that leaving would have been a meaningless escape for him and not a healing or learning process. "For you," he wrote, "obviously the opposite was true, and I don't feel bad about that or resent it in any way." It had never occurred to me until I read that line that Tim would resent me for leaving. That's how pervasive my magical thinking was.

Tim wrote about his stoicism in the face of emotional pain, something learned when he was a boy and his father went on drunken rampages, beat up his mother, and wrecked the house. He wrote: "My stoicism got me through a lot of bad things, but it was a tradeoff. I'm sure in many ways it closed me off emotionally. But Jack's death floored me. I knew life would never be the same for me. I took it as a personal failure that I wasn't able to figure out what was going on with Jack and how to help him."

In the days and weeks after Jack died, when I had sunk into the Green Chair and couldn't seem to escape its upholstered arms, Tim carried on. "Every day I felt like I was staggering up a mountainside carrying a crushing burden on my back," he wrote. He went to work again within a couple of weeks of Jack's funeral but would "often shut the door to my office and sit weeping quietly at my desk."

"I never showed the depth of my pain to you, the kids, or anyone," Tim wrote. "I think you probably felt that I didn't grieve in the same way as you and perhaps you resented it, although I don't think we ever spoke of it."

Gwen, who was only twelve when Jack died, has had a very hard time during the COVID-19 lockdown, especially when she and the other Ithaca College students were sent home from their dorms and had to learn online. She told Tim that it was overwhelmingly depressing being at home, with constant reminders of Jack. She couldn't cope with it and had to drop out for a semester when her college life was confined to her room in the Pink House. Now that she has moved into her own apartment, gotten a job, and bought a car, she feels much happier and has signed up to take online courses through Ithaca College in the spring. "She credits you with encouraging her to do this," Tim wrote to me, "and not giving in to her anxieties."

When Tim spoke to the girls prior to writing this letter comparing his experience and theirs he thought it reawakened the grief that exists in all of them. But what struck him most about the conversation was that they all agreed that they've come through a long, dark passage and were on the other side of it now. They can all envision a future. "And I think all of us, including you, are closer than we've ever been," he wrote. "We all love spending time with each other. I'm so happy and grateful for that."

Well, there it is. We are like pieces of fabric in an old quilt that have become threadbare or worn through to the backing. Like that old quilt, we remain stitched together in such a way that those seams have become stronger than the fabric they connect. I can't give those girls back the lost years. My hope is that they understand and ultimately forgive me.

The Truth about Selfishness

When Jack died at age seventeen, I fell into an almost catatonic state and stayed there for months after his death. Even then, I was so desperate to escape from the Pink House that I went on several trips that I had no business going on. I knew I should have stayed home to be with the girls, who were suffering. I didn't. My selfishness—my need to make Jack's death completely personal—excluded my family.

Years later, Tim told me that in a conversation with the girls, they all said that they felt I abandoned them. They said that when they lost their brother, they also lost their mother. I knew that to be the truth even in 2012. But for some reason, I didn't think they knew it. The fact that they did, and that they all cried when they shared that experience with Tim, cuts me to the quick.

How can I tell them that the only reason I'm alive today is because of them? That when I was sitting in the backyard and thinking and feeling like I had plunged into a bottomless dark hole, what kept me from giving up entirely was the thought that I would be doing an unthinkable thing to my daughters. It would be the ultimate act of selfishness and cruelty.

Deep within me, I knew that traveling away from the Pink House would keep me alive. I knew that living and staying in the house where my son killed himself was pushing me toward that bottomless dark hole. Oddly, sitting in the Green Chair, which is placed directly beneath Jack's room, also kept me moored to life. I constantly picked the emotional scab so that the feelings stayed raw. I could not bring my daughters or my husband into my emotional space for fear they would fall down the dark hole as well, and I knew I wouldn't be able to bear that. So I was either in the Green Chair or traveling far from the Pink House. In both cases, even if surrounded by people, I was by myself.

I wish I could reclaim those couple of years when I was emotionally unavailable. If I could, I would try to do things differently. But I don't know if it would have made a difference; if I would have been able to let the girls into my world. On some level, by keeping them out, I think I believed I was sparing them the worst kind of sorrow. But that, of course, is what a selfish person would think.

The Present

I can't project him into the future anymore. When he was frozen in time at seventeen, and all of his friends and his siblings were around that age, I could see him everywhere—in the past, the present, and even a speculative future. But now that almost a decade has passed, he is no longer their peer. He does not age with them. He remains stuck in time.

I also can't project myself into the future. I've grown comfortable with being in the present even though the present is unbelievably strange. As I write this, the country hangs poised between Donald Trump, determined not to leave office even though he lost both the electoral college and the popular vote, and president-elect Joe Biden.

I can't project myself into the future. People are dying from COVID-19, and we live with masks and hand sanitizer and social distancing. There will be no Thanksgiving as we've known it this year. We are to stay in our homes and eat with those in our households, which would be Tim, Gwen, and myself.

I can't project myself into the future. My aches and pains are in abeyance at the moment. I wish to keep it that way. I don't want to know what lies ahead.

I can't project myself into the future. The rules of comportment have so changed over the last half-decade that many of us don't know how to behave anymore. There is meanness in our country that frightens me. Perhaps it was always there but now that the rules have changed, many believe it's okay to behave badly in the open and rely on false narratives to bolster incorrect claims. The January 6, 2021, insurrection at the United States Capitol is a perfect example of this.

I can't project myself into the future. I don't want anything around me to die—animals, people, scraggly house plants. I am living in an O. Henry short story, assigning power and meaning to dropped leaves and missed connections. My world has again shrunk to the geography of the Pink House.

I still drive through the countryside, aware of the comings and goings of nature, the cycle of the seasons. The leaves are gone except for the stubborn bronze leaves that cling to the branches of the giant white oak tree that stands in the meadow above our old farm. Birds are passing through on their way south. Rafts of buffleheads and hooded mergansers bob on

Cayuga Lake. Tundra swans drop in to Dryden Lake to pay a visit. And common loons have been flying above Cayuga Lake in massive numbers. Everything's heading south.

I take snapshots of the present: the magnificent walnut tree in the backyard with the sun trying to break through gray clouds behind it; the metal towers and wires of the electric power plant several miles down the road juxtaposed with brown autumn trees and blue sky strewn with wispy cirrus clouds; the houses in the village in their various stages of unbecoming as paint fades and flakes, and siding pulls away from structures. I document the five square miles of my tiny world with my iPhone.

I sit at my worktable in the Pink House and paint pictures of tableaus I've assembled from whatever lies in my line of sight. I combine in clever arrangements that which will rot over time with durable objects from my past—apples or oranges or boiled eggs in a favorite bowl that I remember children eating cereal from, a tablecloth used at big family gatherings, a teacup from my mother's house. Then I never paint what I have arranged. Colors morph and backgrounds change under my brush. Still-life becomes abstract. I am documenting my filtered present.

Jack will remain in the past. In several generations, when all who knew him are gone, his short life will be remembered through the pages of a book where his mother has pulled strands of his being through a scrim of grief. The family and friends Jack left behind were all affected by his act of self-violence. Most of us have moved beyond the white-hot fury that accompanies a suicide. Have moved beyond our own self-destructive moments in response to Jack's final act. But his suicide had an impact that spread like widening ripples in a pond. His teachers, his classmates, people in the village, his extended family all carry his death around with them, and the memory of it periodically makes its way to the front of the brain and causes a moment of sadness or a pause in their present. He will be forever known but not known.

The Corncrake

THE CORNCRAKE

When I was forty, I made a journey to Scotland to visit Iona again—this would be my fifth visit to this island in the Inner Hebrides. I'm drawn to the *story* of Iona because I've always been fascinated by and curious about those who search for different ways to explain the world. It would be fair to call me a spiritual dilettante. Maybe I will never find whatever that undefinable thing is that I'm searching for, but that realization has never kept me from trying.

As I began my journey involving planes, trains, buses, and ferries—I thought about how, 1,600 years earlier, Saint Columba and twelve monks crossed the wild Irish Sea in a leather boat to land on the same shores. The first time I visited Iona was when I living in Scotland for a year after college. After several later trips to Iona, I still yearned to return, partly because it's beautiful and remote, and partly because it's a spiritual sinkhole, having been steeped in some form of Celtic Christianity for one and a half millennia. This time I decided to stay for a week at Iona Abbey, the rebuilt thirteenth-century Benedictine monastery, and take part in a workshop run by an ecumenical group called the Iona Community.

A tiny island, only three miles long by one and a half miles wide, Iona lies in the Inner Hebrides off the west coast of Scotland. Iona has a year-round population of about 120. During the summer months, when the weather tends to be fine, thousands of people find their way there each day to visit the birthplace of Christianity in Scotland. My workshop was in mid-June.

When you take the foot ferry from the Isle of Mull to Iona, you can see the abbey. Set about a mile north of the village, the massive stone church and its outbuildings loom above all else on the landscape. Yet because they're made of the native stone, the buildings all but disappear into the hills behind them. There are few trees on the island, and those that manage to survive tend to be stunted and sheltered around the houses of the village. The tops of the hills are craggy, and a soft green down covers their flanks. As the ferry drew closer to the pier, I had the odd feeling that I could reach out and stroke the hillsides.

Three or four farms lie scattered about the island, but most islanders live in the village strung along the road on either side of the pier. The islanders—who pretty much keep to themselves—either farm or fish or are connected to tourism. They seem to barely tolerate the onslaught of visitors as they sell you dry goods from the store or a beer from the pub.

After getting off the ferry, I joined the dozens of visitors drawn to the abbey. We trudged along the cobblestone path called the Road of the Dead, some of us making a stop at the ruins of the thirteenth-century Augustinian nunnery where wildflowers and meadow grasses lean against the stone walls as if holding them in place. As I stood inside the remnants of the nunnery (which was closed during the Reformation), I noticed the jackdaws and rooks calling from the roof of a nearby house. Then I hustled to rejoin the crowd and we all paused to admire several eight-foot-tall eighth- or ninth-century stone Celtic crosses that rise next to the road, their relief carvings almost effaced by a millennium of sun, wind, rain, and snow. Next to the abbey lies a graveyard holding the remains of four dozen Scottish kings—including Macbeth and Duncan—eight Norwegian kings, and four Irish kings: a remarkable necropolis of royalty and a legacy of sixteen centuries of history connected to this Hebridean island.

It was here, on Iona, that Colm Cille, the monk we now know as Saint Columba, after his exile from Ireland, began to build his monastery and abbey in 563 CE. Colm Cille had led an armed insurrection against King Díarmait in which three thousand of Diarmait's subjects were killed. Rather than being put to death, Colm Cille was exiled as retribution for the three thousand deaths and ordered to convert an equivalent number of souls for the church. Colm Cille and his monks were enormously successful in converting the Picts of what is now Scotland to Christianity. For several centuries, Iona was the seat of scholarship and political power in the region and became the most important monastic institution in the British Isles. The monks produced beautiful illuminated manuscripts in the monastery's scriptorium. Mostly they were copies of religious texts with gorgeous illustrations in the margins and illuminated initials painted in jewel-tone colors and gold.

Iona became part of Scandinavian Scotland—called the Kingdom of the Isles from the eighth to the eleventh century—which explains why eight Norwegian kings are buried next to the abbey. Vikings conducted numerous raids on Iona, the most deadly occurring in 806 CE, when sixty-eight monks were slaughtered on the beach, a broad strand of sand below steep cliffs now called Beach of the Martyrs. But then the Norse began to colonize the north and west of Scotland. Men and women immigrated from Norway, and within generations, the entire region spoke Norse. In the ninth century, most of the relics and valuables associated with the abbey were relocated to Ireland for safekeeping—including Saint Columba's bones—as the monks abandoned the monastery ahead of the Viking raiders. This is when a manuscript begun in Iona ended up in the Abbey of Kells and is now called the Book of Kells. It's breathtaking.

When I visited in the summer of 2001, Historic Scotland had recently assumed ownership of Iona Abbey, but the Iona Community, the group that rebuilt the thirteenth-century abbey in the last century, still had access to the dormitories, the refectory, and the church. I sensed an uneasy détente between Historic Scotland, which paid the bills and ran tours through the property, and the Iona Community, which felt stung by the loss of control of the buildings they had, over the generations, maintained.

The ecumenical Iona Community, headquartered in Glasgow, is devoted to changing society through social and political justice. The workshops held at the abbey are a way for the community to support themselves and their projects. I jumped at the chance to attend a weeklong workshop having something to do with spirituality—I'm forgetting the specifics—because it meant I could spend time on this along-the-edge-of-the-world island.

I stayed with forty-five other people in a dormitory connected by the cloisters to the abbey. My room, which I shared with three other women, was slightly larger in size than my dining room table. My roommates were in their early twenties, making me old enough to be their mother. I'm a good sport, but when I saw the two bunk beds, I played the age card and announced, "I don't do top bunks."

In an attempt to foster community, the abbey staff divided us into chore teams. Some teams got to sweep and mop the refectory floor, peel onions in the kitchen, or clean the common room. My group was given bathroom duty. Eight of us had to clean about ten toilets, six showers, and twelve sinks every day after morning church service. I yearned for any other chore, even onion peeling, because I didn't want to feel resentful of people who used the last of the toilet paper and didn't replace the roll.

The workshops drew people from Scotland, England, America, and Australia, with a good third of the participants from the clergy—ministers, Anglican priests, and lay leaders. We represented the curious and the seekers. I didn't know anyone and spent much of that first day feeling awkward and phony. I was there out of spiritual curiosity rather than a desire to better understand the scripture. The other participants seemed to me to have more defined agendas. Later that first day I wandered down to the pier where the ferry from Mull docked and began to look at the birds. I had a pair of binoculars around my neck and my guide to the birds of Britain in my pocket, and began ticking off the species we don't have at home. Wagtail. Check. Rook. Check. Jackdaw. Check.

Workshop participants arrived on the ferry, which made continuous trips between Mull and Iona. When I was trying to identify some gulls, I noticed two men getting off the boat carrying duffel bags and with binoculars slung around their necks. They saw me, and within moments we began looking for and enthusiastically talking about birds. One was an Anglican priest, originally from South Africa, who now had a church in Manchester, and the other was an American Southern Baptist minister, and they were both in Iona to attend the workshop. The priest was tall and thin and anxious-looking with a graying head and beard, and the minister was short and stocky with glasses and an easy smile. They were

Mutt and Jeff, and I was their sidekick. We very quickly became an inseparable trio, spending all of our time either birding or anticipating the activity.

On our first full day on Iona, the three of us headed out right after morning chores. We had an hour before the workshop session and there were birds to be seen. We hadn't gone ten feet from the back of the abbey when we heard *crake crake . . . crake crake* coming from the field that led down to the sea. It was the sound of someone running a thumb down the edge of one of those old ten-cent pocket combs.

We stopped short, binoculars raised, straining to catch a glimpse of whatever made that peculiar noise. My birding pals looked expectantly at me because I had the coat pocket large enough to carry the field guide.

"Wow, that must be the elusive corncrake," I told them. A summer visitor to Scotland and Ireland, the corncrake (*Crex crex*) was rapidly disappearing from the British landscape on account of loss of habitat; a foot in length, they require meadows with tall grass for their nesting. At that time, only an estimated 650 nesting pairs remained. Having heard their distinctive call, we figured we'd spot them right away. *Piece of cake*, I thought as I scanned that first field, to no avail.

Searching for the corncrake became our obsession. They were terribly difficult to spot because they were secretive, lowering their heads after calling and then standing stock-still. After every meal we'd head out. Between workshop sessions we'd head out. Rain. Wind. Sun. We'd head out. We'd hurry past the black sand beach, and the beach of beautiful sea-scoured pebbles. We'd rush through the odd golf course with its shaggy grass and grazing sheep. We'd hurry past the remains of the marble quarry with its beautiful chips of green-and-white marble littering the quarry floor. We were always in a hurry because we had to get back for workshops, meals, and church services. No one minded our excursions but lateness was frowned upon.

By midweek we had identified at least three fields around the island where we heard corncrakes calling. We'd stand at the edges of these fields with the long grasses swaying in the wind and hear that damned call, *crake crake . . . crake crake*. We began to skip some of our workshops because of our obsession with the search for our grail bird, each of us explaining privately to our perplexed instructors the dilemma we found ourselves in.

We also found time to look at other birds. Wagtails, ringed plovers, European goldfinches, oystercatchers, jackdaws, rooks. Once I heard a beautiful birdsong that seemed endless in duration and cheeriness, and the Anglican priest pointed to a bird ascending into the clouds. A skylark. A bird I knew only from poetry. And as I stood, transfixed by what was now a dot in the sky, I thought of William Wordsworth's 1805 poem "To a Skylark":

> Up with me! up with me into the clouds!
>   For thy song, Lark, is strong;
> Up with me, up with me into the clouds!
>   Singing, singing,
> With clouds and sky about thee ringing,
>   Lift me, guide me till I find
> That spot which seems so to thy mind!

While we wandered the island, we'd often talk about the elusive corncrake—about its habit of standing on stones and stretching its neck up and tipping its head back before calling *crake crake . . . crake crake*. And we'd talk about how we'd feel when we finally saw it. How we'd be fulfilled in some basic way. It became clear that we all loved the thrill of the hunt and the ephemeral nature of birding. We also talked about our lives: About my four children and my peripatetic nature; about the priest's unhappiness in his working-class parish outside Manchester and his deep homesickness for South Africa; about the minister's meteoric rise from pastor of a church to administrator within the American Southern Baptist Convention, and about his misgivings in straying too far from the pulpit. These two religious men were at Iona because they wanted more of something, but they couldn't quite identify what that *more* might be. They were both sure in their devotion to Christianity but had struggles over how best to serve their churches and themselves.

One night I dreamt of Saint Columba and one of the many miracles he is said to have performed in Scotland. In the miracle, Columba comes upon a ferocious water beast trying to eat one of his disciples, so he banishes it to the River Ness. In my dream, Columba was riding upon the back of Nessie, like a cowboy riding a bucking bronco in a rodeo, as he drove her to exile in the river that courses through Inverness. When I woke,

I wondered if this was how Columba converted the pagan Picts to Christianity. Did he jazz up his miracles with showmanship to increase his flock?

To me, there was something just beyond the obvious on the island. I could understand why ancient and modern-day Druids were drawn to Iona during particular times of the year. When we stumbled across a stone circle on Iona, that made sense to me. When I heard that Iona was on a ley line—a notion developed in the 1920s identifying alignments of religious sites and ancient monuments in Britain—that confirmed my intuitions. But that's not the kind of thing I mentioned to my birding companions. Or to anyone. When we were out in the field searching for the corncrake, our energies were split between spiritual yearnings and questions, and the vagaries of nature. I am not averse to believing in a thin barrier between this world and some other dimension and, when I was on Iona, I realized I was not the only one who thought that way. Maybe we were all riding on the back of the serpent of the unknown.

I felt guilty about not being more engaged in the workshops. Today I can't even remember what my workshop was about but I do remember that it seemed to hold great meaning for the earnest spiritual seekers. I knew I was searching for something as well, but the second I heard that bird, I knew part of my quest lay beyond the walls of the abbey and the sober teachings of the Iona Community. I was always in a hurry. I fidgeted during workshops, I wolfed down my food, and I rushed through my chores just so I could be outside.

One evening, as we sat in the abbey after singing another forgettable hymn, the warbled song and buzzy calls of a starling filled the church. The small dark bird flew up and perched on a windowsill high above the congregation. It was a sign to those trapped in a ritual that held no meaning. *Look up*, I thought. *Listen to what nature has provided us!* Then I worried about that bird all night—about its being trapped in the church when its home was the sky above the meadows and hills and beaches of Iona. Early the next morning, I went to the church before breakfast and opened the side door that led into the cloisters. It startled the bird, which flew from one window to another as I entered the sanctuary. Leaving the side door wide open, I went to breakfast and willed the starling to go toward the outside light and freedom.

The priest, the minister, and I spent our last day of workshops searching for the corncrake with the kind of desperation you feel when you know you are leaving a place with unfinished business. We raced from meadow to meadow, crisscrossing the island several times. *Crake crake . . . crake crake.* We passed curious sheep, which scattered when we got too close. We didn't pause to raise our binoculars to identify birds flying overhead. *Crake crake . . . crake crake.* Monomaniacal, we were determined to accomplish this one thing while on the island. We needed to go home with a victory to justify our sojourns and our miserable failure as community members.

We headed back to the abbey, close to disconsolate at our inability to find the corncrake, in time for the evening service. As we followed the cobblestone Road of the Dead we didn't talk much because our collective failure weighed us down like stones shoved into our pockets. We had not seen the bird. We had blown off our workshops and behaved badly because we had formed a clique, like we were in high school. We didn't pay attention to those who couldn't understand our pursuit. We ignored those who didn't own binoculars. *What would Saint Columba think of us?* I wondered as we trudged on the same path he had walked 1,600 years earlier. I thought about how intrepid he was as he sailed across the Irish Sea to establish his church in Pict territory. Then it struck me that he acted in a single-minded fashion, much as the three of us had. He was seeking out and pursuing souls to convert for his church and to compensate for the souls he brought to slaughter. We were seeking out and pursuing the corncrake, which we viewed as a symbol of hope. If we saw the corncrake that meant there was still one of the highly endangered birds left to see. We all wanted to believe in something, be it the power of the church or the power of nature, or in the case of the priest and the minister, the power of both.

Our last night on Iona coincided with the summer solstice. At 10:00 p.m., I headed out of the abbey with my young roommates to get a good vantage point for viewing the sunset, which wouldn't occur for another hour or so. We climbed over fences and walked through pastures of sheep where the lambs called *maaaa, maaaa* if we got too close. We began the short climb of the tallest hill on Iona—Dun I—which is only a couple of hundred feet above sea level. Roommate Elsbeth from Inverness pointed out bog cotton, birdsfoot trefoil, spongy bits of moss, a slimy black slug, and a mushroom on our way up the hill—a dedicated spiritualist and, I now saw, a skilled naturalist. She led us through a meadow covered with buttercups and little daisies that looked so soft in the twilight that we stopped and lay down on our backs to look at the darkening sky above us. When we reached the top of Dun I, we stood next to the four-foot-high cairn made of rocks that had been collected and then deposited by pilgrims over the years. We could see water in three directions. We spotted a bonfire flickering on the beach below where modern-day Druids had assembled to celebrate the solstice.

For a moment, time collapsed, and I imagined Columba and his monks standing on this very spot in the early years of their exile, looking wistfully toward home in the southwest across what is now called the Irish Sea.

We were joined by two Scottish men on the summit—brothers-in-law who had been coming for years to Iona to vacation. The small wiry guy dressed in neoprene shorts began to tell us the names of the islands we could see jutting out of the sea. He had kayaked to most of these places and spoke of them with an affection that comes from working hard to get somewhere. "That's Coll, and there's Colonsay. And, of course, there's the Dutchman's Cap and Staffa," he said. "Those rugged hills over there are on Uigg; and that mountain over there on Mull is a Munro," which, he explained, was a Scottish mountain over three thousand feet high. We followed his finger around while he pointed to silhouetted shapes catching the golden rays of the setting sun.

I knew of Staffa and its sea cave—Fingal's Cave—that was big enough to row a boat into. The uninhabited island was made of towering hexagonal basaltic columns with a grassy surface. At one end of Staffa was the cave and at the other was a puffin colony where, in the summer, you could visit and lie on your stomach on the grass and watch the puffins fly into their burrows right below you. Queen Victoria and Prince Albert visited Fingal's Cave, as did Wordsworth, although he was not impressed. Robert Louis Stevenson stopped by. And Felix Mendelssohn was so moved by the sounds of the waves slapping against the basalt that he subsequently wrote the *Hebrides Overture,* op. 26.

The girls and I sat with our backs to the abbey and looked out over the islands to the north and west, and we watched as the horizon gently streaked orange and purple. I felt the collapse of time and space as the day waned and it was neither dark nor light. With one foot in spring and the other in summer, the boundaries between past, present, and future blurred. Maybe the future lay behind us in the rebuilt medieval abbey with its New Age community, which was snug up against the village that had managed to drag itself into the twenty-first century—coexisting with a graveyard filled with kings, meadows hiding secretive birds, and fields full of sheep.

Writing this two decades later, what I couldn't see as I gazed from Dun I were the deaths of my parents, which lay in the future, as well as the death of my teenage son by suicide. My aunts would die one by one over those two decades and my family would spasmodically contract after each loss. For some family members, illness and sorrow dragged us down. Others were able to take a more pragmatic stance and soldier on. When I think back on that night, I remember feeling at peace while watching the orange sparks rise from the Druids' bonfire on the beach below.

What I realized on Dun I was that even though I never saw a corn-crake, didn't wholeheartedly embrace the Iona Community workshop, failed to perform my morning chores with gusto—none of that mattered. My searching for something had led me to spend a week with two deeply spiritual men as we engaged in a quest for a sign of hope—hope that humans hadn't doomed yet another creature to extinction because of our inattentiveness to nature and outright greed. Maybe that was enough. My companions and I were silent as we sat on Iona's tallest hill. The waves crashed against the cliffs, and gulls and terns wheeled in the half-dark, half-light world.

ACKNOWLEDGMENTS

In the years since Jack's death, I've been surrounded by loving individuals who have patiently tried to ease some of my pain. They've been members of my extended family including my sisters Anne and Amy Dickinson; cousins Jan Smith, Nancy Carver, Lorraine Buonviri, and Vicki Pearson; and my lovely aunts Mildred Sherwood, Jean Pearson, and Anne Murray. Two friends, in particular, made the past decade bearable: Marian Van Loan and Marcia Eames-Sheavly. Walking partner Heather Sheridan-Thomas and her dogs Gigi and Winnie made the mornings a little brighter. My online writing and friend group—Jane Boursaw, Bobbi Dempsey, Kristin Ohlson, Gwen Moran, and Barbara Benham—provided invaluable support and friendship. Local writers and friends Amy Reading and Leslie Daniels read early versions of many of these essays and offered generous and invaluable critiques.

Right after Jack died, the Dryden Central School district and the Freeville United Methodist Church provided the kind of support one finds when tragedy strikes a small community, and for that I'm grateful.

The Goucher College MFA community has enriched me in numerous ways, especially by introducing me to my lovely, talented friends Memsy Price, Ginny McReynolds, Neda Toloui-Semnani, Stephanie Gorton, Jean Guerrro, and Kristina Gaddy.

Audubon's artist-in residence program on Hog Island provided me with two weeks when I developed the bones for the essay "Called Back." I loved the two months I stayed as an artist-in-residence at Gullkistan in Iceland, where I painted and wrote the essay "Beside the Volcano." The Constance Saltonstall Foundation for the Arts provided several off-season stays at their artists' colony, where several of the essays in this collection were written.

I will always be indebted to Jack's friends—particularly Will Sheavly and Isabel Richards—for staying in touch with me over the years.

Three Hills editor Michael McGandy was an early supporter of this essay collection and managed to create order out of the chaos. For that, plus his sage advice and friendship, I am grateful. Kudos as well to the production team at Cornell University Press.

The landscape of home has offered both anguish and solace over the years. I am so very grateful to my daughters, Railey Savage, Clara Gallagher, and Gwendolyn Gallagher, for always being there when I most needed them. And finally, my husband, Tim Gallagher, never questioned my penchant for periodically running away from home in search of a way to navigate the world without Jack. Tim's love and dedication to keeping the family together even when fault lines appeared were and are absolute.

ILLUSTRATIONS

All illustrations drawn in pen and ink by the author